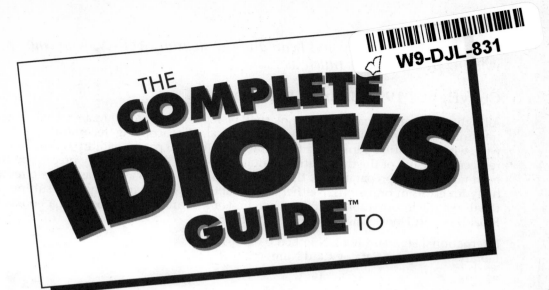

THE COMPLETE IDIOT'S GUIDE™ TO

Starting a Home-Based Business

by Barbara Weltman

alpha books

A Division of Macmillan General Reference
A Simon & Schuster Macmillan Company
1633 Broadway, New York, NY 10019

To my daughters Emily and Leah and my stepson Geoffrey, who enjoy my working from home as much as I do.

Copyright ©1997 Barbara Weltman

International Standard Book Number: 0-02-861539-5
Library of Congress Catalog Card Number: 97-071172

99 98   8   7   6   5   4   3

Interpretation of the printing code: the rightmost number of the first series of numbers is the year of the book's printing; the rightmost number of the second series of numbers is the number of the book's printing. For example, a printing code of 97-1 shows that the first printing of the book occurred in 1997.

Printed in the United States of America

Note: Reasonable care has been taken in the preparation of the text to ensure its clarity and accuracy. This book is sold with the understanding that the author and the publisher are not engaged in rendering legal, accounting, or other professional service. Laws vary from state to state, and readers with specific financial questions should seek the services of a professional advisor.

Publisher
Theresa Murtha

Editorial Manager
Gretchen Henderson

Editor
Nancy Stevenson

Production Editor
Laura Uebelhor

Cover Designer
Mike Freeland

Illustrator
Judd Winick

Designer
Glenn Larsen

Indexers
Nadia Ibrahim
Sandra Henselmeier

Production Team
Angela Calvert
Daniela Raderstorf
Laure Robinson
Susan Van Ness
Pamela Woolf

Contents at a Glance

Contents

9 Paying the Bills While Paying Your Dues   95

10 Hunting for Money: Tracking Down Your Financing Options   107

Foreword

If you're thinking about starting a business in your home, there's no better time to start than right now! The opportunities are unlimited. Many home-based businesses can even be started with very little money. Nearly 30 million Americans currently operate some type of business from their homes. Many of your neighbors are already enjoying the benefits of working from home. Why not join them?

The Complete Idiot's Guide to Starting a Home-Based Business is a wonderful blend of frankness, facts, honesty, and humor. It balances the how-tos with the what-nows. It answers your question, often before you ask it. And it offers easy to follow, practical advice to set you on the road to success.

Admitting you do not have all the answers places you ahead of the crowd. This is the first step toward creating success. With knowledge, all things are possible. If you are the least bit afraid, intimidated, or skeptical about starting a home-based business, here is a book that will take you step-by-step through this process by showing you what it takes personally, financially, and emotionally to make it work.

Working from your home can provide countless benefits. Never lose sight of why you want to work from home. Whether you are working part-time or full-time; whether you are forced to work or choose to work; whether you have small children or are retired; whether this is a career or a hobby—whatever your personal situation, by reading and following the advice in this book you'll learn how to start and operate a home-based business.

Flexible hours, less restrictive work attire, and no lost time in traveling to an office are just a few of the benefits that you will gain.

Besides the many benefits, working from your home can produce obstacles that other business owners don't experience. Barbara Weltman presents these challenges in a straightforward manner that allows the reader to identify, solve, and move past these situations. These problems don't go away simply by ignoring them. Closing your eyes only makes matters worse. Follow her advice; don't become an ostrich with your head buried in the sand. Instead, learn how to confront and manage these situations.

As I read through these pages I was reminded of my own journey working from home. It is one I still enjoy today. I left the corporate world because it did not provide the opportunities I wanted. Being my own boss had been a reoccurring dream. Like many self-employed Americans, I chose to become a consultant and work from my home. There was minimal start-up capital required; beyond a computer, fax machine, and printer, the major investment was my time. This opportunity allowed me to combine my education, work experience, and passion in order to create a career tailored for me.

The ride hasn't always been smooth, but I wouldn't change a day in my life for working for someone else. I just wish everyone could be so fortunate.

Working from home has taught me a lot about myself. It has made me learn how to say "no" to the countless demands and interruptions on my time. I have learned how to be a self-starter; how to work most efficiently around my body clock, my attention span, and my creative spirit; and how to get support from outside the traditional paths. There are no reviews, raises, or promotions to reinforce my work habits. Instead, I look for friendships or business associates to provide encouragement through their positive comments, recommendations, or referrals. The avenues may be different, but the feeling of personal accomplishment is still the same.

Some days are long. Some days are short. No two days are ever the same. Corporate America wanted me to conform to its box, follow its rules, and be measured according to its standards. Working from home allows me to focus on the end results without being bogged down to restrictive rules, conformity, or someone else's standards. As a home-based entrepreneur, individuality is both encouraged and rewarded. Your motivation is what makes it happen.

If working from home has been your lifelong dream, read through these pages, follow the expert advice, and take the plunge. Failure comes from never trying.

Vickie Montgomery

Author of *The Smart Woman's Guide to Starting a Business* and *The Woman Manager's Troubleshooter.*

Introduction

I can't help but be excited about the tremendous growth in home-based business. Today more than 25 million people run their own businesses right in their houses, condos, and apartments. Why am I excited? You see I'm one of the pioneers in home-based businesses, having worked from my home for nearly 15 years. I've watched the movement grow and have benefited from the changes I've seen.

I didn't think much about working from home back when I started. I never sat down and consciously decided to start a business from home. For me the decision was sort of thrust upon me. I'd been working in the suburbs where I live for a company that was bought out on a Thursday. If I wanted to keep my job I had to show up in New York City on Monday. But having two small children, I didn't want to commute over two hours each day. I didn't want to be so far away that I missed class plays, ballet recitals, and gymnastic meets. With one major account lined up, I hung up my shingle that Monday (instead of enjoying all the New York City transit authority has to offer a commuter) and started working from home.

Just to give you an idea about how things were back then in the stone age of home offices, personal computers were just coming into popular use. There was no such thing as a fax or using the Internet from home. The first year in business I operated with just an electric typewriter and a phone—no computer, no copier, no nothing.

I've moved along with the technology. I'm on my fifth computer, upgrading every few years. The old telephone answering machine is now supplemented with e-mail.

And my family's moved along too. My small kids are small no longer. They're off to college; I'm still in my home office.

In 1974 *New York* magazine devoted an entire issue to what seemed to be a growing phenomenon—home-based businesses. Twenty-five years ago, the home as a business location was limited to famous writers and unknown freelancers, artists, and other well-known personalities—composer Jerry Herman, cookbook writer James Beard, and news anchor Walter Cronkite. Over the years I've seen more and more ordinary people become foot soldiers in the home-based business revolution. These people have all kinds of businesses—consultant, greeting card designer, electrician, financial planner, and messenger company.

Seeing this change and knowing what I know about working from home, I've taught dozens of people how to get started and realize their potential by working from home. These people come from all kinds of backgrounds—corporate America, blue collar, housewives, and professionals. All share something in common—the desire to earn money in a business all their own. Being your own boss means never having to hear the words "You're fired" (or "You're a commuter"). Now I'd like to share my ideas with you.

How to Use this Book

Want to know how to start a business from home and make sure it succeeds? Of course you do; that's why you're reading this book. Over 5 million people are expected to start up new businesses in 1997, many of these from home. But not everyone who tries to run a business from home will succeed. There are no guarantees for success. There are, however, certain things that are guaranteed to make you fail. Not knowing the pitfalls is the first mistake you want to avoid.

This book will guide you, step-by-step, in creating your own home-based business. It'll help you choose a type of business to run, organize it, and run it. The information in this book can help you whether you want to start a sideline business or go into one full-time.

This book contains six separate parts. Each part covers some aspect of running your business.

Part 1: There's No Place Like Home...to Start a Business shows you how to join the millions of others who've chosen their home as their base of business operations. You'll see that there's safety in numbers—the numbers of those who've already succeeded in becoming their own boss while working from the den or spare bedroom. You'll learn the positives of working out of your home as well as the drawbacks (yes, it's not all a bed of roses).

Part 2: Finding Your Perfect (Business) Match shows you the different ways to create a business, from buying an existing one, a franchise, or a business opportunity to going into network marketing. You'll also see how you can turn your own idea into a solid business concept. You'll test your business abilities to see if you have what it takes to put your idea into action. And you'll learn about the legalities of organizing your business—should you incorporate or find another way to go?

In **Part 3: Raising Dollars with Sense,** you'll come face to face with one of the most difficult jobs of a new business owner—finding the money to start or grow a business. Working from home doesn't mean you can't convince others you're worth investing in, if you know where to look and what you have to do to get the cash. First you'll learn to write a dynamite business plan. Then you'll find out how to estimate the amount of money you need. You'll see the different ways to get money and learn which one is best for you.

Part 4: Let's Get Physical: Setting up Your Office gives you the nuts and bolts of getting started, from setting up your office and deciding on telephone tactics to buying or leasing a computer and finding other equipment you need to run your business.

Part 5: Running Your Business. Once you've gotten started, the next step is a lulu. You can have the best idea and the best-equipped business but still not succeed. Why? Because you just don't know how to run your business. Marketing is, perhaps, the most vital part of running your business—letting the public know you exist and selling your products or services. But selling may not be enough. You have to manage your finances and taxes, as you'll see. You can really benefit from the tax breaks for home offices. And you should know how to get help when you just can't do it all. Finally, be sure that you're protected with the proper insurance from fire, theft, and other business losses that can be devastating.

Part 6: Up Close and Personal Issues exposes what goes on behind closed doors and what you can do about problems that are unique to people working alone at home. You'll learn about staying connected with the outside world. You'll also find out how to separate business from pleasure by keeping your family life out of your home office. And organization—a key to a successful business—is particularly important for home business owners with limited space and limited time. Finally, after you've followed the steps outlined in this book, you may just turn out to be a success. Maybe you're such a success that you can no longer fit your business inside your home and you have to move out. You'll see how you can stay at home as long as possible and how to move out with the least headaches when the time comes.

Road Signs

As you travel through the pages of this book, you'll see special elements signified by little pictures to guide you. They'll give you a little extra help in navigating your way through the steps of forming and running your business.

The Educated Entrepreneur

This box is a catchall: It gives you facts and figures and explores the fun of running a home-based business.

Business Buzzword
Definitions of terms and expressions used by business-people that may be new or confusing to you.

Homegrown Tip
Added info—a phone number, Web site, or idea—that can help you do a job just that much better or easier.

Home Hazard
Warnings about things you should avoid if you want to stay out of trouble.

Acknowledgments

Thanks are due to the people who've taken my courses and kept me on my toes with questions, questions, questions. They've taught me what they wanted and needed to know about starting and running home-based businesses, the very information I've included in this book. Thanks also to my friend Elliott Eiss, editor of the J.K. Lasser Tax Institute, for reviewing the tax material in this book. And I'm especially grateful to my editor, Nancy Stevenson, who patiently and skillfully helped me get my material into shape.

Special Thanks from the Publisher to the Technical Reviewer

The Complete Idiot's Guide to Starting a Home-Based Business was reviewed by an expert in the field who not only checked the technical accuracy of what you'll learn here, but also provided insight to help us ensure that this book tells you everything you need to know about home-based business success. Our special thanks are extended to David Rye.

David Rye is one of America's leading consulting authorities on the development and implementation of strategic management plans and strategies. He is also a dynamic speaker, writer, and author of several books, including the national best-seller, *Winning the Entrepreneur's Game*. He is currently the CEO for Western Publications.

Part 1
There's No Place Like Home...to Start a Business

You know what? Great-great-grandma and great-great-grandpa were probably home businesspeople: They might have run the farm or doctor's office from the front parlor. Could be they lived in a cozy apartment right above the family butcher store. But in the past several generations, things have changed: Home has become the place where a family lives and takes refuge from the outside world, a place where people go to get away from work.

But what goes around comes around: Today, for a growing number of people, home is again becoming more than just a residence. It's a marketplace to start a business and earn a living.

Your home is an ideal nest in which a business can be hatched. Working at home gets you out of the tedium of the commute and makes you your own boss. You set your own working hours, and nobody can downsize you out of a living. And all you need to get started is a great idea, right? Not quite. Oh, you need a great idea, but you also need a lot of information about things like financing, franchises, zoning, marketing, and taxes. In short, you need this book.

In this part of the book, you'll start to gel that great idea of yours. You'll find out how home businesses stack up against outside ventures. You'll see the pros and cons of starting a business from home. And you'll come to understand what special problems you may face when you run a home-based business.

The Home-Based Business Revolution

Home-based business is drawing more attention than an elephant in a shopping mall. The reason? Because home-based business is the fastest growing segment in our business community today. Ideas, products, jobs, and wealth are being created in spare bedrooms, basements, lofts, and even at the kitchen table.

The growth of home-based business in the past several years is nothing short of a revolution. Already more than 27 million strong, new home-based businesses continue to sprout up and flourish.

Only a decade ago, someone working from home might have tried to disguise his work status. It wasn't considered "professional." Folks working from home were often viewed as dabblers, not serious entrepreneurs. Home was the place for housework, not for making money. A home-based business owner in the '80s or earlier hid the fact that he did business from the basement like a mob member hides his connections.

But now the growing number of home businesspeople are just too cool: they've left the rat race behind and sit on the beach with their laptops and answer to no one. You, too, can join the growing movement of running your own business from the comforts of home.

Look Who's Working from Home

The largest enterprise in the world, the U.S. government, is run from a home office. Each day the president sits in the ultimate home office—the Oval Office—and conducts affairs of state. But the president isn't alone in working from home. Millions of individuals have already set up shop from home. Within 10 years it's predicted that one out of every three households in this country will harbor someone working from home.

The Educated Entrepreneur

A new home business starts up nearly every 10 seconds—more than 8,000 new businesses every day! That means almost 3 million new businesses in the coming year (and some experts predict as many as 5 million new home-based businesses).

Who's running these businesses? Some start working from home by choice. Others are virtually forced to begin working at home—a company relocates but a worker can't make the move, or some Fortune 500 company downsizes to Fortune 1,000 and people are lost in the shuffle.

Many home businesspeople dream of being their own boss. Others are the victims of corporate downsizing and use what they have—skills from the corporate environment and a home—to start a new career. Some home-based business owners are young, with children to care for. Others are retirees starting on second or even third careers. In other words, home-based business owners come in all shapes, sizes, and with every color dream in the rainbow.

What kinds of businesses are being run from home? Professionals—doctors, lawyers, accountants, architects—continue to swell the ranks of home-based business. So, too, do traditional home-based businesses such as child care, music lessons, interior design, crafts, and freelance writing.

New types of businesses are also being run from home. Kitchen table–based consultants can be found in just about every field—including computers, marketing, and public relations. Mail-order selling, medical billing, travel agencies, and network marketing of all kinds are just some of the newer enterprises to move into the home office.

Life in the Information Age

The growth of home business has been made possible by technology. The personal computer, photocopier, fax, modem, and, of course, the telephone allow any Jack in a bedroom in a city apartment or Jill in a den in the suburbs to become an entrepreneur.

The experts tell us that we live in the Information Age. Manufacturing is no longer the driving force of our economy. Instead, we share information via the computer and other technologies. The person running a home business can get just about the same information as any Fortune 500 company. Computers themselves have spawned more business opportunities than Edison's light bulb. Computer consultants now advise individuals and businesses on software applications. There are others who are into software development. And there are some who offer repair services for hardware and software problems.

Even if the business isn't technologically oriented (for example, craft or housecleaning businesses), computers have become an integral part of keeping a business afloat. Computers are being used for bookkeeping, marketing products and services, finding supplies, e-mail, faxing, and more.

Homegrown Tip
Being computer literate is almost as essential to succeeding in a home-based business as being able to dial a telephone. If you're not computer literate, you can get the training you need at computer stores offering training courses, special computer-training schools, adult education classes, or even at your local community college.

What Are Your Chances for Success?

Home isn't only where the heart is. It's also where the money is. Statistics show that home-based businesses are surprisingly successful. According to *Entrepreneur* magazine, the average annual income from a home business is more than $50,000; over 1.7 million home-based businesses earn six figures or more. Should you get in on all this wealth? Of course you should!

Home businesses also seem to succeed at a greater rate than non-home businesses. Some sources put the home business success rate as high as 95% after one year. According to the same sources, after three years 85% of these home businesses were still in operation (compared with just 15% of non-home small businesses). Only 5% of home-based businesses seem to fail each year.

The Birthplace of Major Corporations

The vast majority of home-based business owners who succeed continue to operate from home. But a number of hugely successful enterprises had humble beginnings in a spare bedroom or garage turned office. Lillian Vernon launched her catalog business from her kitchen table. Steve Jobs and Steve Wozniak began Apple Computer in Jobs's parents' garage (and no, I don't think he pays them a royalty to this day). Michael Dell started his computer company from his college dorm room. Calvin Klein and his partner started the apparel line in Klein's living room.

The lesson: Even if you don't intend to remain there forever, and whatever room you put your desk in, home is still a good place to get started.

Predicting the Future of Home Businesses

Home-based businesses aren't a fad. They're here to stay and the ranks should continue to swell. All age groups are represented in home businesses.

People reaching their 50s are ripe for starting their own businesses. If these hardworking boomers are laid off from their high-paying jobs, they are, for the most part, too old to re-enter the ever-shrinking pool of high-paying jobs. What's more, there's a desire to be your own boss that's stronger than the whim of salmon to swim upstream. And even those who continue to work for a paycheck may be inclined to start a sideline business to get extra cash to meet living expenses, pay for a child's education, or save for retirement.

The Educated Entrepreneur

The average age of a self-employed individual working from home is 43 years old. Women own 66% of all home businesses, but men have caught on to a good thing: ownership by men is growing fast.

Seniors who want or need to earn additional income, to feel productive, or to channel their creative and entrepreneurial impulses are starting businesses from home. Many are into their second or third career!

And, increasingly, Generation X-ers are turning to home businesses in surprising numbers. They've seen the writing on the wall and know that job security is a contradiction in terms. Instead of waiting to get a pink slip from a corporate employer, they're launching their own business ventures from home. And their youth makes it easier to take the risk of business ownership and still have time to run back to the corporate fold if things don't work out.

The Least You Need to Know

➤ The number of home-based businesses continues to grow at an impressive rate.

➤ Home business offers the opportunity for full-time or part-time work.

➤ Home-based businesses have a higher success rate than businesses started outside the home.

➤ People of all ages are getting into home-based businesses.

Chapter 2

Why Start from Home?

In This Chapter
➤ Saving time and money with a home-based business
➤ Gaining flexibility by working from home
➤ Benefiting from part-time employment
➤ Understanding the drawbacks of working from home

As you learned in Chapter 1, home-based businesses are overwhelmingly successful. In this chapter you'll learn some of the business reasons for this success. You'll also see some of the reasons why working from home can be the best personal lifestyle around.

But nothing, even working at home in sweats and munching cookies while you work, is perfect. You'll see that not everything about a home business is positive. There are drawbacks you should consider before launching your own home-based business. Understanding the disadvantages will prepare you for the less attractive consequences of working from home.

You're Already Paying the Rent (or the Mortgage)

Starting any business costs money. But the amount you need to launch and run a business from home is less than if you had to rent office space in the local office complex. You're already paying rent or the mortgage on your home. You're already heating and cooling it. It generally doesn't cost you any more to use a portion of your home for business.

Homegrown Tip
You may be able to write off the costs of using your home for business on your personal tax return (which further reduces your costs) as explained in Chapter 22, "Home Office Tax Shelter."

Low overhead may be the prime reason why home-based businesses are so successful. They can afford to be! Low overhead—what it costs to pay for space and utilities—means that you don't need to earn as much to cover expenses. The earnings from your home business that don't go into office overhead can go into your pocket. You can reinvest that moolah in the business in the form of advertising, travel and entertainment expenses, equipment, and inventory. It didn't cost me anything to start my business from home. I used what I already owned—a small office, a typewriter, and a telephone—to get rolling.

Short Commute: From Bedroom to Boardroom

This is one of the big benefits of a home business. When you run a business from home, you don't board a train or bus, or get caught in gridlocked traffic to get to work. You simply get dressed (if you want to) and go down the hall or up the stairs to your office when you're ready to get to work.

Eliminating the commute saves you in two ways. First, you save time. Many who hold jobs outside the home commute 30 minutes, an hour, or more each way every day. The commuting time you save can be used in other ways. You can use it in your business, for your personal stuff, or even to get an extra 40 winks.

Getting rid of the commute also saves you money. The cost of commuting—the commuter ticket, gas for your car, parking, tolls, cab rides—can be steep. Over the course of a year they can total over $1,000—not to mention the aggravation of choice words and gestures from less-than-polite cab drivers. You paid for the cost of commuting while you were working outside of your home with a portion of each paycheck. And you couldn't even deduct it on your tax return!

The money saved by not commuting, just like the time saved, can be used in other ways. You can put it into your business, take the family out to dinner once a week, or save it for a rainy day. Use the worksheet below to see how much you now spend on working outside of your home. This translates into what you'd save by working at home. Enter your costs on a monthly basis. Then multiply by 12 to see your yearly costs.

What You'd Save by Working at Home

Item	Cost
Commuting Cost	
Car expenses (gas, tolls)	$_____
Train fare	$_____
Bus fare	$_____
Taxi fare	$_____
Clothing (additional cost)	
Suits, dresses	$_____
Panty hose, other accessories	$_____
Food	
Coffee breaks	$_____
Lunches out	$_____
Other	
Day care	$_____
Total	$_____

Combine Work with...Whatever

A lot of people find it difficult to leave home for work when there are children (or elderly parents) to care for. In situations like this, you have to deal with the emotional and financial costs of day care. Some may be lucky to have a parent or in-law available to come over and watch the kiddies during the day, but many don't. Most are forced to hire private help to care for their children. The cost of good child care runs from substantial to outrageous. Some people simply can't afford to work because of the high cost of day care. When the cost of day care is added to the cost of commuting, working outside the home may make about as much sense as buying an Edsel.

And even if money isn't the issue, many parents don't like to be separated from their children all day. If you, too, want to be near the kids, then working from home might be for you. You may be able to earn money from home *and* take care of your children yourself.

Even if you're not *required* to stay home to watch the children because they're old enough to fend for themselves, you may *prefer* to work from home. The heck with the V-chip: you'll be there to see them off to school in the morning and welcome them back at three o'clock when they return from school. Working at home may even allow you the flexibility to go to a school play or watch an after-school game.

The Educated Entrepreneur

According to some surveys, the majority of people working from home—female and male—do so in part because of the kids.

Care of children is not the only at-home responsibility faced by the modern working man or woman. Increasingly, there are elderly parents to care for. In fact, statistics show that women spend on average not only 17 years as caregivers for their children, but also 18 years as caregivers for parents. (The statistics don't say what the guys are doing with this spare 35 years.)

With demographics supporting the graying of our population, this parent-care responsibility can only be expected to grow. The cost of hiring someone to care for an elderly parent can be much more than the cost of child care. People who can't afford to pay this high cost might be forced to quit a job to help out mom or dad. If you have to provide care for an ill or infirm parent, working from home might just be a great way to have it all.

More than 2 million Americans, mostly women, are caught in the double whammy of caring for both their own children and their parents at the same time. These aren't easy situations, but you may just be able to juggle all this and relieve some financial pressure by working from home.

Flexibility

Working from home usually gives you greater flexibility in your schedule. You can work when it's convenient for you and take care of your life when you want. Of course, the demands of your home business don't *always* permit this kind of freedom. Many people find they work *longer* hours when they run a home business. This is especially true when you are just getting started. But generally speaking, even if you work long hours, you can pretty much schedule your time the way you want to.

Working from home might also give you the time you need to stop and smell the roses. You may want to join a health club, take classes to improve your business skills, or do volunteer work—things that just wouldn't be possible for you if you held a 9-to-5 job. For example, Jonathan is a financial planner who runs his business from a basement office. Johnny was able to train for the New York City marathon by arranging his client appointments around his training schedule. The time he saved by not having to commute, combined with the fact that he's his own boss, let him run around New York City for the sheer pleasure of it.

Home Hazard
Flexibility means *more* planning, not less. Those with a 9-to-5 schedule know they have to clean the house and do the shopping after work. When you run a home-based business, what do you consider "after hours"? Be sure to give yourself separate times for work and family.

Test the Waters by Starting Part-Time

Starting any business is risky. Even with the success rate of home businesses, there's no guarantee against failure. But starting out part-time can offer you a leg up. You can begin your business on a part-time basis to see if you can cut it. Does somebody need your product or service? Can you provide it?

Part-Time Business, Full-Time Salary

There's an important financial payback to starting out part-time from home. You still get your paycheck to cover your personal expenses. This takes the financial pressure off. The nest egg you need to get going is reduced considerably because you don't have to cover your rent or mortgage. You might even be able to use some of your pay to cover the expenses of your home business.

Staying Part-Time

Many people who start a home-based business have no intention of having it take over their lives. They look upon the business as a nice sideline. The part-time business can provide a little extra cash for those extra expenses.

A part-time sideline business can also be an outlet for something you like to do but can't do full-time. For example, if you love kids, you might enjoy having a sideline day care business from home with no intention of developing it into a full-time activity.

Don't Be an Ostrich!

Sure there are a lot of advantages to working from home: cost savings, an end to the commuting rat race, and greater flexibility. But it's not all gravy. If you want to run a business from home, go in with your eyes open. It'll save you from heartache down the road.

The Price You Pay for Working from Home

When you work from home, your house is no longer just your castle. It's also the place you get calls from annoying clients, create clutter with stacks of paper, and go nuts when a project falls through. This means that your work life begins to spill over into your personal life. There are several consequences.

You may be bringing the business public—clients, customers, or patients—into your home on a regular basis. This means a certain loss of privacy. Your family, your pets, your lifestyle (and even your dirty laundry) may be visible to strangers. You have to be comfortable with this change. If you're the private type, think twice about giving up your day job.

But giving up privacy is just one consequence of working from home. The other, for some, may be the loss of space. Before starting the business your family had the run of the joint. Now you have to use a room or two for business. Whatever was going on in the space now used for your office has to be pushed into other parts of your home. If you convert a spare bedroom into a home office, where will the in-laws stay when they're in town?

Now, personally I like the quiet and solitude of being alone all day, with my interruptions limited to an occasional phone call. But not everyone's like me. Being tied to your home virtually all day long may drive you right up the wall. You may be the kind who thrives on a daily change of scenery. You may feel like living and working in the same place is akin to being handcuffed in a very small closet. If so, you have to deal with the problem. Of course, just because your business is home-based doesn't mean you necessarily have to work at home all the time. For example, a plumber might use her home to schedule appointments, order supplies, and bill for jobs. But basically she's out in the field all day long, banging on pipes and playing with snakes.

A Lifestyle Change...for the Better?

When you work in an office you basically have a 9-to-5 focus on business. Of course, many jobs require travel and a lot more hours than just 9-to-5. But essentially, all jobs outside the home more or less stay outside the home. However, when you work at home, you're never far from your business. The work is always there. You can leave your office, but you can only go so far.

A change in lifestyle involves not only you but also those near and dear to you. Your family may know very well that you're in business, but they may continue to treat you as if you're on 24-hour call. My husband still wanders into the office just wanting to chat from time to time. You need to educate the folks who live with you to the fact that during working hours you're basically not there.

Starting a business from home is like being a double agent. First, you have to get used to working where you live and having the work always there. (Separating work from pleasure is discussed in Chapter 23.) Second, the change from being someone else's employee to being your own boss can be a difficult transition. Because you're starting a business, you're now in charge. You have to get to know every aspect of running a business—which is discussed throughout this book. This is more than just a technical orientation. It's a psychological one as well. You have to get used to the idea of shouldering all the responsibility for your business.

Homegrown Tip
Make sure household members—your spouse, your children, and your dog—know the rules when you're working at home. A closed office door shouldn't be opened without knocking. Interruptions for simple questions should be kept to a minimum (or, preferably, held until after working hours).

Learning to forego the social aspects of working outside the home is another lifestyle change to consider. No longer will you learn the latest scoop while at the office water cooler. Working at home means you're more or less alone for the greater part of the day. (Creative solutions for dealing with isolation are discussed at length in Chapter 25, "Working Alone and Loving It.")

But with all the changes you'll go through, starting your home-based business can still be the most rewarding way to live, and if you want to do it, you can make it happen.

The Least You Need to Know

➤ It's less costly to start a business from home than from outside the home.

➤ Working from home saves you time and money by not having to commute.

➤ Working from home lets you combine earning a livelihood with child care (or parent care).

➤ Starting out part-time from home can help to ensure business success.

➤ Working from home may require a few adjustments on your part (for example, giving up living space and privacy).

➤ Working from home means the business is never far away.

➤ Working at home can be lonely.

Part 2
Finding Your Perfect (Business) Match

You may be sold on the idea of running a business from home. But do you have what it takes? Only you can answer that important question. You need to have the entrepreneurial skills, the emotional mettle, and the energy to run your own business. You also need to have the support of your family and friends.

But once you're satisfied that you're up to the task of being a business owner, it's time to pick your poison—the type of business you'll go into. What do you like, and what are you good at? What does the public want, and what kind of business can you afford to start? And, of course, what kind of business can you run from the spare bedroom?

In this part of the book, you score your business abilities to see where they can take you. You get direction in focusing ideas you may already have. And you learn about prepackaged businesses—franchises, existing businesses, network marketing opportunities, and more. Finally, once you figure out what type of business to start, you learn about options for organizing it from a legal standpoint.

Chapter 3

Do What You Love and the Bucks Will Roll in

In This Chapter

➤ Finding your entrepreneurial IQ

➤ Developing a business idea from what you already know

➤ Turning a passion into a product or service

Wherever you go people are the same, but they're also really different: What they like and don't like is often a mystery. Where one person may be a people person who'll do well in sales, another may shun public contact like the plague. To know what type of business you're best suited for you have to take a good hard look at your personality and skills.

In this chapter you'll learn to recognize your strengths and weaknesses to help you determine whether business ownership of any kind is right for you. Once you're convinced that you want to be your own boss and have what it takes to succeed, you'll also find out about how you can make the skills you already have work for you.

What's Your Entrepreneurial IQ?

Do you have what it takes to succeed in business? Education, experience, desire, and luck are all things that can determine the success or failure of any business. There's no magic

> **Business Buzzword**
>
> An *entrepreneur* is someone who organizes and directs a business, assuming the risk in the hopes of making a profit.

formula. Still, by taking a close and honest look at yourself, you can at least be assured that you're not doomed from the start. You can discover your strengths and can be alert to your weaknesses.

Let's assume you have what it takes to be an entrepreneur. Now you need to be brutally honest with yourself about your strengths and weaknesses so you can determine the *type* of home-based business that's right for you.

Take Your Personal Inventory

Take the following inventory of your personal traits and abilities. Check one box beside each question to indicate whether you agree with, disagree with, or aren't sure of each statement.

	Agree	Disagree	Not Sure
1. I want to be my own boss.	☑	☐	☐
2. I can readily make decisions.	☑	☐	☐
3. I can take responsibility.	☑	☐	☐
4. I can plan ahead.	☑	☐	☐
5. I'm a leader.	☑	☐	☐
6. I like competition.	☑	☐	☐
7. I'm organized.	☑	☐	☐
8. I'm a hard worker.	☑	☐	☐
9. I'm physically able to work long hours.	☑	☐	☐
10. I can handle stress.	☑	☐	☐
11. I'm prepared to make financial sacrifices.	☑	☐	☐
12. I have the know-how to run a business.	☐	☐	☑
13. I'm a fast learner.	☑	☐	☐
14. I have the education to run this business.	☐	☐	☑
15. I know how to sell my product or service.	☐	☐	☑
16. I'm a good communicator.	☑	☐	☐
17. I work well with people.	☑	☐	☐

Now look over your answers. Add up those answers where you checked "Agree." The more of these boxes you checked, the better your shot at entrepreneurial success. There's no magic number that you needed to check to "pass" the test. Just be honest with yourself about your shortcomings and work on them.

Your Personality Can Make the Difference

Wanting to run a business is just the first step in deciding whether you have the personality to give it a try. The test you just took shows you whether you have the characteristics that will serve you well in business—desire to succeed, leadership, being comfortable with risk taking, and the ability to tackle hard work.

Here's a list of other words that are often used to describe the entrepreneurial type. See how many of these words you think can be used to describe you:

➤ Confident

➤ Determined

➤ Disciplined

➤ Innovative

➤ Optimistic

➤ Positive

You may not have *all* these traits. Don't let that stop you. You can pick up some of this stuff as you go along. For example, if you've never been a manager or supervisor, how can you know whether you have leadership ability? Obviously, you can't. But by *assuming* a leadership role you may be surprised to learn how well it suits you. Or maybe you've taken a leadership role outside of the business world—heading up the PTA or running a community fund drive—and you don't even recognize it.

Maybe taking risks gets your knees knocking and your heart pounding. Again, as you begin to run your business and learn to take setbacks in stride, your tolerance for risks may rise.

And even if you're sure you'll never be a great communicator, you can always choose a business that plays down public contact. You don't have to go in for selling a product where razzle-dazzle presentations are the order of the day; you may be able to perform a service, like bookkeeping or medical transcription, out of the limelight, in the privacy of your kitchen.

Your Skills (or Who Are You Today?)

If you think your current job has you wearing a lot of hats, be prepared to open a hat superstore when you start your own business. First, you have to have the technical skill for your particular business (for example, computer knowledge to run a computer-based business or artistic ability to run an interior design business).

Homegrown Tip
Even if you don't have a specific skill to base your business on, you can learn one. There are more courses offered by colleges and continuing education programs than fish in the sea. For example, you can learn medical coding (the codes used by insurance companies to identify and pay doctors for specific procedures or treatments). Once you've learned the coding, you can then set up a home business to work with doctors in making insurance claims.

But whatever business you run, you also need *many* other skills. You need to become an entrepreneur. You need to be able to market your business, whether it's a service or a product. You need to be able to juggle finances—raising capital to start up and grow, managing cash flow, and purchasing. You need to work well with others—hiring employees or subcontractors, working with professional advisors, and keeping customers happy. If you really want your own business, you can always buy another hat (I mean, acquire a new skill).

You can teach yourself in a number of areas. The different chapters in this book will add to your knowledge on accounting, taxes, and many other topics. Reading magazines, newsletters, newspapers, and books will help you keep up-to-date in the area of your business and in business developments in general. You can also take classes. In the adult education class I teach for people starting up a home-based business, taxes, insurance, and finding money for the business are the main topics of interest to almost all students. If you've never operated a computer—an essential today for running most every business—you may want to take an adult education course or a course at a local college. And, of course, experience is the best teacher. You'll become a better salesperson, for example, with every sale you make.

Homegrown Tip
Don't hesitate to turn to experts for help. For example, SCORE (Service Corps of Retired Executives), a volunteer organization under the auspices of the Small Business Administration, provides free advice to budding entrepreneurs. You can find the SCORE location nearest you by calling the SBA at 800-827-5722 or by checking your phone directory.

Your Experience

You may know more than you think you know. What kind of experience do you have? Whatever business experience you have may prove helpful in starting your own business.

Have you ever run a business before? The more experience you have, the better off you are. But even if you've always worked for a weekly pay stub, you may still have enough business experience to be successful. By simply working for a business you may have picked up valuable information on how to run a business (or, as many disgruntled employees claim, how NOT to run a business). And even if you lack business experience of any kind, if you've run a household, budgeted to buy a new car, or coached Little League, you've already picked up some important business skills in the areas of budgeting, purchasing, and personnel.

Even if you have general business experience, what do you know about the particular business you're considering? Have you ever worked in the field—even as an employee—before? Obviously, the more you know about the field, the better off you'll be. But even if you've never set foot near someone who has done this kind of work, you may be able to translate your experience in a related area into valuable help for your business.

For example, you have experience in a retail clothing store. Now you want to start your own mail-order business to sell clothes you design. You don't have experience in mail order, but you might be able to use your knowledge of selling clothes to research fashion markets and create a catalog. You know clothes; you know selling. Don't sell your experience in any other business short.

Your Financial Picture

Your personal financial picture, rosy or not, will affect how you view your home business—how much you can afford to put into it and what you expect to get out of it. For example, if you're retired and living on a pension, then a home business may only have to supplement your income. The same is true if you have a full-time job and only expect the home business to be a sideline for generating extra cash. But if you've been laid off, your home business may just be your bread and butter. You'll learn how to estimate what you think you'll need to live on while your business gets going in Chapter 9, "Paying the Bills While Paying Your Dues."

The kind of business you choose is influenced—a lot—by your bank book. How much do you have to invest? How much can you borrow? Some businesses require a small endowment to get started. It may cost thousands of dollars to buy the equipment or inventory needed to get up and running. Are you in a financial position to come up with the bucks you need to get going? Many other home businesses—day care services, cleaning services, and even consulting businesses—can be started with a few hundred dollars.

Start with What You Know

You want to start a business in the worst way, but you're not sure what that business should be. How do you find a business marriage made in heaven? Start with what you know. The idea for a business might be right in front of your nose. Your real world interests and skills may easily translate into a business concept.

For example, you may love kids and be great at taking care of them. You might consider a day care business right in your home. (This may make very good sense if you're already caring for your own children.) Or you may be a shrewd shopper and know the malls better than you know your in-laws. For you, a business as a personal shopper—for clothing, gifts, home furnishings—might make sense.

Downsized but Upgraded

If you've been laid off because the company you worked for relocated or downsized, you may already have chosen your business—even if you don't know it yet. Your old job may be the basis for your new business.

Home Hazard

More than 5 million workers have been laid off from Fortune 500 companies in the past 10 years. Don't wait to be a statistic. Begin thinking about starting your own home-based business now.

Suppose you worked in personnel and have been offered an early retirement package that you couldn't refuse. You might be able to use all the tricks you picked up in the corporate world to run your own business. Consider starting a personnel agency or a head hunting firm to find jobs for other people. Or you might want to start a temporary agency.

Consider the skills you've learned at a corporate job and then look to apply those skills in your own business. If you were in marketing, maybe you should start your own advertising or promotion agency. If you were a secretary, you might be able to start your own transcription business. The opportunities are limitless.

The Educated Entrepreneur

Of managers laid off over the age of 40, 87.5% choose to start their own businesses. Many of these businesses are home-based.

Everybody's a Consultant

It seems that today nobody is just out of work; everybody's a consultant. Many of the skills learned in the corporate world lend themselves to consulting. This is a popular home-based business activity.

As a consultant you're providing a service to others. Maybe you're a whiz at computers. You can offer your services in a variety of ways: helping people buy and set up equipment, teaching software programs, setting up Web sites, and designing software applications.

The Educated Entrepreneur

Business consulting is, perhaps, the most popular home-based business activity with more than 5 million individuals calling themselves *consultants*. These people offer services in almost anything: information management, dog psychology, human resources, and software development.

Consultants can command high hourly rates for their services. But don't expect to be an overnight success. It may take months or even years to build up a consulting business to the point of equaling or surpassing corporate pay for comparable work. And, when you add in corporate benefits—health insurance, a retirement plan, an expense account—it can be even longer for self-employment to match that weekly paycheck. It takes time to develop business contacts. If you go into consulting, be prepared to use your savings, a spouse's income, Aunt Edna's inheritance, or a loan to carry you for as long as three years before the business is fully profitable.

Some start their consulting work on a part-time basis, moonlighting with their day job. If you choose to begin part-time, you'll get the opportunity to develop your business contacts (which can take considerable time) without having to rely on the income from consulting to buy the groceries.

If you begin a consulting business as your full-time occupation, be prepared for working long hours—even longer than when you had a full-time job. And, again, it may take time before you'll see big bucks.

Business Buzzword

The *Internet* is a worldwide computer network that you can access with the right equipment (a computer, a modem, and a telephone line) and an online service (America Online, CompuServe, Prodigy) or an Internet service provider. Even if you don't own the necessary equipment, you may be able to gain access for free at your local library.

Turn a Hobby into a Money Maker

According to some experts, many people start home-based businesses so they can have more interesting work. And what is more interesting than doing what you love? If you have a hobby, it's an activity that you already love and know about. You may be able to turn your hobby into a full-fledged business.

Love antiques? You may be able to become an antique dealer without leaving home. The Internet allows you to buy and sell your wares virtually worldwide. Have a special craft skill? Produce your art at home and sell it at craft shows, flea markets, or in local gift shops.

The Educated Entrepreneur

According to one home-based business franchise's literature, craft manufacturing accounts for about 4% of the home-business market.

The Least You Need to Know

➤ Understand your personal strengths and weaknesses.

➤ Make sure you have the personality to be an entrepreneur.

➤ Make sure you have the skills to run a business.

➤ Use skills learned in the real world or the corporate world as the basis of your business.

➤ You can turn a hobby into a business.

Create a Business Concept

Once you've determined that a home business is something you want and will be good at, you have to narrow down the field to find *the* business that's perfect for you. Here's where your creativity and ingenuity pay off. In this chapter you'll find out about starting a home-based business from the ground up. You'll learn how to develop a business concept by bringing your idea into razor-sharp focus. You'll also learn how to find out whether there's a need for your business concept in the marketplace. Finally, you'll learn about the all-important business of writing a business plan.

Fine-Tune Your Idea

You know you want to start a home-based business. Great. You may even know what type of business you want to run—a consulting business, selling products through catalogs, or whatever. Even better. But these vague ideas have to be fine-tuned before you can proceed. You have to work out all the particulars. So let's get specific.

You can't simply decide to be a consultant or start a catalog business. You have to clearly define the service you'll be offering as a consultant or products you'll be selling through a catalog. If you plan to be a consultant, presumably you know the general area you'll be consulting in (for example, management advice or computers). But you have to get even more specific. For example, as a consultant for computers, will you be providing advice to individuals or to corporations? Will you write a newsletter about computers or service them door-to-door?

This might seem like a simple exercise, but give it a whirl: To help you focus your idea, try explaining it to others. You might see that in your first few explanations you're about as clear as mud. Try to be specific. Try to address the four Ws: What, Who, Where, and When.

➤ *What* will you be doing? What product or service will you be offering? Why would anyone pay good money for this?

➤ *Who* will you be selling your product or service to once you run out of friends and relatives? The guy on the street? Fortune 500 companies?

➤ *Where* will you be selling your product or service? Are you going to bring every Tom, Dick, and Harry into your home for the sale? Will you put an ad in the paper? Will you sell through the Internet? Via mail order?

➤ *When* will you be selling your product or service? Are you starting part-time? Full-time? Are your sales seasonal?

The more concise you can get in your answers, the better off you'll be. As soon as you can describe your business concept in one or two sentences, then you have a place to begin.

Test Your Concept

After you think you've clarified your idea, then make sure it will fly. Take the time to investigate the marketplace and find out whether there's room for you in it. It could take months to complete this phase of preparation for your business. But the time you take to do the legwork is time well spent. After all, why put the money and the effort into something that has no chance to succeed? Find out at the beginning whether your concept is a winner.

But Will It Fly?

Is your idea for a business practical? It may sound great as a concept, but when you get into some of the specifics—looking at cost, how you'll reach the marketplace, and other considerations—does the business really make sense? One business my husband and I tried to start but never really got off the ground was a mail-order prescription drug business. After some investigation we learned that to run the business we needed a licensed pharmacist and pharmacy space that met state code requirements. Since my husband isn't a pharmacist and neither am I, the whole concept collapsed. It just wasn't practical for *us* to run this type of business (but it might work for you if you're a pharmacist). Your business idea has to be one that's doable. You have to be able to have a realistic expectation of making a profit, if not immediately, then sometime in the foreseeable future.

But Will It Fit in the Spare Bedroom?

In figuring out if your idea is far-fetched or the real thing, be sure to take into account your base of operations—your home. Can this business succeed from a kitchen table? If your business has more people coming and going from your house than attend the World Series, it may simply not be possible to accommodate that traffic because of zoning laws or lack of parking. Here are some factors to consider:

➤ Space in your home. If, for example, you plan to run an inventory-intensive business, do you have the storage space for the inventory?

➤ Suitability of the space for the business. If you want to bring clients or customers into your home for business, is there a room that can be used for this? If, for example, you have young children, how will your major client react to squeaky toys underfoot and wet diapers in the bathroom?

➤ Zoning restrictions. Local zoning ordinances might frown on the kind of business you want to run from home. For example, zoning rules might say you can't have employees (other than family members who live with you), you mustn't post signs, and you absolutely can't run certain types of businesses from home. Zoning (how to check out restrictions and get around them) is discussed in Chapter 13, "Office Space in Your Place."

➤ Parking availability. If you need to have a constant flow of clients and customers coming to your home, is there enough parking space? Will you be violating any zoning laws?

But Will Anyone Buy It?

You may think that your idea for a product or service sounds like the best thing since MTV, but will the public agree? Don't bet the farm solely on your opinion. Do a little market research to find out if the idea will fly. Here are five things you need to learn in order to assess demand:

➤ Who will be buying your product or service? Try to develop a *customer profile*. For example, if you plan to offer personal shopping services to busy executives, define who will fit into this category. Include age ranges, sex (if limited to a single sex), income level, and any other relevant factors.

➤ How many people would be able to use your product or service? Try to fix some number for the *market size*. Statistical information, such as a local census, is readily available at your public library. If you want to sell customized children's books in your neighborhood, find out how many children between the ages of two and ten (or whatever the ages for which the books are suitable) are in your area. There may be 1,000, 10,000, or more. Remember that even the best salesperson will only capture a certain percentage of the potential market. If your market size is only 1,000, you may not be able to make a profit even if you sold to every single one of them; if your market size is a million, maybe sales to 5 or 10% would be enough to make you money (5% of a million is 50,000, and that ain't hay).

➤ Where will you sell your products or service? Be practical in setting your *market area*. Be sure to consider what it will cost you to travel, ship goods, and otherwise service your clients or customers.

➤ What are you up against in terms of *competition*? Check out your phone directory and the local papers to see who is offering a product or service similar to yours. In assessing the competition, be sure to take into account *pricing, quality, and service*. You'll learn more about this in Chapter 16, "Marketing Magic."

➤ What *special factors* might influence demand? For example, you may be offering a trendy product. Remember that trends come and go. Read up on your industry to learn more about trends and predictions for the future.

Business Buzzword

Test marketing is introducing a product or service to a limited area, measuring sales interest, and then projecting what demand would be if the product or service were available to a larger area.

If you have a product that you want to sell, try to forecast what the demand for that product will be. You can do this by *test marketing* that product.

It's a sad fact, but true, that many people don't take the time to do any market research. I confess I've occasionally been one of them. I just jumped into my home business without first checking out my market size or even the competition. But I was lucky. You may not be as lucky, and lack of preparation can doom you. There are many ways in which you can do free or low-cost market research to determine demand. Here are some ideas:

➤ Write your own questionnaire. Look for feedback about the product or service you're planning to offer. Distribute the questionnaire to prospective customers and clients. For example, mail them out to those within your neighborhood. Or even hand them out in the parking lot of the local mall.

➤ Use existing market research. Use your computer to find information, or go to your local library and ask the reference librarian to help you out. Even your local chamber of commerce may have existing market studies it will share.

➤ Talk to some local bankers who make business loans. They're familiar with similar businesses in the area and might be able to tell you how well businesses like yours are doing.

➤ Contact industry and trade associations. Typically they have their own market studies that are available for a fee.

➤ Run a "test" ad in your local newspaper. See what kind of interest in your product or service is generated by the ad. Of course, don't dabble in false advertising by making promises in the ad you won't be able to keep (such as delivery within two weeks when it would take you longer just to get the product in from your supplier). If you have only 50 samples on hand, offer them to the first 50 ad responses.

Homegrown Tip
Even if you can't satisfy all who respond to your "test" ad, take names and numbers or addresses. You can use these names to build up a future customer list.

Finding Your Niche

Suppose you conclude that your idea is just dandy. That's great. But now you have to go one step further and continue to refine your business concept so that you can find your niche.

In your front hall a niche is a little cut-out recess in the wall that's set apart from the rest of the area. That's sort of what a business niche is: it's what sets you apart. Let's say, for example, you determine that your area can support another travel agency that you plan to run from your home. How do you plan to distinguish yourself from the competition? Are you going to offer lower prices? Are you going to offer better service? Are you going to confine your business to a particular specialty of travel, such as the cruise ship business or bus tours? Whatever you can do to separate yourself from your competitors will work to your advantage. Don't think that specializing, which trims your market size, is necessarily bad. There may be plenty of room for your specialization, and it might just help you target your potential customers much more accurately.

Sizing Up the Competition

To help you define your niche, you must size up the competition. What are they doing right? What could you do better? What's the competition failing to do that you may be able to do?

The market research that you conducted to determine whether there'd be demand for your business may have already exposed the strengths and weaknesses of the competition. If not, you can size up the competition by becoming a consumer yourself and sampling what's out there. For example, suppose you want to start a residential cleaning service. Call the competition and see how they respond. Did they get back to you promptly? Were they friendly? Helpful? Responsive to your needs? Their negatives can be your positives. Try out their service in your own home (even if you don't learn much, at least you'll get the windows cleaned). Did you like their work? Their price? Where the competition failed to measure up to your expectations, you can design your business to shine. You may find that they're very good. In that case, you may have to specialize (offering only carpet and rug cleaning rather than general cleaning services or offering 24-hour scheduling).

Positioning Your Prices

Think about the last time you made a major purchase, say a car, a dining room set, or a TV. The price tag was important, but that wasn't all you considered. If it was you wouldn't have had to spend three hours making your decision: you'd have just asked for the cheapest one right off the bat.

Pricing won't be the only thing that separates you from your competition either, but there's no doubt it's important. Most consumers today are price conscious. Your price for your goods or services must be realistic; you have to be able to make a profit from what you sell. And the public must understand your pricing policy.

If you charge lower prices than the competition—something that home-based businesses can often afford to do because of lower overhead—you don't want to come off as offering inferior goods or services. The public can become suspicious and worry they're not getting quality merchandise. You may even have to explain *why* you charge lower prices. For example, if you can buy more economically than your competitor (because you have some special connection with a distributor), then tell the public that "we pass our savings on to you."

If you charge higher prices, make sure the public understands what additional benefit they're getting. Many are willing to pay higher prices for something if there is added value, such as a personal service, a longer warranty, or a money back guarantee. Learning how to set your price is covered in more detail in Chapter 16.

Put Your Idea in Writing

The best way to formulate your business concept is to put it in writing. This means writing a *business plan*. The details on how to write a business plan are discussed in Chapter 8, "So, Why Do I Need a Business Plan?"

A lot of folks start a home-based business as a casual sideline. This is a mistake. If you fail to take the business seriously, others may not take you seriously. Writing a business plan shows serious intent. There are several other important reasons to write a business plan:

> **Business Buzzword**
> A *business plan* is a written report of varying length (typically five to ten pages) in which you describe what your business is all about and where you want it to go in the future.

➤ Organize your ideas. You may *think* you have things straight, but until you put them in writing you can't be sure. For example, you may have thought about how you'll sell your services, but maybe you haven't thought through the money you'll need to meet your advertising budget. To complete your report, you may even have to do additional research on your idea.

➤ Learn the strengths and weaknesses of your business concept. As you develop your plan you'll find what aspects of your concept are real winners. You'll also learn where your idea just doesn't hold water. In the plan you'll be addressing all aspects of business operations—personnel, marketing, finance. By writing the plan, you'll find out what areas you need to learn more about. For example, when you put everything in writing you may discover that you just can't do it all yourself. You may have to hire a clerk, hire an assistant, subcontract out, or bring in a partner.

➤ Have a road map for the future. You wouldn't drive from Orlando to Des Moines without a map: why venture into the world of home business any less prepared? Having an idea will only bring you so far. You have to be able to put that idea into action. How will you take your idea and turn it into a working business? What will you do first? What will you do next? A business plan can serve as your road map to bring you from point A to point B. The business plan will not only serve to get you started, but it can also help you grow your business in the first few years.

➤ Have a presentation package to raise money. Banks and just about anyone else who's thinking about loaning you money or investing in your business will want to see that you know your business, have thought through your needs, have considered your problems, and have put it all together in a businesslike way.

The Educated Entrepreneur

Less than half of all businesses have taken the time to write a business plan. This factor alone may account for some business failures. Don't be among them! While having a business plan is no guarantee of success, it does provide a structure to build on.

The Least You Need to Know

➤ Clearly define your business idea.

➤ Take time to research your prospective business idea.

➤ Check out demand for your product or service.

➤ Find your niche in the industry.

➤ Size up the competition to position your business.

➤ Write a business plan.

Chapter 5

The Franchise Option: Business in a Box

In This Chapter

➤ Franchising your way into business

➤ Finding a franchise just for you

➤ Protecting yourself as a franchise consumer

In the previous chapter you learned how to develop a business concept from scratch. But why reinvent the wheel if somebody's already created your dream business? You may be able to *buy* a concept that's already been developed. What's more, the concept has already been tested. The existing concept comes prepackaged in something called a franchise.

In this chapter you'll learn all about franchises. You'll find out what they are and how to find the right franchise for you. You'll also learn how to protect yourself if you decide to buy and operate a franchise.

What Is a Franchise?

More than 125 years ago, Isaac Singer developed the idea of franchising to sell his sewing machines. Nobody really lugs sewing machines door-to-door anymore, but the concept of a franchise has endured and prospered. You probably go to a franchise on a regular basis. When's the last time you went to McDonalds, perhaps the most successful franchise in the world, for example? Well, you can't install golden arches on your front lawn, so that's not quite the ticket for a home business. But there are many money-making franchises that can be run from home, as you'll see in a few minutes.

Before you can select a franchise, get to know the players. A *franchise* is a business arrangement that gives you the right to sell a product or service in a particular area. The company that sells the concept is called the *franchisor*. The person who buys the concept—you in this case—is the *franchisee*.

Business Buzzword

A *master franchise* is the right to a large territory such as a state, a country, or even a portion of the globe—for example, the North American area. (Get the North American area for McDonalds and you can retire tomorrow.)

By buying a franchise, you get a "name" and the public recognition that goes along with it. You pay for the right to sell the product or service under this name by paying an up-front fee to the franchisor and a percentage of your sales each year. In some cases you also have to buy goods or services that generate additional payments to the franchisor. If the franchise has been around for a number of years, you're assured of getting a proven business concept.

The Educated Entrepreneur

There are between 3,000 and 5,000 franchise options currently available to you, and many of these can be run from home. Franchises account for 33% of all retail sales in this country.

When you buy a franchise you're essentially buying structure in exchange for some of your operating freedom. Why the loss of freedom? You generally have to run your business by the rules of the franchisor. For example, with a service franchise the franchisor can essentially dictate *how* a service is to be provided. Also, with a franchise you can only do business in the location where the franchisor gives you the nod (called a *territory*).

What a Franchise Can Offer

So, what do you get out of this? A good franchisor can offer you a proven track record of success in getting people started. Here are some of the things you can and should expect to receive when buying the franchise:

➤ Training. The franchisor may give you training on how to run the business. This training may be at the franchisor's headquarters. Or it may be in the form of training manuals, audios, and videos. For example, if the franchise is for pet-sitting, the training would probably involve exactly how you keep Fido happy (how many visits should you make to feed and walk each "client," what duties should be performed, and what should you do in an emergency).

➤ Procedures. The franchisor provides step-by-step information on how to run the business. The franchisor should instruct you on the administrative end of the business: advertising your services or product, writing the paychecks, and keeping the books.

➤ Product. Here's where franchisors make a lot of bucks. The franchise provides the products you'll sell. You may also have to purchase ancillary products (not the product you're selling to the public but products you may also use in your business, like uniforms). They've basically gotten you as a lifetime customer.

➤ Advertising. When Merry Maids Inc. runs an ad on prime-time TV, your local Merry Maids reaps the benefit. (You may pay advertising fees, or a *surcharge,* for this service.) This advertising generates name recognition for the franchise that helps you sell what your business offers. But you may also have to spend extra advertising dollars to bring clients or customers to your specific company.

➤ Other support. One thing that appeals to some people about franchises is that you're not entirely alone: You may be able to get ongoing advice and guidance as you run your business. The franchisor may also provide some financing to help you buy the franchise. It may offer some legal assistance if problems arise (if you bite Fido or vice versa during a tense pet-sitting session, for example).

No Guarantee to Success

This all sounds just ducky: built-in concept, built-in products, advertising, and systems. But wait a second: You should understand that buying a franchise is no guarantee of success. It's just like starting up any other business. The only difference is the fact that the concept has already been developed and tried. You still have to learn to run the business efficiently. And nothing's free: you have the added burden of paying annual franchise fees.

The Educated Entrepreneur

According to a 1993 study quoted in *Business Week* magazine, franchises have a higher failure rate than non-franchise businesses: 35% for franchises compared with 28% for non-franchise businesses. Note that there are no specific statistics on the success rate for *home-based* franchise businesses, which may prove to be higher than non–home-based franchises.

Finding a Franchise Just for You

When you hear the term "franchise" it may conjure up images of KFC and Subway in the malls and on Main Street. Obviously, these enormously successful and familiar national franchises aren't suitable for home-based operations. But there are many other lesser known franchises that can easily be run from home. The hottest franchises today include office and home cleaning, dance/exercise lessons, windshield repair, and modular tools.

Franchise Options You Can Run from Your Living Room

Cleaning services are just about the hottest franchise opportunities available. While they may be very popular, there's actually a great variety of franchises. Here are some areas you might consider investigating. Each area listed has an existing franchise or franchises:

Advertising Services:

Direct mail couponing (distributing coupons through the mail)

Telephone directories (selling advertising space)

Business Services:

Accounting

Bookkeeping

Payroll

Tax services for small businesses

Miscellaneous Services:

Baby announcement products

Child security/ID service

Cleaning services

College financial aid planning

Computer enrichment programs for children

Fitness classes at schools, churches, etc.

Home inspections

Résumé preparation

Youth/sports photography

Referral Services:

Apartment rentals

Day care

Domestic help

House-sitting

Nanny placement

In-home pet care

Home Hazard
Before you decide to start a business smelting metal at home, check your local zoning laws to see if you can run such a business from the den, as explained in Chapter 13, "Office Space in Your Place."

Which One's Right for You?

Having a lot of choices is great, but those choices bring their own challenge. How do you pick the franchise that's right for you? Here are some of the factors to consider when choosing a franchise:

➤ Take into account your skills and interests. If, for example, you don't like working directly with the public, be sure that the franchise you consider doesn't depend on you meeting and greeting people all day. If you're good with numbers, you may want to consider a franchise in the area of business or tax services. If you hate to clean, the Merry Maids may be for Robin Hood, but they ain't for you.

➤ Consider the amount of time you expect to devote to the business. Some franchises are suitable for part-timers; others aren't. You may not be able buy a particular franchise unless you agree to devote your full time to it.

➤ Look at the costs involved. These include both the *franchise fee* (explained later) and other costs to get started (equipment, fees to lawyers, and so on). Franchise fees can run to $15,000 or more, making them much more expensive than just hanging a shingle out over the kitchen door. But you can also find many franchise opportunities for $6,000 (and some for much less).

39

➤ Popularity of the franchise. Remember bell-bottoms? I didn't think so. Trends come and go in business just as quickly as in fashion. What may have been a "hot" franchise in the '80s or even '90s may not be quite the thing for the 21st century, which is just around the corner. Try to project where the economy and the population is heading and see whether the franchise you're considering will go the way of the tie-dyed shirt or be a perennial classic.

Find a Franchise in Your Own Backyard

Finding the right franchise for you—if you decide to go the franchise route—may be easier than you think. You may already be familiar with a particular franchise because you've eaten its product or used its service in your own area. But if you don't know of a specific franchise to investigate, here are some sources to find a franchise:

➤ Advertisements in newspapers and in the backs of magazines.

➤ Trade shows for small businesses often have franchisors there eager to sell their concepts.

➤ Reference books in your local library have directories listing all the national and international franchisors you can contact for more information.

➤ Listings on the Internet.

Franchisees Have Rights, Too

What are you getting as a franchisee? Be sure you understand up front your rights as well as your obligations. Ask yourself (and the franchisor) these questions before you write out a check:

➤ What are your territory rights? Where can you sell your product or service (your sales territory)? Are there enough potential customers there to make a go of it? Is the franchisor prevented from selling other franchises within your territory? Obviously, you don't want the guy next door starting up exactly the same franchise one month after you do.

➤ What do you have to do? Are you required to generate a certain level of sales? Is there any time period for meeting the numbers? How flexible are these terms?

➤ What do you pay to the franchisor? What's the up-front fee (the initial franchise fee)? What's the amount (generally defined in terms of a percentage of sales) of your ongoing franchise fee? When do you have to pay this fee (monthly, quarterly, annually)? Are there any additional fees you may be required to pay (a renewal fee, an advertising surcharge)?

➤ What do you get for your payments? Will they train you? Will you benefit from any local and national advertising? Do you have to buy products from the franchisor and nobody else?

➤ What's the termination policy? Suppose after you become a franchisee, you find you like it about as much as you like cold coffee. How can you terminate your franchise agreement? Check to see whether there are any penalty clauses and whether you may be entitled to a partial refund of the franchise fee. Many franchise agreements are like signing a contract with the devil: they don't allow a franchisee to terminate unless the franchisor commits fraud or files for bankruptcy. On the other hand, suppose the franchisor wants to cut you loose. Make sure that the franchisor doesn't have the right to do so easily (such as by giving a measly 30 days notice).

> **Homegrown Tip**
> Have a money person—an accountant—review the numbers in the franchise agreement to see that it makes financial sense. Then make sure you have an attorney versed in franchise law review the franchise agreement *before* you sign it.

If you're seriously interested in a particular franchise, you don't have to take the first offer. You can negotiate to get terms that are more favorable to you.

Make sure that you get *everything* in writing. If a franchisor makes a promise, put it in the franchise agreement. It may be unenforceable unless you have it in writing.

You're Crazy If You __Don't__ See a UFO (Circular)

No, you haven't wandered over onto the set of the *X Files*. If you, as a franchisee, are required to spend at least $500 in the first six months and the franchisor has agreed to provide goods or services, you're entitled by law to see a *Uniform Franchise Offering (UFO) Circular*. This circular is a disclosure document that contains required information about the franchise and the franchisor.

The circular isn't exactly a fun read, but it's a necessary one: It should include an *audited financial statement* about the franchisor. This is a statement prepared by a certified public accountant who is warranting the authenticity of the financial information provided in the statement. If the circular makes claims about what franchisees can expect to earn, these claims have to be supported by separate written proof.

You're also entitled to receive a list of existing franchisees. Ask for a list of at least 10 names in or close to your area. When you talk to or visit these franchisees—and you absolutely should contact them before going forward—make sure that they're not just shills for the house. Some disreputable franchisors may use *singers* (liars paid by the

Home Hazard
If the franchisor balks or refuses to provide you with the UFO circular, walk away immediately. This is an indication that the franchisor may not be on the level or may be trying to hide something.

franchisors to support their claims). After all, you don't want to become a *moocher* (a victim of a franchise scam). See, there's a seedy side to franchising and you're now fully equipped to avoid it!

In general you want to look for a franchise that has a proven track record. The longer the franchisor has been in business, the better for you. Keep in mind that franchisors, like any other business, can themselves go under (about 5% fail each year). The longer they've been operating, the less chance for failure. (But longevity is no guarantee of success.) Newer franchises may be less expensive, but be aware that you're taking a greater risk.

Franchisee vs. Franchisor: How to Win

Franchises can offer dangerous waters to swim in, but there are also a lot of perfectly legitimate ones out there. However, if you're the cautious type, you'll be glad to know there are safeguards you can (and should) use. If you have a problem with a franchise, you may be able to get help at the federal, state, or local level. Franchises fall under the auspices of the U.S. Federal Trade Commission. If you have any questions about claims made by the franchisor (such as that it's exempt from having to give a UFO circular to you), call the FTC's Division of Marketing Practices at 202-326-3128. Remember, it's this government agency that set up the rules for the UFO circular.

You can also check with the National Fraud Information Center, a nonprofit organization that logs in complaints daily (800-876-7060).

Homegrown Tip
Check out the franchisor *before* signing on the dotted line. Ask your state attorney general about any previous or outstanding violations; call the Better Business Bureau about any complaints against the franchisor.

About half the states in the U.S. require franchisors to register with them before the franchisors can sell their franchises. If your state is in the other half, they may still use general fraud statutes, consumer protection laws, and securities laws to deal with unscrupulous franchisors.

You may also be able to save yourself from scams by seeing whether a particular franchisor was included in the list of more than one hundred companies targeted in a joint federal and state effort, called "Project Telesweep," which can be found on the Internet at http://www.ftc.gov.

The Least You Need to Know

➤ Buying a franchise gives you a ready-made business concept.

➤ With a franchise you exchange freedom for some structure.

➤ Buying a franchise is no guarantee of success.

➤ There are numerous franchises suitable for the home-based environment.

➤ Get expert advice before signing a franchise agreement.

➤ Check out a franchisor thoroughly.

NO. **TURN**KEY BUSINESS.

Chapter 6

Turnkey Business: Up and Ready to Go

In This Chapter

➤ Buying a pre-owned business

➤ Buying a "business opportunity"

➤ Getting into network marketing

You don't have to buy a franchise to get a business in a neat little package. You can buy a *turnkey business*—a business that's either already in operation or, at the least, ready to go. The turnkey business is fully equipped; it needs only you to get it into operation. If you ever took over another kid's paper route when you were 10, you've already had experience with acquiring a turnkey business.

There are three general types of turnkey businesses (in addition to franchises discussed in Chapter 5) that may make sense for you. One is an existing business. In this case you buy the business and take over its operations, stepping into the shoes of the former owner. A second is a "business opportunity." It's similar to a franchise in that you pay for the concept and are essentially ready to go. But, as you'll learn in this chapter, it's quite different from a franchise in several ways. The third type of turnkey business is network marketing, which involves both selling products and making money from the sales of others who are brought into the network by you.

In this chapter you'll learn the benefits and drawbacks of buying an existing business, as well as how to find one. You'll also learn how to complete the purchase, step-by-step. Then you'll learn how to avoid being taken in by con artists who are pros at offering business-in-a-box promises they can't keep.

Buying an Existing Business and Getting a Head Start

If I've learned anything from being a home businessperson, it's why make anything harder than it should be? Instead of building from nothing you may be able to buy an existing business and save yourself all the groundwork of starting from scratch. This enables you to acquire the concept, the existing customer base, a list of suppliers, and a track record. The only thing you change is the location of the business—from the former owner's home or office to your home. When Sam, my neighborhood dentist, retired, moving from the suburbs of New York City to year-round golf in the outskirts of Phoenix, he sold not only his home, but also his dental practice that he had conducted in his home office for over 30 years.

But just because the business seemed to have been successful, don't assume everything's hunky-dory. When you buy an existing business you take the good with the bad. The good may be the business' list of customers or suppliers and good will. The bad may be the business' poor credit rating from paying bills late or a less than favorable reputation for quality or service.

> **Business Buzzword**
> *Good will* is the favorable reputation of a business—an intangible asset. For example, if the seller is charging $10,000 for her business and the value of equipment and supplies total only $8,000, the other $2,000 represents good will.

But even if an existing business has been successful, there's no guarantee that it will continue to do well under your ownership. You still have to learn how to run the business. You have to be able to handle things like finance, promotion, and personnel to get by.

The process of buying an existing or "pre-owned" business takes a lot of time and effort. But it generally costs less to get a business in this way than to develop a concept on your own and get it started, so the time and effort may be well spent.

So, how do you get an instant business? The four basic steps to buying a business are:

1. Locating an available business

2. Investigating the business

3. Negotiating for a sale

4. Closing the deal

For some people there's an additional step: Raising the dough to pay for the purchase. This crucial step is discussed at length in Part 3 of this book.

Step 1: Locating an Available Business

You may not think that existing home-based businesses would be up for sale, but that's not necessarily so. When the owner of a messenger service wanted to retire, he sold his successful business to Angelo, the person who had been managing it for several years. Angelo moved the business into a spare bedroom in his home. The customers were given a new phone number but otherwise they hadn't a clue that the business had changed hands. This home-based messenger service now has a $30,000 a month payroll! Sarah, who had run a successful child care business from home for almost 20 years, moved away. Someone else was able to pick up her young client base and start her own child care business almost overnight.

How can you find an existing business for sale? If you work for a home-based business, you may be able to buy out your boss when she wants to retire or relocate. But these opportunities don't grow on trees. There are, however, other ways to find a home-based business for sale instead of waiting for a home business to find you:

➤ Ask around. Talk to people in your neighborhood who know what's going on. (Neighborhood gossip may prove to actually be a force for good in this case.) Real estate agents selling commercial space can tell you about businesses up for sale. Chamber of commerce members may also have insider info on this.

➤ Check out your local newspapers. In the classifieds portion of the paper you'll see "Business Opportunities" listed. Owners who want to sell their businesses may list them in the classifieds.

➤ Surf the Web. The Internet lists businesses for sale. You can see these listings for free at the National Business Exchange (http://www.director.net/lexis-nexis/sba). If you want to download any of the descriptions, the cost is just 95¢ per contact name and number. (Note that these listings are for *all* businesses, not just home-based businesses.)

➤ Use a business opportunity locator. There are actually companies, listed in the Yellow Pages under "Business Brokers," that can find the business you want (at the price you want to pay). But beware: These companies can charge a hefty fee for their services and may not handle home-based operations.

Step 2: Investigating the Business

Once you locate a business you want, check it over more carefully than you check your dog in flea season. You want to be sure to investigate it from a financial and legal perspective:

➤ Look at the numbers. Get the lowdown by talking with the business' customers, suppliers, employees, if any, and competitors, if possible. Some may be willing to tell you what may be happening behind the scenes. For example, they may note that business has been falling off for some time or that a key customer or supplier has fallen (or is about to fall) by the wayside.

➤ Ask to see the books. Look at the business' account books for at least the past three years. Were the financial statements certified by a CPA? The books will show you exactly how income and expenses have been running.

Homegrown Tip
To complete steps 2 through 4 for purchasing a business, you may need the help of an expert such as an attorney or an accountant, or both. While this help may seem costly, it can save you dollars and aggravation in the long run.

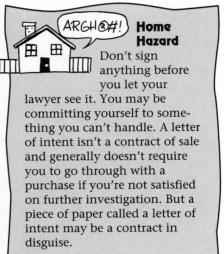

Home Hazard
ARGH@#!
Don't sign anything before you let your lawyer see it. You may be committing yourself to something you can't handle. A letter of intent isn't a contract of sale and generally doesn't require you to go through with a purchase if you're not satisfied on further investigation. But a piece of paper called a letter of intent may be a contract in disguise.

➤ Ask to see tax returns. Like the account books, the business' tax returns for at least the last three years will reveal the company's profit or loss. Also be sure that sales tax returns have been filed on time, so there are no liabilities lurking about.

➤ Talk to the "in" crowd. If the owner gives you permission, speak with the company's bank and learn about how the company's viewed by the loan officer (a good risk? overextended?). The company lawyer can fill you in on any pending legal actions against the business.

➤ Run a credit check of the business. You can do this with a Dun & Bradstreet report (800-234-3867). The cost for this service—just $79 for one report—is certainly well worth the price if it steers you clear of a problem business.

➤ Pour over legal documents. Check out the business' contracts and leases. What's the business already obligated to do? For example, the business may have a contract to provide services through the first of the year. Or the business may have leased equipment that it's on the hook to make payments on for another two years. Rule of thumb: Know what they owe before you buy.

At some point during the investigation stage you may be asked to sign a *letter of intent* stating that you want to buy the business if everything checks out and you can agree on terms. After all, the seller doesn't want to reveal the business' confidential financial matters and other guarded information unless there's a realistic possibility that it can lead to a sale. The seller needs to know that you're serious about your intentions and not merely curious about the business.

Step 3: Negotiating for a Sale

If you pass the investigation step—and you may not necessarily do so with the first business you look at—then you're ready to negotiate for a sale. There are a number of different items that can be the subject of considerable wrangling between you and the seller:

➤ Purchase price. How much are you going to pay for the business? It's not any easier to settle on the price of a business than it is to settle on the price of a new car. Presumably the seller will have had the business appraised (by getting an expert to put a dollar value on the business). But the seller may not be realistic and may want a higher price. You've got to negotiate, just like you do with a car salesperson. Presumably, the seller's got a bottom line and so do you.

➤ Part of the purchase price may be based on projections of what the business is expected to earn over the next year or a set number of years. Again, make sure these projections are realistic.

➤ Payment method. How does the seller want to get paid for the sale? If the seller wants all of the purchase price in a lump sum and you have the cash on hand (or can easily raise it), you may be able to negotiate for an even lower purchase price than if you paid in installments.

➤ If the seller's willing to accept payments over a period of time—an installment sale—then you must hammer out the details. You have to agree on the number of installments (for example, annual payments for five years). You also have to set a reasonable interest rate. Because the seller's financing the sale for you, the seller is acting like a bank and will be paid for the service.

➤ Where the seller is flexible—willing to take a lump sum or installments—then you must decide which method is better for you. Weigh the cost of coming up with the cash up front against the added cost of interest on installments. Where you must borrow to get the lump sum, there may be no difference in cost between borrowing from a lender to make the

Home Hazard
Arranging to pay for the business in installments doesn't give you any protection if the business fails. You're still obligated to pay off the balance of the purchase price—out of your own pocket.

lump sum versus paying interest to the seller on the installments. However, the installment method may hold an advantage: If the business is profitable, you can use funds from the business to pay off the installments. Sources of capital are discussed in Chapters 9 through 12.

➤ Type of purchase. If the business you're buying is incorporated, there are two ways to structure the purchase: the Wall Street method (a stock purchase) or the Garage Sale method (an asset purchase). With a stock purchase you buy the seller's stock and, as a result, own the corporation with all its assets and liabilities. Or you can purchase the assets of the corporation, from filing cabinets and computers to leases. You then run the business through a corporation you set up or as an unincorporated business. If you're buying an unincorporated business, you're automatically buying the assets. (Of course, you can always decide to make the business a corporation yourself.)

➤ Sellers typically prefer stock purchases. They are simpler to arrange. A price is set for the stock and that's all. The sellers are completely finished with their connection to the business.

➤ Buyers typically prefer asset purchases. This type of purchase enables them to choose which assets they want. For example, they may not need five dented metal filing cabinets, so why pay for them? Generally, it also enables them to avoid the business' liabilities.

➤ Tax allocations. If you and the other guy agree on an asset purchase, then you have to negotiate how the purchase price will be broken out among the different assets of the business. The reason: An allocation determines what amount you'll be able to write off through depreciation or amortization.

Business Buzzword
Fair market value is what a willing buyer would pay and a willing seller would accept, if neither one had a gun pointed at his head and each had full knowledge of the facts and circumstances of the transaction.

➤ The way you divide up the assets also affects how the seller's gain is reported (how much is capital gain, which is taxed to individuals at a more favorable tax rate, and how much is ordinary income).

➤ The allocation is made on IRS Form 8594 according to the fair market values of the assets. I know you love reading IRS publications: After you translate the IRSese, these instructions basically specify the order in which the fair market values are allocated. It's critical for the parties to agree on this allocation because it's binding upon them (even though the IRS isn't bound by anybody's rules and can challenge the allocation).

Step 4: Closing the Deal

You can talk all you want, but it ain't over till the fat lady sings. The last step in buying an existing business is closing the deal. This means legal stuff: drawing up a contract and then finalizing the deal by paying for the business and transferring ownership.

In drafting a contract be sure that it includes the following:

➤ A description of what you're buying (stock in a corporation; trademarks, copyrights, patents, and so on; assets of a business; what these assets are; what liabilities, if any, you're taking on; what contracts or leases are being transferred to you; and so on).

➤ The terms of the purchase (the purchase price; the time for payment; interest rates; balloon payment; payment penalties; and other details).

➤ Allocation of the purchase price in the case of an asset sale (as described earlier).

➤ Seller warranties. You want to be sure that what the seller told you was fact and not fiction. If anything he disclosed turns out to be inaccurate (or fraudulent), you want to be covered. Also, there may be hidden liabilities that may not surface until after the sale. You want the seller to make good on these liabilities.

To be sure that everything's on the level, the contract may require a portion of the purchase price to be held in *escrow*. For example, the funds may be held in escrow for one year against the possibility that somebody comes after you for something the seller did. If nothing happens during this time and all is as the seller said it was, then at the end of one year the funds are paid out to the seller. But if an unexpected liability arises, the funds in escrow can be used to cover it so your neck's not on the line.

> **Business Buzzword**
> *Escrow* is an arrangement in which a third party (typically a lawyer) holds on to money until certain conditions are satisfied and then forks the money over.

➤ Risk of loss until closing. You want to define who's at risk of loss until the business finally becomes yours. Generally, some risk may be assigned to the buyer and some to the seller.

➤ Miscellaneous factors. If the seller has made any other promises, like providing you with some training or advice, be sure it's included in the contract. Spoken promises aren't worth the air behind them. As the buyer you want to be sure that the seller won't immediately go into a competing business (taking all she knows about YOUR business with her). Therefore, a contract typically includes a *covenant not to compete*. The seller agrees not to run a competing business within the same area (such as your town, your part of the city, or some other area defined in the covenant) for a set time (for example, one or two years).

51

➤ The seller may be willing to work for you or with you for a period of time after the sale to help with the transition. Be sure that the details of this are clearly spelled out in the contract. These terms would include whether you'll pay him for his help, how it's to be set up (as a consulting agreement; employment agreement), and how long he'll hang around.

➤ Closing procedures. The contract states the time and place for closing the sale. Typically a sale is concluded at a lawyer's office or at the seller's place of business. If you're arranging outside financing to complete the sale, give yourself enough time to get the check from the bank before you have to attend the closing.

Once you have the contract in place, then you follow its terms to conclude the deal. After closing, that's it: You're the proud new owner of a bouncing baby business.

Buying a "Business Opportunity"

Ideas are a dime a dozen, right? Sort of. Ideas may be cheap, but good ideas can be rarer than free diamonds. If good ideas were that easy to come by, why didn't you invent the personal computer, CDs, or Velcro? 'Nuf said.

So, consider buying a good idea for your business. Besides buying a franchise or an existing business, or starting a business from scratch, you can buy a business concept. You may see some of these concepts referred to as "business opportunities."

With a franchise you're buying a name and concept by paying an up-front franchise fee *and* a continuing percentage of your earnings. With a non-franchise business opportunity you also buy a concept by paying an up-front fee. You may also pay the seller for equipment and supplies. You don't pay a continuing percentage of your earnings.

While you get a business idea that is a turnkey business and you can immediately begin your operations, you *don't* get many of the things that come with a franchise. Sometimes these things are good; sometimes not so good. Here are some things you *don't* get with a non-franchise business opportunity. First, the positive aspects of non-franchise businesses over franchises:

➤ No requirement to pay any ongoing fees. Once you pay for the business opportunity, you're basically on your own. You may continue to order supplies from the seller, but there are no other fees. With a franchise you have a continuing obligation to pay franchise fees.

➤ No restrictions. With a non-franchise business you aren't required to conform strictly to a franchisor's code of operations. You have more flexibility to run the business as you see fit. And because you don't have the ongoing fees of a franchise, you have more money in your pocket to do with as you wish.

Not all differences are positive. Here are some drawbacks to non-franchise businesses compared with franchises:

➤ A trade name. With a non-franchise business you get the concept, such as college scholarship matching in which you help students locate scholarship opportunities, but you probably won't get the trade name, such as American College Planning Service®, a franchise providing the same type of service. Although you can negotiate to keep the current business name, in most cases you run the non-franchise business under the name you select. You must establish your own name recognition.

➤ A protected territory. Unlike a franchise, the seller of a non-franchise business may sell the same business opportunity to your next-door neighbor, unless you have a non-compete clause in your contract.

➤ Extensive training. You may get some reference guides or tapes to instruct you in how the business operates, but the seller of a non-franchise business opportunity will not show you how to run a business in general. You have to pick this up on your own. There may be a trade association that covers your business type that can help (you can find one through a national directory of trade associations in your library).

➤ National advertising. You must advertise and promote your business entirely on your own. You can't rely on the seller to do this for you. Of course, you don't pay any advertising fees or surcharges to the seller either.

> **Homegrown Tip**
> Because you don't necessarily have a protected territory, check to see whether there are existing competitors in your area. Look at local advertising and the classifieds in your local phone directory. Personally scout the area for competitors. Also ask around.

Locating an Opportunity

So, are these opportunities just waiting around to be snatched up? Surprisingly, yes. Business opportunities can be found in much the same way as finding a franchise (see Chapter 5). You can find them in your local newspapers; in the backs of magazines such as *Business Opportunity, Home Office Computing,* and *Entrepreneur;* through reference material in your local library; or even on the Internet.

Here are some of the more popular business opportunities that can easily be run from home:

Advertising services

Baby shoe bronzing

Birth announcement services

Bookkeeping

Button/badge making

Claims processing

College scholarship matching

Gift baskets

Medical/dental billing

Personalized children's books

Tax return preparation

Travel agencies

Typing services (medical histories; legal briefs)

Vending machines

Avoiding Scams

The growing desire of good, honest people like you to own their own business has spawned hundreds of no-goodniks, just lying in wait to take your money. To avoid becoming a victim, remember non-franchise business opportunities are covered by the same protections afforded to purchasers of franchises. If, as in the case of a franchise, you're required to spend at least $500 in the first six months and the seller has agreed to provide goods or services, you're entitled to see a *Uniform Franchise Offering Circular.* The name may say franchise, but the law applies equally to business opportunities. This circular should include an audited financial statement about the seller. This is a statement prepared by a CPA who is vouching for accuracy of the financial information provided. If the circular makes claims about what buyers can expect to earn, these claims have to be supported by separate written proof.

Make sure you get references before you buy a business opportunity. Ask for a list of at least 10 names of individuals in or close to your area who've already bought such businesses. Be sure to contact them before going forward. Again, make sure that they're not just *singers,* shills for the house who are paid by the seller to lie in support of the seller's claims. You can also ask the seller for personal references as a second check. As in the case of a franchise, check out the seller with your local Better Business Bureau to see if there are any existing complaints against her. Also ask your state attorney general whether the seller's on the books as a con artist.

If you have a problem with a business opportunity, you may be able to get the same help from the federal, state, or local officials as you can for a franchise. Business opportunities fall under the auspices of the U.S. Federal Trade Commission. If you have any questions about claims made by the seller (such as that it's exempt from the UFO circular requirement), call the FTC's Division of Marketing Practices at 202-326-3128. Remember: It's this government agency that set up the rules for the UFO circular (and you might as well get something back from all those taxes you've paid out).

You can also check with the National Fraud Information Center, a nonprofit organization that logs in business opportunity complaints daily (800-876-7060).

Network Marketing

Whether it involves selling cosmetics to shut-ins or vitamins door-to-door, pyramid or network marketing arrangements have worked for some and been disastrous for others. In the recent past, multi-level marketing was the rage for those looking to supplement their income or even earn a full-time living on their own. Many successful, legitimate, multi-level marketing companies (called MLM), such as Amway, Tupperware, and Mary Kay Cosmetics, got thousands of individuals to join their ranks. But in many other cases these marketing programs turned out to be nothing more than pyramid scams where nothing was sold or consumed. People who went in late in the game at the bottom of the pyramid lost all.

The industry has evolved and now is generally referred to as "network marketing." It's still based on the concept of direct (face-to-face) sales to consumers, with participants or *distributors* benefiting both from their direct sales and getting a percentage of the sales of the distributors they bring into the network.

Here's an example: You become a distributor of weight loss pills that you sell through word of mouth in your neighborhood. You also get two friends, Betty and Carol, to become distributors for you, and they go out to sell. You get paid on your sales as well as a percentage of Betty's and Carol's sales. Then Betty and Carol bring in their own people, and, depending on the network marketing organization you're with, you get a percentage of the sales from distributors brought in by Betty and Carol. It can go on and on to become an empire, or crash like a house of cards.

The basic structure of network marketing.

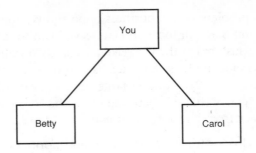

Network marketing is an ideal home-based business. You can sell directly from home (through telephone sales, "parties," or person-to-person contact). You can use your home for all administrative work associated with the business, such as ordering inventory, record keeping, and setting up appointments. You can schedule your sales calls at your convenience and work full-time or part-time in the business.

Is Network Marketing Right for You?

Before going into network marketing be sure you understand exactly what it is and be realistic about what you can earn from your efforts. Network marketing is a method of distribution that brings goods from the manufacturer directly to the consumer by the distributor (which is you). This is why network marketing is called direct sales. (Other types of sales arrangements that don't fall under the umbrella of direct sales include sales in stores and mail-order sales.)

When you become a distributor in network marketing, you're effectively in your own business. You're not an employee of the company. The company typically provides you with a starter kit containing order forms and an explanation of its compensation plan, inventory, and training. You use your supplies to sell products directly to consumers. Also, you try to enlist others to become distributors. You're then paid not only for your own direct sales but also a portion of the sales by distributors brought in by you. The distributors brought in by you are called *downline*.

In addition to understanding how you make money, check the productivity (or "activity") requirements and other things you're responsible for. If you don't perform, you may be dropped from the network.

Becoming a distributor in network marketing is, perhaps, the least costly way to start your own business. The initial fees generally are modest— averaging under $100 (with some as low as $25) for starter kits that include order forms and other materials. Then you probably have to buy some inventory (there may or may not be any minimum order requirements). Again, these costs may be only a few hundred dollars to get started.

When you start in network marketing you can expect most of your money to come from your direct sales. As you bring in other distributors and they produce, you'll begin to reap the rewards and even find that the lion's share of your income is from your share of their sales.

Despite stories by star distributors of spectacular earnings, don't expect to "strike it rich" overnight from network marketing. Being a distributor is like starting any business. You have to pay your dues before you collect a bundle.

Home Hazard

Understanding network marketing compensation can be trickier than predicting the winner of the Super Bowl. Make sure you understand the compensation arrangement you've agreed to. You may see terms like "binary system," "matrixes," "standard Australian," or "two-up." These aren't exotic drink recipes: these terms describe the levels of distributors you receive compensation on. Some arrangements limit compensation to four levels below you; others don't have limits. Also, the pay periods (weekly, monthly) for compensation arrangements can vary, so check this out.

The Educated Entrepreneur

Network marketing statistics to dazzle your friends with: Only about 5% of distributors make more than $35,000, and only 0.5% make more than $100,000. Nearly 90% of all direct sellers do it only on a part-time basis, and nearly 70% have other employment.

To succeed in network marketing you have to be a "people person." You must enjoy talking to people and have an ability to communicate your ideas. This is the only way you'll succeed in direct sales. If your idea of a hot Saturday night is to knit mittens for your cat, this just may not be the route for you.

Finding a Network Marketing Company

Because distributors hope to make a significant portion of their income by bringing in other distributors, you may not have to look for a network marketing company; one may be looking for you. A relative, a friend, or even a stranger may approach you and ask you to become a distributor.

If the idea of becoming a distributor appeals to you and you haven't been "recruited," there are lots of ways to find the right match for you. Look in your local phone book for distributors in your area. You'll find companies selling things like vitamins, beauty supplies, artwork, toys, cleaning products, and even financial services.

Also check out opportunities through the Internet:

➤ Network Marketing Mall™
(http://network-marketing.com/nmm/nmm.htm)

➤ Network Marketing Yellow Pages™
(http://www.network-marketing.com/nmyp/nmyp.htm)

➤ *PROFIT$ Online* magazine
(http://profitsonline.com)

To get a listing of national companies, call the Direct Selling Association (a trade association of leading firms that manufacture and distribute goods directly to consumers) at 202-293-5760.

Protecting Yourself from Network Marketing Scams

Unlike franchises (see Chapter 5) and business opportunities, network marketing *isn't* given protections. For example, there's no *Uniform Franchise Offering Circular* requirement for network marketing businesses. So it's up to you to do your own investigations. If you look into a particular company's claim and it sounds too good to be true, it probably isn't true. Here are five things that should alert you to steer clear of a prospective company:

➤ The company promises you the financial moon or guaranteed profits.

➤ The company requires you to pay an up-front fee that greatly exceeds the value of the profits, kits, and any training given in return.

➤ The company makes claims that high income is "easy" to achieve.

➤ You have to make a huge payment *before* you get anything in return.

➤ You're pressured into signing up as a distributor.

Understand what you're agreeing to if you sign on as a distributor. Here are some high-lights from the Direct Seller's Association Code of Ethics to help you out:

➤ No member company of the Association shall engage in any deceptive, unlawful, or unethical consumer or recruiting practice.

➤ Pyramid or endless chain schemes shall constitute a violation of this Code.

➤ The company will repurchase on reasonable commercial terms currently marketable inventory in the possession of that salesperson (with "reasonable commercial terms" defined to mean inventory within 12 months from the salesperson's date of purchase of not less than 90% of his/her original cost).

➤ No member company shall misrepresent the actual or potential sales or earnings of its independent salespeople. Any earnings or sales representations...shall be based on documented facts.

If you have a problem with a seller, you may find help from the U.S. Federal Trade Commission (Division of Marketing Practices at 202-326-3128). There are no specific federal regulations dealing with network marketing (as there are in the case of franchises and business opportunities), but the FTC will investigate claims using general regulations against unfair or deceptive trade practices. In some cases, the Securities and Exchange Commission can also be brought in to investigate problems.

Again, you can also check with the National Fraud Information Center, a nonprofit organization. They log in network marketing complaints daily (800-876-7060).

Home Hazard
While promising to follow the Code of Ethics is voluntary, it might be wise to avoid companies that aren't members of the Direct Seller's Association (a trade association for companies involved with person-to-person sales). These guys don't even make the promise to adhere to an ethical standard.

The Least You Need to Know

➤ A turnkey business is fully equipped and ready for operations.

➤ Buying an existing business is no guarantee of success.

➤ The process of buying an existing business can be long and involved.

➤ Buying a non-franchise "business opportunity" is less costly than a franchise one, but you're also getting less.

➤ Network marketing involves the lowest initial costs with the opportunity to earn a good return.

Chapter 7

Forming Your Business

In This Chapter

➤ Running your business by yourself

➤ Working with partners

➤ Incorporating your company

➤ Electing special tax treatment for your corporation

➤ Using a limited liability company

➤ Getting your identification number

Having an idea for a business is great, but it's just the first step in starting that business. Now's the time to consider all that legal mumbo jumbo about how to set up the company. All businesses are not created equal: in fact, there are five ways in which businesses can be organized. Starting a business without knowing how to structure it is like beginning to write a novel without a clue about the plot.

In this chapter you'll learn what each type of business organization is and how to set it up. You'll also find out about the consequences of the different forms. These consequences will influence which type of form you choose. Finally you'll learn how to get your company's identification number so that you can begin doing business.

Flying Solo

You're on your own and ready to go. You can incorporate your business. You may even be able, as a sole owner, to set up a limited liability company (it depends in which state you live). But if you take no legal steps at all, you're automatically a sole proprietorship. When you hear the term *proprietor* you may picture the guy running the luggage store downtown, but the term applies to people in all kinds of businesses. It doesn't matter whether you have a product or service to sell. Whether you're a dentist, an accountant, or even a member of the oldest profession, if you're in business alone and haven't incorporated, you're a sole proprietorship.

As a sole proprietor you're also called a self-employed person because you're not an employee of your business. You may sometimes see sole proprietorships referred to as *unincorporated* businesses because they haven't taken the legal steps required by state law to become a corporation. Consultants who work as *independent contractors* are also considered sole proprietors.

A sole proprietorship is the easiest form of business to set up and the least costly to get started because you basically don't have to do anything. Keep in mind that you can start a business as a sole proprietor and become some kind of corporation later on. Steven, a financial consultant in my neighborhood, set up his consulting business by himself, becoming a sole proprietor. A few years later when he was very profitable he incorporated and became an employee of his corporation. People often do that to take advantage of certain fringe benefits that are only available to corporate employees or to limit the amount of personal liability they might have (translated, that means the wolves can only go after the corporation's nest egg if you screw up).

While it's easy to become a sole proprietor, there are legal and tax consequences for this form of business organization.

> **Business Buzzword**
> An *independent contractor* is a person who contracts to provide work according to her own methods and with-out being under the control of the business for whom the work is being performed; not an employee.

Legal Consequences: Tell It to the Judge

As a sole proprietor your business is your alter ego: you're virtually one and the same for both legal and tax purposes. Legally, you're responsible for any debts of the business. Say you sign a lease for a photocopier for your business so you can keep duplicates of invoices and make copies of your face when business is slack. After a few too many of those slack times, you can't keep up the lease payments. The leasing company can come after your house, your savings, your collection of face photocopies, and any other personal assets they want to pay off the remaining balance. Just because you have the potential for legal wrangles doesn't mean you have to go unprotected. Some states give partial or full homestead protection for your home, which means you won't lose your home if you lose a lawsuit. Other assets may also be protected by state law from the claims of creditors (such as retirement plans and, in some states, IRAs). But the only practical and easy way to keep all your personal assets from the grasping hands of lawyers is to carry insurance to cover all possible liabilities. (Insurance coverage is discussed in Chapter 19, "Be Sure to Insure.")

Ever heard that government encourages small business? Think again. If you decide to go out on your own, just when you need Uncle Sam's help most, you may find yourself out in the cold. Because a sole proprietor is a self-employed person, he can't get the same protections offered to employees. This means that a self-employed person can't get workers' compensation or unemployment insurance. As a self-employed person you can't be covered under these programs, period. Even if you have employees and provide coverage for them, you're on your own.

Opening Shop

What do you do to become a sole proprietor? Really there are no legal steps to take. You decide to be in business, say abracadabra three times, and you are *automatically* a sole proprietor.

Check to see whether you have to register your business with city hall. This registration is called a *DBA* (doing business as) in which you notify the local authorities of the name of your business and that you're the owner. There may be a small filing fee for registering your name, but the good news is you don't need an attorney to file your DBA. Call your town or county clerk for more information. That office should be able to give you the right form and reasonably intelligible instructions for filling it out. You can generally file the DBA in person or by mail.

Even if you're not required to file a DBA as a condition of doing business in your area, registration may still be a good idea. It protects the name for your business by preventing anyone else in your area from using it. When you go to register your business name you'll find out whether it's already being used by another company. It can also come in handy to have a DBA to open up a business bank account.

Teaming Up

Astaire and Rogers, Abbott and Costello, Bonnie and Clyde: Two heads are better than one (sometimes). Instead of starting a business by yourself, you may want to go in with another person. When two or more people join together in a business with the intention of making a profit, they've formed a *partnership*. Owners of the partnership are called, aptly enough, partners. Partners are self-employed folks; they're not employees of their partnership even though they work for it.

There are good reasons why you might want to team up with someone when starting your business:

➤ Skills. You may be good in one area but lack skills or expertise in another area. Here's where a partner can be useful. Jake and Bill were college friends. Jake, a computer whiz, developed software to manage those phone menus we all get annoyed at. But that's where Jake's abilities ended. It took a partnership with Bill, a real people person, to sell the software to companies all across the country.

➤ Responsibility. Running a business requires a great amount of time and responsibility. If you can share these burdens with a co-owner, you can take a vacation once in a while without worrying about who's running the business.

➤ Capital. Starting a business can run into big bucks. You may not have the money or the good credit necessary to get started. But if you pool your resources with someone else who does, you may be able to get up and running without losing the ranch.

The Educated Entrepreneur

Thinking of partnering with your hubby or wife? Nearly 20% of all those with businesses in network marketing are husband-wife teams.

Legal Consequences

A partnership has many of the same legal consequences as a sole proprietorship, but as with any marriage, in tough times, things can get ugly. Partnerships in disarray can be a lawyer's fantasy and your worst nightmare: The partnership gets sued; partner A loses his house to the lawsuit and sues partner B to get his share; partner B in turn sues partner C and so on.

Example: A man I know invented a new flavor of ice cream (bubble-gum chocolate chip); he joined with his neighbor to form a partnership. They spent $3,000 leasing a 300-gallon ice cream maker, then went to the store one day and found Ben & Jerry had beat them to it. After one year, the business didn't make it and there was still $3,000 remaining on the lease.

In this scenario, the leasing company can go after *either* partner to pay the rest of the lease. If this happens to you, either you or your partner can be out on the limb for the full $3,000. Should the leasing company win and you pay the $3,000, you can try (with a polite request or a lawsuit) to get the other partner to cough up her $1,500 share of the obligation. Good luck.

Not all partners have full exposure for personal liability, though. There's a special kind of partnership that limits the liability of some owners. It's called a *limited partnership.* In this type of organization, there must be at least one owner who is a general partner with unlimited personal liability. Other owners may be limited partners whose liability for partnership debts is limited to the amount of their contribution in the partnership, and so they're called *limited partners.* Limited partners are simply investors who have nothing to do with the day-to-day operation of the business.

Example: In the preceding example, you're the general partner while your partner is a limited partner. In this case, the leasing company can go after you, the general partner, for the entire $3,000. Your partner, the limited partner, can lose just her initial investment of $2,500. As long as she's already made her full investment, you can't get any more money from her.

What's a partnership without partners? A partnership, by its nature, exists only while the partners are in it. When a partner retires or dies, technically the partnership automatically terminates. But as a practical matter, business can go on. As you'll see later in this chapter, when you set up the partnership, you take care of these contingencies. You also address what happens to the business when one partner simply wants out.

Like sole proprietors, partners are not covered by either worker's compensation or unemployment insurance. If you're injured on the job or if work dries up, no one is protected by a government program.

Partnerships are also similar to sole proprietorships for income taxes. Income is taxed directly to the owners, not to the partnership. A partnership never pays any tax—only the partners themselves.

Getting Up and Running

You and your friend talk for hours on end about someday going into business together—no partnership. Then one day the two of you draw up a flyer that you put on the windshields of the cars in your local shopping center to offer car detailing in your garage—instant partnership! This coming together and getting started is all that's needed to make the partnership come into existence from both a legal and tax perspective.

Like a sole proprietorship, you may have to register your business with your town or county clerk. There may be a small filing fee for the privilege of registering your name.

While nobody puts a gun to your head to do anything legal to form a partnership, it's still not a bad idea to take legal steps and make a formal *partnership agreement*. This agreement spells out all of the understandings between you and your partner (or partners). Remember that a partnership is like a marriage. When things go well, formalities don't matter. When things go badly, many couples wish they'd had a prenuptial agreement to decide what happens when they split up. A partnership agreement might cover who gets paid what, who's responsible for doing what, and what happens if one of you wants out. You don't have to use a lawyer to draw up a partnership agreement, but you may want a lawyer's expertise. The cost for this service is generally a few hundred dollars or more, depending upon how complicated you want to make the agreement.

Here are some of the points you should be sure to include in your partnership agreement:

Home Hazard

Limited partnerships work a little differently than regular partnerships: they *must* follow formalities and organize under the laws of the state in which they're formed. Limited partnerships *must* have a formal, written partnership agreement that conforms to state law.

General Terms

➤ What's the name of the partnership? (You'd be surprised how many businesses never got started because no one could agree on a name.)

➤ What are the names and addresses of the partners?

➤ What type of business will the partnership run?

➤ What's the place of business (your den; your partner's garage)?

➤ What's the duration for the partnership (a set number of years; the completion of a business objective)?

➤ Under what circumstances can new partners be brought into the business?

➤ Optional: A statement prohibiting partners from selling, assigning, pledging, or mortgaging their partnership interest without the consent of the other partners.

Partnership Capital

➤ What will each partner put into the partnership?

➤ Will property contributed to the partnership be returned at some point (for example, who gets the coffeepot?)

➤ If the partnership will need more money in the future, what's each partner going to ante up?

Management

➤ Who's going to run the business?

➤ How will differences of opinion be resolved?

➤ Will a unanimous vote be required to take certain actions, such as selling the business?

➤ Will you use binding arbitration to settle important matters that you and your partner can't agree on?

Services to the Partnership

➤ What will your duties (and your partner's duties) be for the partnership?

➤ Will you be working full-time or part-time?

➤ Will you get paid for what you do? In a partnership this isn't salary since you're not an employee. However, you may receive guaranteed payments. You may have an expense account you can draw against to wine and dine clients (or buy paper clips). Be sure that the agreement details any compensation arrangement, including the amount and the time for payment.

➤ Will the partnership carry liability insurance to protect you when debtors come huffing and puffing at your back door?

> **Business Buzzword**
> *Liability insurance:* If your partner does something while carrying on partnership business and you and the partnership are sued, liability insurance protects you if you are required to pay for your partner's mistakes.

Allocation of Partnership Items

➤ Will you divvy up the profits or losses equally? Generally in an equal partnership, they're allocated equally. So, if you are a 50% partner you're entitled to 50% of the profits.

➤ Will there be special allocations? Sometimes you might go 60/40 or 75/25. The partnership agreement can spell out when different splits of partnerships items will be made.

Accounting and Tax Matters

Home Hazard
From a tax point of view, special allocations will be respected only if there is some economic effect to the business. For example, say your partner is in a high tax bracket. You can't just decide to give your partner a huge chunk of losses to offset his high income even though it would help him out at tax time. There's no economic effect for this allocation.

➤ What *tax year* will you use for reporting the annual revenues and expenses of the business? You have a choice between a calendar year ending December 31 or a fiscal year ending on the last day of any other month but December. (However, as you'll learn in Chapter 20, there are limits on the use of a fiscal year.)

➤ What *accounting method* (the cash basis or the accrual basis) will you use to report your income and expenses? Accounting method determines when you record money coming in and money going out.

➤ Where will you keep the partnership's books and records? His basement? Your kitchen?

➤ When do you have a right to check the books?

Changes in and Termination of Partnership

➤ How will you determine when changes need to be made?

➤ What happens if one person wants to leave the business?

➤ What happens if one person becomes disabled or dies?

➤ How much notice does a partner who wants to leave have to give?

➤ What kind of settlement can a partner who's leaving expect?

➤ Does a partner who leaves have to agree to a non-compete clause?

Me, Inc.

When a home-based businessperson incorporates, it's like having another person move into the spare bedroom. That person is the corporation, and it's very independent. It sits back there filing its own tax return and paying its own taxes. Oh, and if it's not careful, it can get itself sued, too. The corporation has a life of its own independent from its owners. It stays in existence until it's formally dissolved in accordance with state law. This means that even if an owner sells his interest or dies, the corporation goes on.

Okay, pay attention: Here's your basic corporation dictionary. Owners of a corporation are called *shareholders* or *stockholders*. A corporation is governed by its *by-laws*. The people who see that its by-laws are followed (or changed when necessary) are called *directors*. The day-to-day operations of the corporation—its business activities—are carried on by *officers* (a president, secretary, and treasurer).

In closely held corporations the same person typically wears more than one hat. If you're the only owner and you incorporate, you'd be a director as well as president of the corporation (and just a tad schizophrenic on managers' day). You may want to bring in outsiders (non-shareholders) to serve as directors with you, but it's not required.

Any person can form a corporation. You can incorporate as a one-person business or have co-owners. You print up pretty shares of stock showing your ownership interest. The number of shares is spelled out on a stock certificate. If you own the entire corporation, then you own all of the corporation's outstanding stock and you can paper your bedroom with the certificates. If you have co-owners, the number of shares owned by each owner will reflect his or her ownership interest. So, if you and a friend contribute unequal amounts of cash or property to start the business and you want the ownership interests to reflect this fact, then the shares must be divided accordingly.

> **Business Buzzword**
> A *closely held corporation* is a privately owned corporation whose stock is *not* traded on any public exchange. If you form a corporation, you're considered a closely held corporation. In contrast, General Motors and IBM, whose stock is traded on the New York Stock Exchange, are public corporations.

Incorporation is a big step. In deciding whether to take it, think about these things:

➤ Cost of organization. It costs more to set up a corporation than an unincorporated business. There are state filing fees and attorneys' fees for organizing the corporation.

➤ Cost of operation. Because a corporation is a separate entity, there's more formality to operate it. You have to be careful what money you put into which bank account—yours or the corporation's. Formality can translate into extra costs. Accounting costs for filing corporate tax returns may be higher than fees for processing returns for unincorporated businesses.

➤ Personal liability. One of the big plusses of having a corporation is that you're protected from the business' problems. Anyone who does business with the corporation can only go after corporate assets to satisfy claims. So, if the corporation buys a fax machine and fails to pay for it, the seller can only sue the corporation, not you personally (although there are some situations where shareholders can become personally liable for corporate debts, which I'll get into later).

➤ Tax issues. It's not easy to say whether taxes will be higher or lower if you incorporate. There are just too many variables to generalize. The potential exists for *double* tax on the same income—once at the corporate level when it's earned and again at the shareholder level when the corporation (called a C corporation in tax parlance) pays out a dividend. But as a practical matter, you'll probably be pulling out most of the profits in the form of salary and benefits (not dividends). This means the corporation can deduct these amounts (and so, won't pay tax on them) and you'll pay tax on your paycheck at the same rate you would have if you hadn't incorporated. Other tax issues are discussed in Chapter 21, "Sharing Your Profits with Uncle Sam."

Business Buzzword

A *personal service corporation* is any corporation engaged in the fields of health, law, accounting, engineering, architecture, actuarial science, performing arts, or consulting that meets certain ownership and service tests. PSCs are subject to special rules (primarily limitations) in the tax law. Once you've incorporated, you're automatically a personal service corporation if you meet this definition.

➤ Other considerations. Being a corporation can add a veneer of professionalism to a business. The public may have more respect for a corporation than a company being run under Joe Blow's name. A corporation may also be in a better position to get loans and buy property or equipment. That's because the lender or seller knows that the corporation's life is independent of its owner or owners. A corporation also makes it easier to bring in new owners. The new owners buy shares in the corporation (from the corporation itself or from the existing shareholders). This means that it's easier for owners to get out when they want to by selling their shares to other owners or to outsiders.

The Law, a Corporation, and You

As you've seen, a corporation provides its owners an important legal protection—limited personal liability. The corporation is a separate legal entity that makes its own contracts and can be held responsible for them. You incorporate your mail-order maternity wear business and order 200 dresses. They come in damaged and you refuse to pay for them. The dress company sues for the cost. It has to sue the corporation, not you personally. If it wins, it can collect only from the corporation, not from you.

While a corporation *technically* provides personal liability protection for owners, when it all hits the fan, there are circumstances in which you may still be responsible. Banks typically will not make loans to small corporations unless the owners co-sign the loans. This makes the owners personally liable for the debt if the corporation goes under and fails to repay the loan. Leasing companies (for example, car leasing companies) may also make you personally guarantee a lease to your corporation. In Chapter 21 you'll learn about situations where the good ol' U.S. government can hold owners of a corporation responsible for tax liabilities.

Home Hazard
Once you start a corporation, you can't just walk away if things don't work out. You have to take legal steps to end the corporation—formally dissolve it under state law.

Starting Up

A corporation is a creature of state law. It does not exist until it's formally set up (incorporated) under that law.

Corporations are also not a cheap date: It costs more to create a corporation than other types of businesses. You may spend several hundred dollars in state incorporation fees and attorneys' fees. Generally attorneys' fees for incorporation are modest and cover not only incorporation but also help in preparing the corporation's minutes book and in issuing the stock.

If you're not exactly flush with cash, you can self-incorporate using special software or online incorporation services. If you decide on the do-it-yourself method, contact your state's Department of Commerce or Department of State for further information.

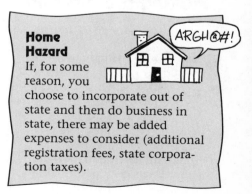

Home Hazard
If, for some reason, you choose to incorporate out of state and then do business in state, there may be added expenses to consider (additional registration fees, state corporation taxes).

Have you ever noticed that some large corporations, especially public corporations, incorporate in Delaware or Nevada? It's not that these states have better incorporation forms, football teams, or lawyers: the laws in these states favor the corporation's management (officers and directors) over outside shareholders who may want to challenge management decisions. Closely held corporations don't need the same protection for management because the same guys who run the corporation are the guys who own it. So, you probably want to incorporate in the state where you'll be doing business (where you live).

Casting Your Vote for S Status

You say you want to have all the advantages of a C corporation, such as limits on personal liability, but you also want to avoid double taxation? Luckily, I have just the thing for you. You can elect special tax treatment. This election is called an S election, and once it's made the corporation is called an S corporation.

> ### The Educated Entrepreneur
>
> Way back in 1958, Congress introduced a new concept into the tax law: a corporation that would be a regular corporation in all respects—except how it was taxed. In 1982, the law was completely revamped to end old restrictions, making S corporations more usable by you and me. Again in 1996, rules were further relaxed. Today, S corporations are very popular for small businesses. According to the latest IRS statistics, there are over 2 million S corporations in this country. Of these, nearly 90% have only one shareholder.

Making the Election

Homegrown Tip
You may also be able to make an S election for state tax purposes. But be sure to use the correct state form. The state figures if the feds get a piece of paper out of you, they should get one too.

It would be nice if you could just go to the local school gym, close yourself in a little booth, and make an S election, but that's not quite how it's done. An S election can be made only by an existing corporation. So, even if you decide you want S status, you first have to set up a corporation under state law.

You make an S election by having the corporation, with your consent as shareholder, file a special form with the IRS (you knew there'd be a form in here somewhere, didn't you?). The form is IRS Form 2553, Election by Small Business Corporations to Tax Corporate Income Directly to Shareholders. You can get the form from the IRS by calling 800-TAX-FORM. Among other things, the form asks you to include your *employer identification number* (explained later in this chapter).

Don't be lax about the filing deadline. You have to file the form no later than the fifteenth day of the third month of the corporation's tax year (generally March 15) for the election to be effective for the current year.

Home Hazard
When filing the S election be sure to use certified or registered mail or a private carrier designated by the IRS so you'll have proof of the date that you sent the election.

How the Law Sees an "S"

If you're an S corporation, just think of yourself like a C corporation. There's no difference from a legal perspective.

An S corporation is a separate entity that can sue and be sued. Like a C corporation, owners have protection from unlimited personal liability. And, to end the corporation if things don't work out, you have to take the same legal steps as you would with a C corporation.

You're the owner of the corporation, but you're also its employee. You can take a salary and be covered by worker's compensation and unemployment insurance.

Limit Your Liability with an LLC

News flash—a new kind of business organization is sweeping the country! All states and the District of Columbia now have laws allowing for the creation of a new type of business organization called a *limited liability company (LLC)*. (Hawaii's law finally went into effect on April 1, 1997.) An LLC isn't a corporation and it isn't a partnership. It's a new hybrid business entity (sort of like when a Klingon and a Vulcan have a kid together). Like a corporation, an LLC is a creature of state law, and the laws vary from state to state.

Homegrown Tip
Professionals (lawyers and accountants) may also be able to form limited liability partnerships (LLPs) for their practices. Right now the majority of states have laws on the books allowing LLPs to be set up within their borders.

Owners of an LLC are called *members*. (State law—for example, New York—may allow the formation of a one-person LLC but, as you'll see shortly, there may be little reason in opting for this type of setup.) An LLC is governed by its *articles of organization* and *by-laws*, written documents that are similar to a corporation's articles of incorporation and by-laws.

A limited liability company is very much like an S corporation: It combines the best features of a partnership and a corporation. Like a partnership or S corporation, the income and deductions pass through to the owners so there's no possibility of the double taxation whammy you can have with a C corporation. But like a corporation (C or S), the owners also have limited personal liability. Look at the table below to see how an LLC stacks up against the other kinds of business organizations.

Comparison of Business Forms

Type of Entity	Name of Owner	Limited Personal Liability	Tax Form Protection	One-Person Business
Sole proprietorship	Owner (proprietor)	No	Schedule C of Form 1040	Yes
Partnership	Partner	No	Form 1065	No
C corporation	Shareholder	Yes	Form 1120	Yes
S corporation	Shareholder	Yes	Form 1120S	Yes
LLC	Member	Yes	Form 1065	No*

One-member LLCs may be permitted in some states, but they're not taxed as partnerships under federal income tax law.

LLC, the Law, and Thou

So just what is an LLC? An LLC is more like a corporation than a partnership from the lawyers' point of view. It can be set up to have *continuity of life*. This is sort of like life support for a company. The business continues unaffected by the death, retirement, or withdrawal of a member. It can also be set up to make it easy to sell or give interests in the business to your children or other people without the consent of current owners. Like a corporation, it's generally run by a board, with day-to-day operations in the hands of one or a small group of members who function as managers.

As the name implies, a limited liability company, like a corporation, means that owners have personal liability protection. Owners don't put their house and BMWs at risk when they start an LLC. However, also like a corporation, members may become personally liable for company debts in some circumstances (when they co-sign loans and leases to their LLC and when the LLC fails to pay the IRS withheld income and payroll taxes on employees' wages).

Organizing as an LLC

You have to set up an LLC according to the laws of your state. The cost of setting up an LLC is pretty much the same as incorporating: there are filing or registration fees and the lawyer takes a cut (if you use one). But there may be other fees for organizing an LLC. In New York, newly formed LLCs are required to place public notices in local newspapers for a certain number of weeks. And there may be ongoing annual fees as well.

Get Your Business Identification Number

Name, rank, and serial number? Well, to run your business, it's actually just name and serial number (rank is only for military types). The federal government requires businesses to have identification numbers just like regular people have Social Security numbers. After you've selected *how* you want to organize your business, then, as if you didn't have enough numbers to remember, you need to get an *employer identification number* from the IRS. The form you file to get your number is reproduced on the next page.

You need an employer identification number to:

➤ Open a business bank account (unless you're a sole proprietorship)

➤ Elect S corporation status

➤ Make deposits of employment taxes

➤ File tax returns

➤ Set up company retirement plans

To get your employer identification number you file IRS Form SS-4 according to the instructions that come with the form, which, yes, are as clear as any other IRS instructions. You can get a number over the telephone by following the special instructions with the form. There you'll find a list of telephone numbers to call for an immediate number assignment in case you have a hot need for this and just can't wait.

Homegrown Tip
You don't need an employer identification number if you meet these three requirements: (1) you're a sole proprietorship, (2) you don't have any employees, and (3) you aren't setting up a retirement plan. In this case you can use your personal Social Security number to open a business bank account and to file your tax return.

You may also need a state employer identification number to report state unemployment insurance. Or you may simply be able to use your federal employer identification number on state forms. Check with your state's Department of Taxation or Revenue as well as your state's Labor Department for requirements on state identification numbers.

Form **SS-4**	**Application for Employer Identification Number**	EIN
(Rev. December 1995) Department of the Treasury Internal Revenue Service	(For use by employers, corporations, partnerships, trusts, estates, churches, government agencies, certain individuals, and others. See instructions.) ➤ **Keep a copy for your records.**	OMB No. 1545-0003

Please type or print clearly.

1 Name of applicant (Legal name) (See instructions.)

2 Trade name of business (if different from name on line 1)

3 Executor, trustee, "care of" name

4a Mailing address (street address) (room, apt., or suite no.)

5a Business address (if different from address on lines 4a and 4b)

4b City, state, and ZIP code

5b City, state, and ZIP code

6 County and state where principal business is located

7 Name of principal officer, general partner, grantor, owner, or trustor—SSN required (See instructions.) ➤

8a Type of entity (Check only one box.) (See instructions.)
- ☐ Sole proprietor (SSN) _____
- ☐ Partnership
- ☐ REMIC
- ☐ State/local government
- ☐ Personal service corp.
- ☐ Limited liability co.
- ☐ National Guard
- ☐ Estate (SSN of decedent) _____
- ☐ Plan administrator-SSN _____
- ☐ Other corporation (specify) ➤
- ☐ Trust
- ☐ Federal Government/military
- ☐ Farmers' cooperative
- ☐ Church or church-controlled organization
- ☐ Other nonprofit organization (specify) ➤ _____ (enter GEN if applicable) _____
- ☐ Other (specify) ➤

8b If a corporation, name the state or foreign country (if applicable) where incorporated | State | Foreign country

9 Reason for applying (Check only one box.)
- ☐ Started new business (specify) ➤ _____
- ☐ Hired employees
- ☐ Created a pension plan (specify type) ➤
- ☐ Banking purpose (specify) ➤ _____
- ☐ Changed type of organization (specify) ➤ _____
- ☐ Purchased going business
- ☐ Created a trust (specify) ➤ _____
- ☐ Other (specify) ➤

10 Date business started or acquired (Mo., day, year) (See instructions.)

11 Closing month of accounting year (See instructions.)

12 First date wages or annuities were paid or will be paid (Mo., day, year). **Note:** *If applicant is a withholding agent, enter date income will first be paid to nonresident alien. (Mo., day, year)* . . . . ➤

13 Highest number of employees expected in the next 12 months. **Note:** *If the applicant does not expect to have any employees during the period, enter -0-. (See instructions.)* . . . ➤ | Nonagricultural | Agricultural | Household

14 Principal activity (See instructions.) ➤

15 Is the principal business activity manufacturing? . . . . ☐ Yes ☐ No
If "Yes," principal product and raw material used ➤

16 To whom are most of the products or services sold? Please check the appropriate box. ☐ Business (wholesale)
☐ Public (retail) ☐ Other (specify) ➤ | ☐ N/A

17a Has the applicant ever applied for an identification number for this or any other business? . . . . ☐ Yes ☐ No
Note: *If "Yes," please complete lines 17b and 17c.*

17b If you checked "Yes" on line 17a, give applicant's legal name and trade name shown on prior application, if different from line 1 or 2 above.
Legal name ➤ | Trade name ➤

17c Approximate date when and city and state where the application was filed. Enter previous employer identification number if known.
Approximate date when filed (Mo., day, year) | City and state where filed | Previous EIN

Under penalties of perjury, I declare that I have examined this application, and to the best of my knowledge and belief, it is true, correct, and complete. | Business telephone number (include area code)

Fax telephone number (include area code)

Name and title (Please type or print clearly.) ➤

Signature ➤ | Date ➤

Note: *Do not write below this line. For official use only.*

Please leave blank ➤	Geo.	Ind.	Class	Size	Reason for applying

For Paperwork Reduction Act Notice, see page 4. | Cat. No. 16055N | Form **SS-4** (Rev. 12-95)

IRS Form SS-4

The Least You Need to Know

➤ The easiest and least costly business form to arrange is a sole proprietorship.

➤ Partners are jointly and severally liable for the debts of their partnership.

➤ C corporations give owners protection from personal liability but have the possibility of a double tax—once at the corporate level and again at the shareholder level.

➤ S corporations can offer the best of both worlds: protection from personal liability (like a C corporation) but one level of tax (like a partnership).

➤ Limited liability companies are similar in many respects to S corporations, offering the same personal liability protection combined with the pass-through tax treatment.

➤ New businesses should get their employer identification numbers (unless they are exempt).

Part 3
Raising Dollars with Sense

An idea for a business is great, but it won't see the light of day if you can't pull together the money to finance it. Almost all home-based businesses need cash to get started. In the business world, this cash is called capital. Only a fortunate few have the cash on hand to begin a business without having to look for more capital. If you're not so fortunate, then you have to know where to get the money to start your business.

Some business owners require a lot of cash to get going, others not so much. You have to figure out how much money you need to start. You also have to know what kinds of money to look for.

Undercapitalization is a fancy term for being too broke to make it, and it's one of the main reasons why businesses fail. Don't let your business be one of them! You can see to it that there's not only enough money to get you started but also to help you grow.

How much is enough? How do you put a price tag on your business? As you'll learn in the chapters that follow, there are simple ways to figure what your expenses will be so that you can budget for success.

Finding money sources can be relatively easy. Getting those sources to write you a check is another story. It's often a lengthy and frustrating process. Still, it can be done—with good preparation and an understanding of the process.

In this part of the book, you do the legwork for raising capital to start your business. You find out how to write a business plan—an essential item for raising capital. You see how to project your cash needs to get started. And you learn who has the money and how to get it from them.

Chapter 8

So, Why Do I Need a Business Plan?

In This Chapter

➤ You need a business plan

➤ What to include in your plan from A to Z

➤ Make projections about your needs and about the business

➤ Attachments can make a plan complete

➤ Get help in writing your plan

A business plan is as essential a part of raising money to start your business as bait is to catching a fish. It may seem like an academic chore but, unfortunately, you may not be able to get around it if you need money. And, unless you're flush with enough cash to pay someone else to do it, you'll probably have to write all or most of it yourself.

But don't be blown away by this prospect. Even if you weren't the star in English class at school, you still have all you need to make a plan for your business. After all, when it comes to your business, you're the expert. The trickiest part of the plan, as you'll see, is the *numbers*. These are the financial facts and figures of your business (or what you think they'll be).

In this chapter you get an overview of what a business plan is, why you need it, and a description of its basic elements. You'll find much of the information you need to complete the details of your plan explained in chapters that follow. And remember, don't think you're alone in writing a business plan. There's help out there, if you know where to find it.

Why You Absolutely Need a Business Plan

In Chapter 4 you learned that a business plan is a written report that describes what your business is all about and where you want it to go in the future. A business plan can help you focus your business concept. But what does a business plan have to do with finding money to start your business? Everything!

If you want money for your business from a private investor (someone other than your rich uncle or a close friend), you must have a business plan. These guys will not even talk seriously about giving you money without seeing a professional-looking description of your business, an estimate of how much you need to raise, and how you plan to use the money you get. There's a good reason for making you jump through all these hoops. Writing a business plan shows these people two important things about you. First, that you are serious and professional about your business and, second, that you understand your business.

Having the business plan will open the door to sources of financing, but it's what's in the plan that brings home the bacon. Lenders or investors want to know what they're getting into. The only way to do this is to read your plan and talk to you.

Writing Your Business Plan: 101

Writing a business plan is about as much fun as having a root canal. You need to assemble a ton of information. You need to put numbers together in a way that financial-types understand. The report has to look good when you've finished. All of this takes a lot of time and considerable effort. It may take many weeks or even months (and not a few pots of coffee) to finalize your plan. But in the end you'll have a business, so all this sweat can be worth it.

So, you sit down to write your plan, and there you are; the blank piece of paper or glowing, empty computer screen stares back at you daring you to do something. But how the heck do you start? Before you can begin to write your plan, you must decide how you'll approach the writing process itself. You can select an approach to writing your plan from the three options described here:

➤ You can follow the outline in this chapter. The outline was designed by the Small Business Administration (SBA), the government guardian angel of small business that sponsors a number of loan programs. Following this outline guarantees you'll include all the information a prospective lender needs.

➤ If you own or have access to a computer (and know how to use it), you can use software designed for the very purpose of writing a business plan. This is the fast-food approach to writing a business plan: fast, (relatively) cheap, and easy to get. All the necessary sections of the business plan are included in the program. You simply bring up each section of the plan on your computer screen and then fill in the blanks. The amount of information that you have to type into the plan is minimal. And you get a professional-looking report when you're finished. Jian Biz Plan Builder for Windows, one example of software to write a winning business plan, runs about $90.

➤ If you have the bucks, you can go to experts who write business plans professionally. These plans can cost several hundred to several thousand dollars. If you need a large loan, you may need this kind of professional help. For most home-based businesses seeking modest capital, however, the cost of professional business plan writers may not be justified.

You can, of course, take the Chinese menu approach and combine any of these options. For example, you can prepare your business plan using the SBA outline and then pay a professional to look it over. The professional can make suggestions on how to improve your plan. You can use a computer program to write your plan, modifying it to more closely resemble the SBA outline in this book. If writing isn't your strong suit, you'd probably feel more comfortable letting the software "write" the plan for you; all you do is enter your company name, product or service, and other information when the software asks you to. Whichever way you go, you're not wrong. Just make sure to include all the necessary information.

Homegrown Tip

If you need more detailed help with some of the things asked for in the outline, you'll find whole books in the library on the subject of preparing business plans.

Homegrown Tip

There's even free computer software available for writing a business plan. For example, the SBA has software that it makes available to the public for free via the Internet. There's also shareware (software that you pay a small fee to use and you're on the honor system to pay it). To find a program that will help you with your business plan, go to http://www.sbaonline.sba.gov/shareware/starfile.html.

Regardless of which approach to writing you choose, you still have to put together the information to be included in the plan.

The Ingredients of Your Plan

Like the basic food groups that make up your daily fare, every business plan should contain certain basic information. Also, it's helpful to arrange this information in a logical order. This is where the following outline comes in. It's a recipe for business plan success, containing not only information about your business but also documents that you have to include with the plan. Using the outline also helps with organization. The order of the items in the following list makes sense to loan officers and other sources of capital.

Start with a Cover Sheet

This is the all-important first impression, the first view of your business plan that loan officers and others will see.

Homegrown Tip
Neatness counts! Make your business plan look neat and professional. Use good quality paper. Don't cross out or write in anything. Check for spelling and grammar errors.

On the cover sheet (also called a title page), include the name of your company, its address (your home address), and the business' phone number. If the business has an e-mail or Internet address, put it in as well. Also include your name as owner (plus the names of any other owners).

Some business plans number each copy so the owner can keep track of how many plans are floating around. You should include a date on the cover sheet. This is important if you revise the plan later. A date on the plan helps you distinguish between older and newer versions.

Your Purpose

Write a one-page statement about why you wrote the plan. Generally the statement is your objective of raising start-up capital or a loan for expansion. Be specific about the dollar amount you're trying to raise. For example, you need $6,000 to pay a franchise fee and an additional $4,000 in start-up costs to get your business off the ground.

Put Your Contents on the Table

To help the lender see how your plan is organized, write a table of contents listing each part of the plan and the appendixes (supporting documents at the end of the plan). Include page numbers so readers can find their way around easily.

Part I: Executive Summary

You may sometimes see this called a *summary description.* It's a brief sentence or two about each of the other parts of the business plan. This is your attention grabber, just like a snappy newspaper headline. Make sure it's well written so that they'll want to read on. The executive summary is often the first thing that loan officers and investors read. Unless it's of interest to them, it's the last thing they'll read in your plan. It must be complete enough to describe who you are, what you want, and why they should give it to you.

Homegrown Tip

You may want to write your executive summary after you've written the rest of the plan. That way, you'll be better able to summarize the actual content for the executive summary.

Part II: Business Description

This section of the business plan contains a description of your business. Part II of your business plan should contain all the essentials in the opening of any well-written news article. It should contain the who, what, where, when, and why of your business in the following order:

1. Re-state your company name and address from the cover page.

2. State when your business was formed or that it's being formed.

3. Discuss the legal angles of the business. Include a sentence about the legal organization of your business (sole proprietorship, partnership, C corporation, S corporation, or limited liability company; review the options for business organization in Chapter 7). Also mention any licenses or permits your business needs.

4. Describe (briefly) your business type—product or service. Also, state whether the business is independent, a takeover, a franchise, a business opportunity, or network marketing.

Homegrown Tip

Mention your business hours if this is relevant. For example, Carol, with the help of her teenage daughter, provided day care in her home *whenever needed.* This meant her services could be used by working parents late into the night and even on weekends, which was an important part of its appeal to the buying public.

Part III: Product or Service Description

Okay, now that the guy with the checkbook understands how you've structured your business, he needs to know more about what makes it tick. In this section, explain the core of the business—the product or service you're providing. Discuss how your business operates. Be specific, but concise.

Part IV: Your Marketing Plan

You have to show how you stand out from the competition and why you'll succeed. Describe the market for your product or service. Provide details like the size of the market and existing competition. If you don't know this information, find it out. Discuss your marketing strategies (advertising and promotions). Explain how your prices and sales terms stack up against the competition (higher prices, lower prices, guarantees, free follow-ups, and so on). (You'll find details on developing a marketing plan in Chapter 16.)

Part V: Operating Requirements

This is the physical description of your day-to-day business operations. State that you operate from home. This fact is not an automatic disqualification for getting a loan. And it's the truth about your business. Describe any special equipment you use in your operations. Some of this information may seem self-evident, but it helps to spell it out.

Part VI: Personnel

An idea for a business is one thing, but it's people that make it happen. List the people directly involved in your business. These are the key individuals who are or will be responsible for the business' success. If you own and run the business alone, make this clear and briefly describe any work experience and educational background that might make your business fly. If you have others working with you (either in your home office or behind the scenes), explain how you work together. Describe each person's business function (such as sales, purchasing, or finances). If you plan to use additional people in the future, state who these people will be, why you need them, and when you expect to add them.

> ### The Educated Entrepreneur
>
> Being a sole owner with no employees doesn't mean working alone. You can put together a strong team to help you with your business. Line up professionals—a lawyer, an accountant, and an insurance agent—to advise you. Use consultants to help you with advertising or collections or any activity that you don't have the time or the expertise to handle. Mentioning that team of pros in your business plan can lend it credibility.

Part VII: Financial Data

For lenders, this is the heart of your plan. You have to include a number of different financial projections in your plan. These projections show *how much* money you need and, perhaps more important to a lender, *how* you intend to repay the money (with interest, of course!). Your projections of sales and revenue (the things you'll need to repay the loan) usually should be made for three to five years.

Part VIII: Supporting Documents

I know your eyes are beginning to glaze over with all you'll have to pull together, but stay focused for just another minute. In addition to all of the financial stuff included in Part VII, you may have to include additional financial information as well as other materials—testimonials praising your product, scientific reports, demographic information, and so on. Generally, you gather this information at the end of your plan under the title *Appendixes*. Okay, glaze away.

> **Home Hazard**
> Projections aren't a work of fiction. They are only estimates but should be based on fact. A lender won't believe that the business will start from zero and earn a million dollars in the first year unless you can show that the numbers make sense. The credibility of your entire plan can be placed in jeopardy if you make outlandish claims you can't support.

Financial Statements: The Heart of Your Plan

Now that you've taken a deep breath and accepted the size of the challenge you've given yourself, let's get down to some details. I'll tackle the biggest chunk of your business plan first—financial statements.

The term *financial statements* may conjure up images of a troop of bespectacled accountants with pocket protectors and calculators for brains. Although financial statements are a favorite tool of the financially informed, don't let them frighten you. They are simply a picture of where your business stands financially at a particular point in time. Trust me, even you can write one.

What financial statements you should include with your business plan depends on whether you're just starting your business or have been around for a while and are looking to expand.

> **Business Buzzword**
> *Financial statements* are collections of information about income, expenses, sales figures, and other numbers-oriented stuff. There are a variety of different financial statements, including cash flow statements, balance sheets, and profit and loss statements.

Financial Statements for a Brand-New Business

If your business plan is being used for start-up purposes, include five different financial statements: (1) a statement of projected start-up costs, (2) a projected income statement, (3) a statement of expected profit and loss, (4) a projected monthly cash flow statement, and (5) a personal financial statement. These are briefly discussed below. You'll find a sample worksheet for each in Appendix B and more details on their contents in Chapters 9 and 10.

➤ Projected start-up costs. These are the expenses you expect to have to pay while you begin your business. Think about what it will take to begin to sell your product or service. Generally it's a good idea to budget for the first 12 months you'll be in business. Here's a worksheet that a desktop publishing business might complete.

Sample Worksheet for Projecting Start-Up Costs for a Desktop Publishing Business

Start-Up Item	Estimated Cost
Equipment	$0
Computers, telephones, copiers, faxes	$12,000
Office furniture and fixtures	$0
Inventory (for product-oriented businesses)	Not Applicable
Supplies	$250
Stationery, business cards, office supplies	$200
Professional fees	$0
Legal fees to set up a corporation, obtain a special zoning permit	$600
Accounting fees to set up books and accounts	$500
Insurance	$0
Fire or liability insurance on property and products (separate or add-on to homeowner's policy)	$350
Workers' compensation for employees	$0
Disability insurance for employees	$0
Licenses/permits (e.g., day care facility; home contractor)	$0
Utilities	$0
Advertising and promotion	$2,500

Start-Up Item	Estimated Cost
Occupancy costs	$0
Miscellaneous and unanticipated expenses	$600
Personal living expenses	$3,000
Total Start-Up Cost	**$20,000**

➤ Projected income statements. An *income statement* is a listing of how much money you expect the business to make during the start-up period. If your business provides a service, these *revenues* are the fees you expect to take in. If you sell a product, this is the amount you bring in from selling your product after returns and markdowns.

➤ Expected profit or loss. Lenders aren't philanthropists. Anyone who considers putting money into your business wants to know if that business will have something called a *net profit*. This will affect whether a loan will be repaid and whether an investor will see any return on her investment.

➤ Projected monthly cash flow statement. *Cash flow* is simple: It's the difference between the amount of money you earn and the amount of money you spend. You need to make an estimate of what you think your business' cash flow will be every month for the next year.

➤ Personal financial statement. This is a listing of your assets (stocks, bonds, real estate, and bank accounts) and your liabilities (mortgages, credit card debt, and car loans).

Business Buzzword
Net profits are business revenues reduced by both business expenses *and* taxes.

Business Buzzword
A *personal financial statement* shows your net worth, which is the amount by which your assets exceed your liabilities.

"The Numbers" for an Existing Business

If you've already started your home business but need money to expand, you've got to include different numbers. Obviously, you don't have to describe projections of start-up costs since you have already started. You do, however, have to include all of the other financial projections required for start-ups. In addition, you have to provide a *balance sheet* for your business.

Business Buzzword
A *balance sheet* is a listing of your business' assets, liabilities, and owner's equity (investment) as of a particular date (end of year, end of quarter). The assets must equal the liabilities and owner's equity. A business' balance sheet is like an individual's personal financial statement. It shows the net worth of the business.

You'll find a worksheet for creating your own balance sheet in Appendix B.

Supporting Documents for Your Plan

Some documents—personal tax returns, your résumé, and a business income tax return for an existing business—must be included with *all* business plans used for getting financing. Other documents are included only if appropriate. The following required documentation is based on SBA loan program requirements. Other lenders or investors may want even more paper. Check with them before you send in your plan.

➤ A copy of your personal tax return and the personal tax returns of all other owners for the last three years is always required. If you haven't yet prepared your most recent return, you may need to include a personal income statement listing your income and expenses for the year.

➤ A résumé for you and any other owners is a must. If you're working with any key person who is not an owner, such as a special consultant who is important to your business, you can also include that person's résumé.

Homegrown Tip
Don't hide your head in the sand when writing a business plan. If you have any negative information that prospective lenders or investors should know about, it's better that it come from you. For example, if you have a bad personal credit history, lenders have ways of discovering this. If you bring the issue up, you may be able to explain the reason for the problem—and why it will not be a problem in the future.

➤ An income statement for the business for the past year is necessary if you've been in operation. An *income statement* contains the same information you included in a projected income statement except that it's based on actual (not projected) numbers.

➤ Copies of proposed leases for a warehouse or equipment.

➤ Copies of licenses, patents, and other items you've created (such as a formula).

➤ A copy of the franchise contract (if you are buying a franchise).

➤ Letters of intent from suppliers and manufacturers.

➤ Industry data or demographic information supporting your claims.

➤ Other material that might be helpful in explaining your business. For example, if you're selling a new floor wax, it could be helpful to include a scientific report showing how your wax makes floors shinier than Yul Brynner's head or testimonials from satisfied customers.

Getting Help

Maybe by this time you're feeling overwhelmed and not up to the task of writing a business plan. That's certainly understandable considering the amount of information and what's involved in pulling it all together. This may seem especially difficult if you have only limited experience in writing reports. You may be a whiz at the business you plan to run—say a home contracting business—but have only a passing understanding about finances. Don't despair, you can get help.

When Numbers and You Don't Mix

Some people and numbers make about as much sense together as salsa and bananas—they just don't mix. Even if you're one of these people, you can't avoid the need to get the numbers straight. You might want to work with an accountant for this portion of your plan. You'll have to pay for this help (unless the accountant is your brother-in-law and he owes you a big favor!). But if you're writing the plan to raise money, you'll be wasting your efforts on other parts of the plan and won't accomplish your goal without good financial information.

To give you an idea of where in this book you'll find more information about putting the numbers together yourself, here are areas you may want to check out:

➤ What start-up costs you need to budget for (Chapter 9)

➤ Costs of borrowing money (Chapter 10)

➤ Office expenses (Chapter 13)

➤ Phone costs (Chapter 14)

➤ Equipment costs (Chapter 15)

➤ Advertising budgets (Chapter 16)

➤ Insurance costs (Chapter 19)

> **Homegrown Tip**
> Make sure that when you make your projections on start-up costs you include these accounting fees in your figures.

Making Everything Legal

Don't make claims or promises in your plan you can't keep. But in case you might have exaggerated a teensy bit by mistake, the best way to protect yourself is to have your plan reviewed by a lawyer. Like the accountant, the lawyer will charge you for his or her services. But the expense may be well worth it if it saves you from having problems down the road.

A friend of mine, Chris, is a toy inventor. Chris found out about legal pitfalls the hard way when he claimed in his plan that he had patented a new kind of puppet. In fact, he'd only applied for a patent. He didn't realize that jumping the gun on this in his plan could be a problem, but it was. A toy company looking at him with the intention of producing the puppet dropped him and his puppet like a hotcake when the truth came out. If a lawyer had looked over his plan he would have known that the patent was only pending. Chris might have saved himself a lot of time and might have struck up a deal with the toy company when the patent actually came through.

Homegrown Tip
The lawyer or accountant you choose to help you with your business plan may be willing to negotiate a reduced fee with the promise that she'll get all your business in the future.

Just like accounting fees for help with your numbers, make sure that when you make your projections on start-up costs you include these legal fees in your figures.

Polishing Your Plan: There's Help Out There

If you can provide the financial information, you can always get help in sprucing up your plan. There are many free or low-cost organizations or agencies to help you.

SCORE—the Service Corps of Retired Executives—is a division of the SBA. It's staffed by business pros who've been there before and can provide you with free counseling on your business plan. They can critique your plan and offer suggestions on how you can make it better. In reworking your business plan you may just find that you're also getting a better handle on your business idea. For example, a SCORE volunteer who may have expertise in your business field may suggest marketing strategies you've never thought of. SCORE can also help you by directing you to sources of financing.

Homegrown Tip
Be sure to schedule an appointment so that you won't waste your time waiting for a volunteer to assist you. You can find the SCORE office nearest you by calling 800-634-0245 for a referral.

State agencies may also provide assistance with business plans. Check out your state's economic development office. It'll review your business plan for free, just like SCORE. And also, just like SCORE, it can direct you to people with money to invest. For example, I know one fellow who wanted to start a home business to market products imported from Sweden. Sven took a draft of his business plan to a local state economic development office. The person who reviewed the plan had spent many years in Fortune 500 companies and not only offered some suggestions on how to improve the plan, but also personally knew a loan officer in a local bank. This personal touch paved the way for Sven to get a loan to start the business.

Look for a listing in your local telephone directory. If you can't find a listing for a local economic development office, call your state office and ask for a referral. The number of each state's economic development office is listed in Appendix A.

The Least You Need to Know

➤ A business plan is essential for raising money.

➤ Writing a business plan is a lengthy but necessary process.

➤ The numbers are the key to your business plan.

➤ You can get help in writing your plan.

Chapter 9

Paying the Bills While Paying Your Dues

In This Chapter

➤ Covering your start-up costs

➤ How are you going to cover those personal expenses?

➤ Moonlighting for fun and profit

➤ Planning for those day-to-day costs once you get going

I know you don't want to hear this, but running a business means paying your bills each month. To do this you need to know what you can expect. First, there are costs you'll encounter in your start-up phase. That generally carries you for about the first three months. After that, you need to learn how much it's going to cost you each month to stay in business.

In this chapter you'll see the types of costs you may have when you're just getting started. Then you'll learn to estimate your personal living expenses. After all, you have to eat while your business gets off the ground. You'll also find out how to make an operating budget.

How Your Start-Up Costs Stack up

No more theory or generalities about what it's going to cost you. The time has come to get specific. Like a Boy Scout, you've got to be prepared—prepared for expenses you may face during your start-up phase, typically the first three months of operation.

Start-up costs are different than the costs you'll be paying month in and month out. Start-up costs involve one-time expenses, such as legal fees to have your lawyer review your franchise agreement or deposits you'll have to make on phone lines or storage space outside your home.

Homegrown Tip
Don't go overboard ordering stationery, invoices, and business cards. Get just enough to get you started in case the information about your business changes. You may add a second phone, incorporate, or get an e-mail address that you'll need to include.

Close your eyes and picture your home office and what it will take to get it ready for you to begin. Need furniture? A computer? Stationery? Paper clips? Permits and licenses? Maybe you already have a setup that's usable for a time. But maybe you have an empty room at the moment that you'll fill up with the things you need for your business.

If you're selling children's toys or other inventory, you'll have to estimate what you need to get started. Don't order more than you'll sell in the first few months because your money's tight. But don't order too little. You don't want orders to go unfilled. And you don't want to miss out on better prices that buying larger quantities may give you.

The costs you'll need to budget for when getting started are discussed in detail in the following chapters:

➤ Buying the business (Chapters 5 and 6)

➤ Insurance (Chapter 19)

➤ Setting up your office (Chapter 13)

➤ Computers and other equipment (Chapter 15)

➤ Phones (Chapter 14)

➤ Advertising (Chapter 16)

Make your own grocery list of expenses you'll have to pay to get going. Here are some to get you started:

Professional Fees

Legal

Business purchase	$_____
Franchise purchase	$_____
Incorporation	$_____
Partnership agreement	$_____
Business name search	$_____
Zoning variance	$_____

Accounting

Advice on business structure	$_____
S election filing	$_____
Setting up the books	$_____

Insurance

Health	$_____
Disability	$_____
Liability	$_____
Property	$_____

Materials

Equipment

Computer, printer, etc.	$_____
Copier/fax	$_____
Furniture	$_____
Specialized tools	$_____
Other equipment	$_____
Car/truck	$_____

continues

continued

Materials

Supplies

Stationery $_____

Business cards $_____

Office supplies $_____

Postage $_____

Inventory

Inventory $_____

Office Space

Remodeling costs $_____

Connection fees and deposits
on utilities $_____

Deposits on storage space $_____

Marketing

Company brochure $_____

Yellow Pages ad $_____

Business opening announcement $_____

Personal Expenses

Starting a business takes time. It may be many months before the business generates enough money for you to begin taking a salary or otherwise tap into the cash. Think about how you're going to put food on the table in the meantime.

How to Eat While Feeding Your Business

If you're working on your home-based business on a full-time basis, you need to plan so you have money for things like your rent or mortgage and utilities. (Remember your business is only taking up a portion of your home. The cost of running the other part of your home is not a business expense.) You need money to eat, pay for flu shots, put gas in your car, and even to go out to the movies occasionally.

You have a few options to help you survive while you feed your budding business:

➤ **Live off your savings.** If you've put aside a nest egg, you may be able to use it now for your personal expenses while your business gets started. In this case, you don't have to budget for personal living expenses in your start-up costs.

Some people begin their own business as a result of an unexpected windfall. One corporate executive I know was laid off in a wave of downsizing. Joe got a generous severance package that continued his wages for nine months. He decided to start a home business using marketing skills he learned in the corporate world. He used his windfall salary to pay the mortgage and put shoes on the kids' feet. With careful budgeting, that nine month severance package carried him more than a year!

If you plan to use your nest egg to buy the business, or to purchase needed equipment, then you have to be realistic: Is your nest egg a robin's egg or a dinosaur egg? Your nest egg may not be big enough to cover both business start-up costs and your personal expenses. You may have to borrow additional money.

➤ **Rely on a spouse.** If you have a working spouse whose income can cover your personal living expenses, then you don't have to budget for them in your start-up costs. That's how I was able to get my business started. Sometimes, however, a spouse's income may only cover so much. Be sure to include any other money you need to cover your personal living expenses in your start-up budget.

Homegrown Tip
Figure your personal living expenses for at least six months. Then make a plan for how you'll pay these expenses while your business gets up and running.

Keep Your Day Job

You don't have to burn all your bridges to start a new business. Many people start a home-based business on a part-time basis. By moonlighting, they can continue to earn a salary and benefits. The salary from their day job covers personal living expenses. If you're still employed, you may want to try this approach when starting your business.

In deciding whether to begin part-time, take into account the all-important exhaustion factor. If you work all day, you only have nights and weekends to devote to starting up your business. You may be shortchanging yourself. There may not be enough hours in the day to work your day job and spend the time your business needs to succeed. Or you may just be too pooped to do a good job in your own business.

Don't ignore the impact your decision will have on your family. If you're working day and night, there's little time for anything else, like going to Johnny's soccer game or doing the housework. This work arrangement may be fine for a short while, but it probably won't work indefinitely.

Homegrown Tip
Keeping an outside job while starting up a home business has two positives. Not only are you ensuring that you have enough cash to pay your personal bills, you also avoid the pressure of making your home business succeed right off the bat. You don't need to have it become successful overnight because you're not relying on it for a living.

There are pros and cons to both starting a business part-time and taking the full-time plunge. In making this choice, ask yourself these questions *before* you quit your job:

➤ Will you be able to pay your bills if you quit? Be sure to include the cost of health care in your plans if you're not covered under a spouse's plan. When you leave your job you're entitled under a federal law—COBRA—to continue the same health coverage for 18 months. But you, not your former employer, have to pay the cost!

➤ What happens if the business doesn't work out? Will you be able to go back to your old job or get a new one?

➤ Can your ego handle the drop in income? Are you comfortable relying on your spouse for support?

Just What the Doctor Ordered: Operating Expenses

You've learned about preparing a start-up budget. Now you have to make an operating budget. But how do you know when a business passes the start-up phase and enters the operating phase? There's no magic number. As a rule of thumb it's helpful to look at your start-up budget to carry you through the first three months of business. The operating budget should be designed to carry you for the next three months of business. Some experts suggest you budget for at least the first year.

Many of the items you budgeted for in the start-up phase won't go away in the next phase of your business—the next three months of operations. Let's say you planned for advertising costs in the start-up phase. You have to continue or even accelerate your advertising campaign as you nurture your business. Be sure to budget for expanding your operations.

You'll be glad to hear, however, that some of your start-up costs disappear as you move forward. You don't need to plan for occupancy costs in the operating budget. Once you've put in the new phone and wiring in your office, you don't have to budget for them in the operating budget. These are one-time costs.

There are some items that may have been more heavily budgeted in the start-up phase. For example, professional fees might be a big bite when you're buying a business and working out the legal stuff. But you might still have ongoing professional fees throughout the life of your business. So, if you pay an accountant to do your books and tax returns, you should budget for this service.

However, it's not all good news: There are several new items to include in your operating budget that weren't necessarily there at start-up. These items include payroll, debt service, taxes, dues and subscriptions, and repairs and maintenance.

Payroll

If you hire an employee to work for your business, even your husband or teenage daughter, you have to budget for payroll costs. Payroll costs are more involved than a U.N. peace accord. There are a lot of aspects to consider, and they're discussed in detail in Chapter 18, but here's a brief rundown:

➤ **Wages.** Include the amount of wages you expect to pay. If you're an employee of your own business (your business is incorporated), you can include your own salary in this category. If the business is not incorporated, don't include payments to yourself here (you'll account for the payments in your personal living costs). If you contract out your work, you're not talking about wages, but you'll have to pay a similar amount to get the work done.

➤ **Other benefits.** During the start-up phase of your business you probably won't be providing any fancy fringe benefits, such as retirement plan contributions, for yourself or your employees. However, there may be some additional benefits—car fare when your employee works late, for example—that you want to plan for.

➤ **Workers' compensation and disability.** By law you're required to provide workers' compensation and disability for employees. These expenses may have already been included in your insurance costs. If not, be sure to add them into your payroll costs.

➤ **Unemployment insurance.** You may pay state and/or federal unemployment insurance to cover workers if they're laid off or fired (unless, of course, they walked off with the company petty cash). The amount of unemployment insurance you pay depends on the size of your payroll and your unemployment *experience*. A business with high unemployment experience—people coming and going like a turnover revolving door—will pay higher unemployment insurance than a company that keeps its people around, even though both have the same number of employees.

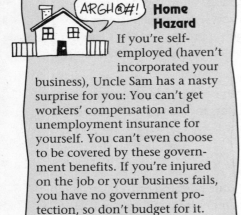

Home Hazard

If you're self-employed (haven't incorporated your business), Uncle Sam has a nasty surprise for you: You can't get workers' compensation and unemployment insurance for yourself. You can't even choose to be covered by these government benefits. If you're injured on the job or your business fails, you have no government protection, so don't budget for it.

➤ FICA. You've seen this little fella on your pay stubs: An employer must pay Social Security and Medicare taxes on employee wages. Social Security and Medicare taxes are called FICA. As an employer you have to withhold a matching amount of FICA from employee wages—the employee's share—and pay this to the IRS along with your employer's share. However, since the employee's share is subtracted from wages, it's not an additional cost for you.

See, I told you there was more to payroll than writing out the checks. Complete this worksheet for figuring your payroll costs. Later in the chapter you'll transfer the total from this worksheet to another one, so keep it handy.

Worksheet for Payroll Costs

Payroll Cost	Total Cost
Wages	$_____
Health insurance, vacation pay	$_____
Workers' compensation and disability	$_____
Unemployment insurance (FUTA)	$_____
FICA	$_____
_____	_____
Total	$_____

Servicing Your Debt Service

If you're one of the fortunate ones who has not borrowed any money to get your business started, then you can skip this section and go get a cup of coffee. But if you have taken a loan to help you get going, you have to plan for paying it back.

Not all loans are equal. You may, for example, have a loan that doesn't call for any immediate repayment of principal. In that case, you include only your interest payments for the second three months that you're in business.

If you have a loan with an interest rate tied to the prime rate or some other rate that moves around more than a rock band on tour, it may be more difficult to budget for your interest payments. Will interest rates rise? Will interest rates fall? If droves of economists with PhDs can't predict this, how can you? If you want to make a conservative budget you may want to include some rise in interest to cover yourself. However, as a rule of thumb, just use the initial interest rate when making your budget.

Taxes, Taxes, Taxes

Here's an understatement: There are a number of different kinds of taxes. In fact, people get postgraduate degrees in this topic, write whole books on it, and go crazy trying to keep up with the constant changes. You've already seen payroll taxes on wages. Now I'll give you the gist of some other taxes (you'll find some more details in Chapter 22).

> **Business Buzzword**
> *Debt service* is a term used to describe the repayment of a loan. It includes the repayment of principal as well as interest on the loan.

For the purposes of budgeting your operating expenses, the most common type of tax your business may face is sales tax. This is a tax you collect from your clients and customers on the product or service you provide—you know, the 27¢ you add to the price of a pen at Kmart. If you're unlucky enough to live in a state with a sales tax, check with your state to find out about your sales tax requirements. Some states might exempt certain goods and services from tax, while others might not.

And lest we forget, if you're fortunate enough to have your business be profitable from the start, then you must also consider income taxes on your profits.

Dues and Subscriptions

As you begin to run your business you might want to join local business groups or trade associations. Despite popular belief, the purpose of these memberships is not to eat a lot of rubber-chicken lunches every month (although you will). These memberships help you network your business with other business owners, learn what's happening in your business community, and deal with some of the cabin fever you may suffer when working alone in a home office.

Check out the cost of membership. Become a member of the groups you can afford to join that will give you the greatest business benefit or personal enjoyment for your buck.

Business newspapers, magazines, and trade journals can also help you stay current and, maybe, even one step ahead of your competitors. You may also want to sign on to the Internet with an online service provider. Investigate your monthly costs for these services.

> **The Educated Entrepreneur**
>
> According to a survey of business owners who succeeded and those who failed, those in the success column overwhelmingly kept up on developments affecting their business and their industry. You want to stay abreast of not only the latest developments in your industry but also developments affecting business in general (taxes, insurance, technology). To do this you need to read, read, read.

Repairs and Maintenance

It's Murphy's Law: If you use equipment of any kind in your business—even a simple copier—you can bet that sometime, somewhere, something will break. Hopefully this won't happen too often, especially if you buy or lease new equipment. But when something does break, you need to get it fixed. Be sure to plan for repair costs.

Even if nothing breaks, you'll save money in the long run if you follow a routine service program and have checkups for your equipment. Most service contracts for your equipment offer an annual or more frequent checkup or service call.

Tallying Your Operating Expenses

After you make educated estimates, transfer the total of all the items in this section and other costs you think of to the worksheet of your operating budget provided on the next page.

Worksheet for Projecting Operating Costs for a Home-Based Business

Item	Estimated Cost
Payroll	$_____
Debt service	$_____
Taxes	$_____
Dues and subscriptions	$_____
Repairs and maintenance	$_____
Equipment	$_____
Inventory (for product-oriented businesses)	$_____
Supplies	$_____
Legal, accounting, other professional fees	$_____
Insurance	$_____
Licenses/permits	$_____
Utilities	$_____
Advertising and promotion	$_____
Miscellaneous and unanticipated expenses	$_____
Personal living costs	$_____
Total Operating Cost	$_____

The Least You Need to Know

➤ Cover the costs of getting started by budgeting for them.

➤ Be sure that you plan for your personal expenses in addition to your business needs.

➤ Consider moonlighting so that your day job pays your personal bills while you start up your business at night and on weekends.

➤ Your operating budget should carry you for the second three months you are in business.

Chapter 10

Hunting for Money: Tracking Down Your Financing Options

In This Chapter

➤ Understand the real price of borrowing money

➤ Sell your (corporate) soul for cash

➤ Get creative about raising money

➤ Make the choice: Go in debt or share the spoils

You've looked at your personal bank account and (once you stopped crying) have decided you just don't have what you need to get your business started. You may have to look to family, friends, or outsiders for help. If you discount robbing your bank or winning the lottery, there are really only two prime strategies for raising money: borrow it or bring in investors. Borrowing money is called *debt;* investment in your business by investors is called *equity*.

There are sound reasons why one strategy may be better for you than the other.

In this chapter you'll learn the pros and cons of raising money with a loan. You'll also find out about the consequences of bringing in investors. You'll discover other sources of financing that you might not have considered. Finally you'll learn which type of financing strategy is best for you.

Borrowing

Okay, a quick course called Borrowing Money 101. When your business borrows money that has to be paid back along with interest, this is called a *loan.* If you borrow from Citibank or another financial institution, you're dealing with a *commercial loan.* If you borrow from your mother-in-law or best friend, you have a *private loan.*

Home Hazard

Loan brokers can help you find a loan. But some loan brokers operate scams. They may, for example, promise to get you a loan if you pay an up-front fee of several hundred dollars plus a loan processing fee. Then, suddenly, they end up in Rio with your money and you don't get a loan. So check out any ads offering loans to individuals based on their "credit worthiness." If you have any doubts, check with your Better Business Bureau.

Home Hazard

The owner of a corporation can be personally liable for a loan to the business because almost all lenders will require the owner to give her personal guarantee for the loan. Incorporation doesn't protect the personal assets of an owner who personally guarantees a loan to the business.

Loans have a language of their own. You (or the business) are the *borrower,* or *debtor.* The bank or other lending source is the *lender,* or *creditor.* The time during which you have the use of the money you borrow is called the *term* or *period* of the loan. This is also called the loan's *maturity.* The amount you borrow from the lender is called *principal.* (You'll be talking like a loan officer in no time!)

You get a loan by making a loan application. Since you're looking for money for your business, you'll probably be asked to show your business plan. The loan application process varies considerably, depending on the type of loan you're going for. Some applications are like skits on *Saturday Night Live*—they are as brief as a page and don't go into great detail. Others are like four-hour feature films—they're much longer and ask many of the questions you already answered in your business plan.

As fascinating as your business is, the lender is not really interested in the intricacies of the product you sell or the service you provide. The main thing a lender wants to know is, will he get his money back? The lender doesn't benefit from your profits (beyond money used to pay back the loan). The lender doesn't own any part of your business. (Of course if you fail to repay the loan, the lender may be able to take your house or car, but let's not even go there.)

While you're looking for a loan for your business, the lender is looking closely at you as much as he is at the business. The reason? As the owner of a small business you'll be asked to co-sign or guarantee the loan. In other words, the cash will go to the business, but if the business goes under, your friendly bank manager will come knocking on *your* front door for repayment. Therefore, your personal credit history will affect whether you can get a business loan.

The time between making the application and hearing the happy news that you've been approved can also vary a great deal. It may be as short as a few days, but usually is a lot longer. For business loans, depending on the loan program involved, it may be several months before you learn whether you'll get the money.

Consequences of Borrowing

Like casual dating, borrowing means that you have a limited relationship with the lender. You make a loan application and, if it's approved, your contact with the lender is basically one of making monthly payments. Some banks are more aggressive in providing counsel and advice to businesses. Some bankers, for example, may try to establish more personal relationships with lenders and help them to make contacts within the community.

At the end of the loan term, when you've paid off your debt, the relationship ends. You may, of course, renew the relationship by taking out another loan with the same lender, but it's not like feelings will be hurt if you go down the street to another bank for the next loan.

Borrowing does mean that you have to come up with the cash each month to pay off the debt, plus a little (or a lot) in interest. Sometimes the loan can be set up as a *balloon* loan. Although balloons may conjure up a day at the zoo, this is a little less fun. The balloon is a great big payment, usually at the end of the loan. Instead of paying back a part of the money you borrowed in monthly installments, you simply pay interest each month. At the end of the term of the loan you must pay *all* of what you borrowed in one lump sum.

> **Homegrown Tip**
> A balloon loan may be a good way to borrow if it's an option. It lets you make smaller payments up front while you're getting started. But don't let your balloon burst. Be sure to put aside enough money to pay off the principal when it comes due.

How Long Will It Last?

Business loans generally fall into two main categories: short-term and long-term. In banking lingo, a *short-term* loan is one that will be paid back in less than one year. Examples of short-term business loans include:

➤ Working capital loans

➤ Accounts receivable loans

➤ Lines of credit (or revolving lines of credit)

Long-term loans are loans that (you guessed it) take a while to pay back. They typically have a payback period of at least one year. Generally, long-term loans don't run longer than seven years. Typically, long-term loans are used for major business undertakings like expansion or the purchase of equipment or real estate.

Loans for start-up capital generally fall in the long-term loan category. So, you can anticipate repaying a loan and saying a fond farewell to the lender in three to seven years.

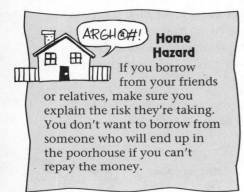

Home Hazard

If you borrow from your friends or relatives, make sure you explain the risk they're taking. You don't want to borrow from someone who will end up in the poorhouse if you can't repay the money.

Borrowing from Family and Friends

If you don't want to (or can't) get a commercial loan, consider a private loan from family or friends. The good news here is that the process can be very informal. After all, the lender knows you, probably quite well. You may not even need to show him your business plan.

Of course, the main drawback to borrowing from family and friends is what can happen to relationships if the business doesn't fly. If you can't repay the loan you might lose a friend, or run the risk of never being invited to the family reunion again.

The Educated Entrepreneur

It doesn't matter that you're borrowing from Uncle Charlie, always put it in writing. In a private-loan situation, drawing up a formal agreement is more for the protection of the lender than for you. If you have a written loan agreement stating the amount borrowed, the rate of interest charged, and the terms of repayment, Uncle Charlie will be in a better position to write off the loan on his tax return if you skip town. Without a loan agreement, the IRS may disallow the write-off, claiming that the loan was really a gift to his favorite nephew.

Giving Away the Business

Instead of borrowing money, which you have to pay back with interest, you may want to bring in an investor. With an investor you share the ownership of your business with someone else. If you have an idea for a business and start it on your own, you own 100% of the business. If you bring in an investor, your 100% is reduced.

The amount of the business you give away depends on how much money the investor brings to you, how much that money is worth to you at the time, and how much the investor's willing to settle for. For example, $10,000 to get your business off the ground may be the difference between getting started and not getting started, so it's very significant to you. You might be willing to give up 10%, 20%, or even more of the ownership to the investor.

Of course, the investor may have other ideas. Paul was trying to raise money to buy more inventory for his foot cream business. One investor was anxious to help—in exchange for a majority interest in the business. Paul may have been needy but he wasn't crazy enough to hand over his business. Instead, he kept looking for the money he needed and found it with another investor who wasn't greedy.

In deciding how much ownership you're willing to exchange for the cash, weigh the possible return to the investor (what you think that share may be worth a few years down the road when your business is profitable) against your current level of desperation (how badly you need the money). A $300,000-a-year business is going to return tens of thousands of dollars a year to a 20% investor, who may have put up only $5,000 up front. Is her investment really worth it?

Here's the real payoff with an investor: When she puts money into your business, you don't have to pay anything back. Nada, nothing, zip. You don't have to make monthly payments of interest and principal. This is a big plus since the money that you would have used to make loan repayments can be used to help your business. The investor benefits from her cash contribution only if the business makes it and becomes profitable.

> **Homegrown Tip**
> You may want to give up part ownership to bring in needed capital even though you give up some control. After all, it might be better to have a smaller percentage of something than 100% of nothing (what you could wind up with if you can't get the money you need to start up).

As a rule of thumb, a private investor (other than perhaps a relative or a friend) is looking for a high return on investment (as much as 25% or more) in a relatively short time (usually less than five years). When Aunt Lottie invests in your company, her expectations might be quite different. She might not be looking for quick profit as much as she's looking to help you out. (Of course, she doesn't want to lose her shirt, either.)

Since you don't have to pay anything back, the investor is less interested in your credit history, but more in the business itself. Is this the best idea since sliced bread? Is it practical? And, most important, will it make money so she's not flushing her money away? The answer to this last question, which the investor must answer for herself, is often the reason she decides to ante up.

Like having a baby, when you take on an investor she is going to be around for a long time. When you bring an investor into your business, it's important that you understand you're beginning a long-term relationship. Just like being a parent, there's no set time for this kid to move out (although it's certainly possible to disown her if you come to a mutual parting of the ways).

When you look for investors, there's no formal or established process like filling out a loan application. However, most prospective investors (outside of your family) will insist on seeing your business plan. If that sparks any interest, then the investor will meet with you before deciding to go any further.

Getting investors interested in your business to the point where they're willing to put up cash may take weeks or even months. Then you generally involve attorneys in the process to formalize your arrangements. This, again, will take time.

Investors Come in All Sizes

Just because you take on an investor, you don't have to give up total control of your business. Investor arrangements are not all the same. There are various ways to set them up:

➤ Partners. If you bring in someone to work with you on the business and you're not incorporated, you two become a partnership. You don't have to be equal partners. A 50/50 split makes you equal partners, but you might prefer something like a 60/40 or 75/25 split of the business (and hence the profits).

A partnership arrangement is the closest thing in the business world to a marriage. Partners must get along and be able to agree on most issues that come up.

There's a benefit to bringing in a partner in addition to the money it means for the business. A partner can bring not only additional capital but also additional talent to the business. You may be a whiz with numbers while your partner is great at sales, for example.

➤ Limited partners. You can share the ownership of the business with a partner without giving up any of the control over day-to-day activities by forming a limited partnership. The limited partner puts in money but is only entitled to receive a share of the profits. He can't tell you how to run the business.

➤ Members. You can form your business as a limited liability company and bring in members who will contribute needed cash. The role of a new member can be defined by you either as a general partner or a limited partner. Make sure that the investor understands whether he will have a say in how the business is run.

➤ Shareholders. If you have incorporated your business and find an investor willing to put money into it, you can sell stock (shares) in the corporation to investors. Investors then become shareholders (or stockholders, the words are interchangeable). How does this affect your ownership interest? This is a little complicated, but bear with me for a moment.

Here's an example: Say your corporation is formed with 200 shares of stock. You issue 10 shares of stock to yourself. You own 100% of the corporation. You want to bring in an investor and decide that the investor should have a 10% ownership interest. You can do this by selling the investor 1 of your 10 shares of stock. You now own 9 of the 10 outstanding shares, or 90% of the company; the investor owns 1 of the 10 outstanding shares, or 10% of the company. Alternatively, the investor can buy 1 share of stock directly from the corporation. In that case, you own 90.9% of the company (10 of 11 outstanding shares); the investor owns 9.1% of the company (1 of 11 outstanding shares). Get it?

An investor who owns shares in the corporation may or may not have a say in the business. As a minority shareholder there's not much an investor can do to tell you how to design your widgets or sell your skin cream. However, as a practical matter, you may want to work with the investor to start up and grow the business, taking his counsel and advice.

Venture Capitalists

Some of you might be saying, "Hey, I've read about venture capital firms that invest in new companies; why not mine?" True. But venture capital isn't all that easy to come by. A venture capital firm is a company of savvy investors who are in business solely to find profitable ventures, invest, and reap (hopefully) huge profits.

As a practical matter, your gift basket business, or most home-based businesses for that matter, aren't attractive to venture capitalists, who are generally looking for the latest technology or the hottest new product. If you're the next Bill Gates developing a new software technology in your garage, you may interest a venture capital firm (which you can find through a directory of venture capital firms in the reference section of your local library). Otherwise, don't waste your time or theirs. Even if you have the right product, most venture capitalists are only interested in existing businesses that are already profitable, which leaves out start-ups.

Free Money: Options for Finding Start-up Cash

Instead of borrowing from a lender or giving up part of your ownership interest in exchange for an investment in your business, you may be able to find *free money*.

Home Hazard

Although a grant is desirable because it doesn't get repaid, it's perhaps the most difficult kind of money to get. You're at the mercy of the people making the grants. They have special interests and you have to fit their mold if you want the money. And, even if you find a grant you may be suited for, then you have to overcome stiff competition for it.

Although money still doesn't grow on trees, grants and awards provide money that doesn't have to be repaid. It's like a prize. There are a variety of grants and awards given to businesses.

If you're lucky enough to get a grant, you'll have a continuing relationship with the grant maker for the term of the grant. You'll generally have to do a certain amount of paperwork, sending in *interim reports* telling the grant maker how things are going and that you're using the money the way you said you would. At the end of the grant term you also have to write a final report. The grant maker will also audit your books to make sure you haven't spent the money on a vacation home in the Bahamas.

Getting Money from Uncle Sam: Government Grants

Although you may think of the government as taking money rather than giving it back, grants are made by the government to businesses in certain industries. There are grants designed for small businesses but typically they're not suitable for start-ups. There may, however, be exceptions for special businesses. For example, Ramona, a retired teacher, was one home-based business owner who saw an opportunity in government funding. She applied for a government grant designed to provide tutoring services to inner-city children. Since the government often supports economic development for depressed areas, this was a great match.

There may be grants for special business owners—women, minorities, or people with disabilities. These grants can also be applied for by home-based business owners.

Homegrown Tip

Look for grants for *seed money* in the bible for grants called "Awards, Honors and Prizes" (published by Gale Research), which you can probably find in your local library.

Foundation Grants

Grants and awards are also made by *foundations*. Foundations are kind of like that guy on the old TV show who went around handing out checks for a million bucks to total strangers. Foundations are basically charitable organizations set up to fund projects they're interested in. Some foundations give out *seed money,* money that can be used to start up a business. Generally, however, like government grants, foundation money is designed to go to businesses that already have a track record.

Granting Your Business Wish

You start the grant process by finding a specific grant you think you might be eligible for. Once you've found the right match, you can begin the application process.

Start by sending the government agency or foundation making the grant a *letter of intent.* This letter informs the grant maker that you want to submit a formal *proposal,* which is just another word for an application. The letter should contain a brief outline of your project—which may be simply to start up a business. Describe your business, your background, and any other key people you work with. Specify how much grant money you're looking for and how the money will be used.

Sometimes your letter of intent will be answered with encouragement to continue and submit a formal application. Other times you might get word not to bother going any further. Still other times you might hear nothing at all and have to forge ahead with no inkling of whether there's a chance for success.

Remember, the government agency or foundation making the grant doesn't know you exist. Your job is to make yourself sound fascinating and convince them that the grant should be given to you over thousands of other applicants.

Home Hazard
Watch out for deadlines. Some grants can be submitted at anytime and will be considered when received. Other grants have an application deadline that's as sacrosanct as April 15 is for the IRS.

What Type of Financing Is Best for You?

Many factors influence which type of financing you should pursue. In fact, there's nothing preventing you, other than the time and effort required, from exploring all avenues at the same time. Friends thought Jim was nuts when he described his efforts to get the money he needed for his software development business. Loan applications to Marine Midland; calls to Arty, his college roommate; begging for cash; and even a grant proposal to a foundation. But he didn't seem so crazy when the bank loan came through and his college roommate Arty anted up. Jim had enough money to start developments on two projects at the same time!

The following table provides a checklist for some things to consider when deciding how to raise money for your start-up. Weigh the plusses and minuses of each type of funding.

Selecting a Form of Financing

Factors to Consider	Debt	Equity	Grant
Limit on funds available	Yes	No	Yes
Application process	Complex	Informal	Complex
Obligation to repay	Yes	No	No
Loss of control	No	Yes	No
Impact of your credit history	Yes	No	No
Applicable for start-ups	Yes	Yes	Limited
Open to home-based business	Yes	Yes	Yes

Notice that this table indicates a limit on funds available through a loan. While there may be high limits on loans available, the amount you can qualify for is limited by your personal financial situation.

The Least You Need to Know

➤ Borrowing means you have to pay back the cash in monthly installments over a set time with interest.

➤ Borrowing from friends or family may take less effort, but it can take a toll on your relationship if things don't go right.

➤ Bringing in investors allows you to have more cash for use in the business.

➤ Venture capital generally is not suited for home business start-ups.

➤ Free money for start-ups is very hard to come by, but might be worth exploring.

➤ One type of financing may be better for you than another.

Chapter 11

Digging in Your Pockets for Cash

In This Chapter

➤ Tap into your savings to start your business

➤ Use the equity in your home

➤ Borrow against your life insurance policy

➤ Use your retirement plan for a loan

➤ Deduct interest on your borrowing

In the last chapter you learned about the options of borrowing or sharing your ownership interest in exchange for investments to give your business a jump-start. You saw that there are upsides and downsides to both choices. But, like Dorothy in the *Wizard of Oz*, you may not need to look beyond your own front door to find the money to get your home-based business off the ground. You may be sitting on a pile of cash you can use to start your business—even if you don't know it yet.

In this chapter you'll learn how to recognize the personal resources you may already have that can be used to start your business. You'll see that it's easy and quick to tap into each of your personal sources of funding. But before you mortgage the farm, it's also important to weigh the pros and cons.

Be Your Own Banker

In the best of all possible worlds, you'd be independently wealthy and wouldn't need anyone's help to start your business. You wouldn't have to borrow or share your ownership or look to outsiders in any way. If you didn't have to borrow then you wouldn't have to make monthly payments and you'd save on interest expenses. If you didn't have to bring in investors, you'd keep full control and enjoy all of that lovely money from your business for your own selfish pleasures.

Yeah, right. Now let's get real. Most of us aren't independently wealthy. But, most of us do have resources we might not have thought of to finance our own businesses. Using those resources keeps control of your business in your own hands, even if you aren't a Rockefeller. So let's look at what you have that you can borrow against or turn into cash for your business.

Emptying Out the Christmas Fund

With personal savings there's no process at all. It's right at your fingertips. So, the best case scenario is to be your own banker and rely on your own savings to get your business started.

The Educated Entrepreneur

Almost 80% of all new business owners don't use commercial loans to get started, says the Small Business Administration. Instead they rely primarily on their savings and other resources. There are no specific statistics available on the financing of home-based businesses, but I'd bet that owners aren't out robbing banks. More likely, they're relying on personal resources to get their businesses going.

Okay, be brave. Open your savings passbook. Do you have enough cash on hand to pay for the things you figure you need to get started? Maybe you're one of those farsighted people who had the idea to start up a business when you were 10. Maybe you had enough foresight and discipline to save your pennies for your goal. (Or maybe, like Howard, a computer technician downsized by IBM, you can use a juicy severance package to start your business. He used his to start a catering business from home.)

But back to reality. We all know how difficult it is to save, and only a select few find themselves in the enviable position of having a bank account flush with enough cash to start a business. Still there might be a way to build personal savings for a business start-up that you just haven't thought about.

Save As You Go

If you keep your day job and start up your home-based business on a part-time basis, you can use part of each paycheck from your job to pay for your business. Say you normally put some of your paycheck into a savings account each month. Use that money to pay for an extra phone line, business insurance, stamps, paper clips, or other business expenses.

Go "On Margin" Against Your Investments

You may not have your savings sitting in cash. Maybe you went the Wall Street route and bought stocks or bonds. That investment can be turned into money for your business, you just have to know how to get at it.

Homegrown Tip

If you incorporate your business, be sure to keep track of all the savings you put into your business. That way you can see whether you're making any money on your investment. Also, for tax purposes, your contributions to the business are added to the cost basis of your stock. That means you reduce your gain if you sell off some of your stock or sell the business entirely.

Suppose you have 100 shares of Boeing. Sure, you can sell the stock and use the $10,000 or so you'd get to help your business. But remember, not all of that money is yours. First, there are selling expenses—commissions to sell the securities. And don't forget federal (and, in some cases, state) income tax on any profit from the sale. In tax parlance, profit is called *gain*. Your gain is essentially the difference between what you paid for the stock and what you got for it when you sold it (less any selling expenses). Uncle Sam eats gain for breakfast.

Instead of selling the stock, why not simply borrow against it? If you let a brokerage firm hold the stock in *street name* (the name of the brokerage firm), you can go *on margin*. On margin is just a fancy Wall Street term for borrowing, with your stock used as collateral for the loan.

You go on margin (get your loan) simply by signing a margin agreement. The margin agreement details the terms of the loan (the interest rate and so on). You can usually borrow up to 50% of the value of your stocks and up to 90% of government securities. For example, say you own $30,000 of Treasury bonds and $20,000 worth of stock that's held in your brokerage account. Your maximum margin loan is $37,000 ($27,000 [90% of $30,000], plus $10,000 [50% of $20,000]). Once the papers are signed, the money's yours when you want it, even the same day!

So it's easy to go on margin, but is it a good idea? Here are a couple of points to keep in mind:

➤ You can get a favorable interest rate for the loan. In many firms, you're charged only a small percentage—historically 1.5%—higher than the *broker call rate* (an index created by the major brokerage firms that's similar to the prime rate). Some firms may even offer rates below the broker call rate.

Homegrown Tip

Since there are almost as many margin rates as there are brokerage firms and since those rates are at the mercy of rising and falling interest rates, be sure to check with your broker if you're considering a margin loan. Your margin interest rate is posted on your monthly brokerage statement.

➤ You don't have to pay the loan back at any set time. You don't have to make monthly payments of either interest or principal. Each month the interest is added to your outstanding debt. The interest continues to be figured on the outstanding balance of the loan. As you pay it back, your interest payments shrink (assuming the interest rate remains the same). If you have the money, you can repay the loan all at once. Or you can pay it back in any kind of installments you want.

While these are good reasons for using a margin loan (as opposed to another type of loan), there's also a downside:

➤ If you don't make payments, you'll begin to pay interest on the interest.

➤ The interest rate can bounce around like that little metal ball in a pinball machine. In times of low interest, the interest on your margin loan is also low. But as the prime rate rises, the interest on your margin loan can be adjusted each month, or even several times in the same month. While the past several years have seen relatively stable interest rates (rises of no more than a point or two), those of us who remember way back to the '70s and '80s recall interest rates zooming into double digits practically overnight. Other types of loans allow you to lock into an interest rate at the start so you know exactly what interest rate you're paying for the privilege of borrowing money, but not when you borrow on margin.

➤ If the value of the securities you borrowed against falls, you may be subject to an unpleasant little thing called a *margin call*. When that happens you might be forced to sell some of your holdings or come up with outside cash to bring the value of your account up to what it was to keep the loan going.

Let's take the same facts as before for an example. If the value of the stock drops from $20,000 to $15,000 and you borrowed the maximum margin loan you could, then you'd have to sell enough to pay off $2,500, the part of the loan no longer supported by the value of the stock ($5,000 drop in value multiplied by 50%, since it takes two dollars of stock for each one dollar of margin debt). Or you'd have to put $5,000 into the account from outside sources to bring its value up to the previous level.

In the past few years we've experienced a continually rising stock market, and the values of many stocks have similarly climbed. But remember, even where the stock market rises, the value of individual stocks can fall.

If nothing else, you can see that this is not a game for amateurs. The discussion of margin loans here is just the basics (for example, there are other complications, such as *house calls,* which have nothing to do with Marcus Welby coming to call). Just keep in mind that you should discuss margin loans with your stockbroker if you think they're the way to go.

Credits Cards for Cash

A tempting source of cash for your business may be those lovely little slivers of plastic in your wallet. Just go to an ATM , slide your credit cards in, one after another, punch a few buttons, and the cash is yours. A good idea? In most cases, it's about as good an idea as sticking your arm in a buzz saw.

Sure, credit card borrowing is easy. There are no forms to fill out and the cash is yours instantly. But the price you pay for the privilege of borrowing against your credit cards is high. Interest can run around 18% a year, maybe even higher. (If the statement says you're paying 1.5% per month, this translates into 18% a year.) Credit card borrowing is just about the most expensive way there is (short of going to a loan shark!) to raise money.

Despite the high interest rate, credit card borrowing can be useful for limited purposes. If you need a computer for your business, you may want to charge it as a way to finance your purchase. If your business earns money (or you have extra cash), you can pay off the credit card immediately, getting rid of any interest charges. If you can't pay the balance in full, you can pay the computer off over time. Just remember: The longer you take to pay off the charge, the higher your interest costs will be.

Use the Nest Egg You Live in

When I needed money to put an extension on my home for my office, I didn't have to look farther

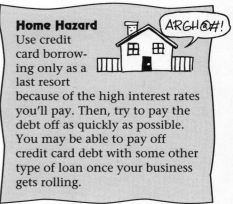

Home Hazard
Use credit card borrowing only as a last resort because of the high interest rates you'll pay. Then, try to pay the debt off as quickly as possible. You may be able to pay off credit card debt with some other type of loan once your business gets rolling.

Business Buzzword
Equity in your home is the amount you'd be able to put in your pocket if you were to sell your house today after paying off any mortgages you already have on your home.

than my own front door. If you own your own home, you're probably sitting on a nest egg you never thought about. This particular nest egg is called *equity in your home.* You can take out the equity and use it in your business.

You can tap into this equity *without* selling your home. You do this by taking out a second mortgage or a home equity line of credit.

Home Equity Loan Process

How much can you borrow? As a rule of thumb, figure that you can borrow up to 75% of the equity in your home (though some lenders will go as high as 100%).

Let's say your home's worth $150,000 and you already have a mortgage with a balance of $100,000. Your equity is $50,000. You can't borrow more than 75% of the value of your home, which is $112,500. Since you have an existing mortgage of $100,000, the limit on a second mortgage or home equity line is $12,500.

Homegrown Tip
If you're planning to leave your job to run your business full-time from home, it's a good idea to apply for the loan *before* you quit your job. Self-employed people have a harder time borrowing money (even a home mortgage) than employees. So keep the paperwork and hassle down by coordinating your job departure with your loan application.

The interest rate you pay on a home loan is usually lower than the rate you'd pay on commercial loans. However, rates vary from lender to lender. You can get fixed rate loans where the interest rate is set from the start. Or you can get a variable rate loan, also called an adjustable rate mortgage (ARM), where the interest rate goes up or down, according to a pre-fixed index and at pre-set intervals.

You usually repay home loans by writing a check every month. The repayment period is long-term, running up to 15 years. The longer you stretch out the payments, the more each monthly payment shrinks. But, remember, the longer you take to pay off the loan the more interest you pay over the life of the loan.

To get a home equity loan you make an application to the bank or other lender. The process is just about the same as getting a first mortgage on your home (and you remember what fun *that* was).

Drawbacks to Borrowing Against Your Home

While there are a number of good reasons to use a home equity loan over other borrowing options, there are some important drawbacks you should know about. I waited more than a month after submitting a wheelbarrow full of paperwork to get approval for a second mortgage on my home. Then I had to sit through a closing and, under New York law, had to wait three days after the closing to get my money. If you used a mortgage to buy your home then you know what I'm talking about.

Getting a second mortgage or a home equity loan is usually no easier than it was to get your first mortgage. You complete a lengthy application form. The lender does a credit check on you. But even if you have a less-than-perfect credit history you'll be able to get a mortgage. That's because the lender is protected if you don't repay the loan: He can just sell your home out from under you and pocket what he's owed. Your credit history may, however, affect the interest rate you'd have to pay.

It may be weeks or even longer before you can *close* (finalize the loan) and get your money.

Also, you may be charged *points* on the amount you borrow. Points, which are a percentage of the loan, are, in effect, additional interest that you're paying up front for the privilege of borrowing money. If you're charged one point on a $100,000 mortgage, you'll pay $1,000. In addition to points, there may be closing costs. These can be modest or quite steep, depending on the lender and the loan program involved. But adding up the points and other closing costs, the fact remains that it's going to cost you money to borrow money.

But let's say the paperwork doesn't get you and you're willing to pay the piper to get the loan. The fact remains that borrowing against the equity in your home puts your home at risk. If you invest money in your business and don't succeed, you still have to pay off the home loan because it's your personal debt. Even if you incorporate your business, you remain personally liable for your home equity debt.

> **Homegrown Tip**
> If you already have a mortgage on your home you don't have to go to the same lender for the home equity loan. Shop around for the best loan possible, comparing interest rates, repayment terms, closing costs, and other loan features.

Take a Loan from Your Life Insurance

Remember Jimmy Stewart's character in the movie *It's A Wonderful Life*? He needed money for a business debt and decided to jump off a bridge so his life insurance could pay for it. Good news. You don't have to do anything that drastic to tap into insurance money. If you own a permanent life insurance policy (a whole life policy or a universal life policy), you may have another source of ready cash. As long as you've owned the policy for several years, you may have equity in the policy. Equity in a life insurance policy is called *cash surrender value.*

Business Buzzword

Cash surrender value is the amount of money you'd receive if you turned your policy in to the insurance company for çancellation.

Of course, you can simply choose to cash in your policy and use your cash surrender value without arranging for a loan. But in that case you lose your insurance protection. What's more, if you later decide to get a new policy, you have to undergo a new insurance physical and pay higher premiums (because odds are you're older and the premiums are fixed by your age when you take out the policy). Or you might even find yourself uninsurable because of recent high blood pressure or another condition uncovered during a physical.

The Educated Entrepreneur

If you own a term policy, which is the least expensive kind of life insurance to own when you're young, you don't build up any cash value in the policy; all of your premiums go to pay the death benefit under the policy (what your beneficiaries get when you kick the bucket) plus the fees of the insurance company (which are built into the policy). Bottom line: Don't look to term insurance (which doesn't build up a cash surrender value) as a source of financing.

There are a lot of reasons why a life insurance loan can look good to you. First, it's very easy to arrange. You don't have to fill out any request forms or loan applications. You just call your life insurance agent or the insurance company that issued your policy and ask for a loan. It can be handled over the telephone (although you'll be asked to sign a loan form that will be sent to you). Getting the loan doesn't depend on your credit rating or what you plan to do with the money. The life insurance company doesn't ask any of these questions. Since the cash surrender value is really your money, the insurance company makes it easy for you to borrow it. You may be able to get your money in a matter of days.

Home Hazard

ARGH@#!

While you have the flexibility of repaying the loan when you can afford to, delaying the repayment can have negative results. If you die before you pay back the loan, the insurance company simply subtracts the outstanding debt against the death benefit it will pay your beneficiaries. Of course, you won't be around to care, but you're reducing the protection you originally planned for your family.

Another good reason for life insurance loans to finance your business is that you get a favorable interest rate. This rate is much lower than the rate you'd pay on a commercial loan.

Need more reasons? You don't have to pay the money back at any special time. While you can't simply *withdraw* the cash surrender value from the policy—it has to be treated as a loan—in effect it's a withdrawal at your option since you don't ever have to pay it back. If you want to pay it back (and stop the interest meter from running) you can do it any time you want and in any size payments. You can pay it back all at once or a little at a time.

Use Your Retirement Plan for a Loan

For many people today, especially those who've stayed in the same job for a long time, retirement plans are a big chunk of their savings. If you or your employer have been contributing to your retirement account, you can tap into this resource without having to pay any current income tax on the retirement benefits. But the tax law has strict limits on loans from retirement plans, so be sure that you know the rules and follow them. If you don't keep the loan within these limits you'll have to pay tax that you could have avoided.

Ken ran an antique business on a part-time basis while working full-time in a Fortune 500 company. He started his business by taking a $60,000 loan from his company's 401(k) plan. Wouldn't you know, he was downsized out of a job just a few months after taking out the loan. To avoid immediate tax on the funds, he had to put the outstanding amount back into the IRA. To do this he had to sell off some of his antique bric-a-brac at a serious loss.

If a retirement plan loan fits your situation, then ask your plan administrator what your *vested benefits* in the plan are. Basically, vesting is a sly form of indentured servitude: The longer you stay in your job, the more of your own money you can have. Vested benefits are yours now; you wouldn't lose them if you left your job today. Your vested benefits affect the dollar amount you can borrow. The limit is 50% of your vested benefits or $50,000, whichever is less. Of course, any loans you've already taken from the plan and haven't repaid reduce the $50,000 limit.

Getting a loan from your plan is easy. All you have to do is ask the plan administrator (if you can find her between meetings). You don't have to complete any lengthy application forms or even tell your company you're taking the money to get out of their lousy job down the road. You just have to sign a loan agreement.

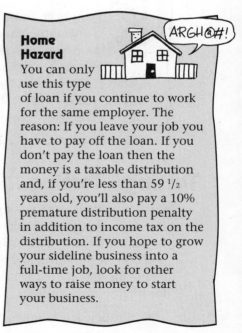

Home Hazard

You can only use this type of loan if you continue to work for the same employer. The reason: If you leave your job you have to pay off the loan. If you don't pay the loan then the money is a taxable distribution and, if you're less than 59 $\frac{1}{2}$ years old, you'll also pay a 10% premature distribution penalty in addition to income tax on the distribution. If you hope to grow your sideline business into a full-time job, look for other ways to raise money to start your business.

The interest rate on a retirement plan loan is usually low (lower than rates charged on commercial loans). What's more, you're really paying the interest back to yourself. So, if you borrow $10,000 from your 401(k) plan to start a sideline business from home and pay 7% interest on the loan, the interest, along with your principal repayment, goes back into your own account.

You have to repay the loan in level amounts over a term of not more than five years. But, as you continue to build up money in your retirement plan (through additional contributions by you or your employer on your behalf), you can take additional loans (subject to the dollar limit explained earlier). This could go on for years, as long as you have the stamina to do two jobs!

The biggest reason *not* to take a loan from your retirement plan to start a sideline business is the fact that you'll be reducing that little retirement nest egg that was growing on a tax-deferred basis. Remember, you don't pay any current income tax on contributions to the plan. And earnings on those contributions are also tax deferred. But if you borrow those funds, there's less in the plan to earn income on. Your retirement plan account will be smaller at retirement time when you'd hoped to move to Florida and golf all day.

> ### The Educated Entrepreneur
>
> If you have an IRA you *can't* borrow from your account. A loan is treated like a distribution and you have to pay tax on it. But there's a way to use money in your IRA on a temporary basis without Uncle Sam biting you in the shorts. You can withdraw the funds and use them any way you want. However, there's a Cinderella clause: You have to put the money back into the IRA within 60 days or the distribution becomes taxable and you turn into a pumpkin. Still, this source of "borrowing" can be helpful in stop-gap situations.

Testing...Testing...Is This Loan Deductible?

If you borrow large sums, you're going to be paying high interest expenses. Are your interest payments deductible? You may already know that you can't deduct personal or consumer interest other than home mortgage interest (within limits). But just because you borrow from personal resources doesn't make the loan a personal loan. Interest is deductible if you use the money for business or investment. Here's how to test your loan for interest deductibility:

➤ Business loans. Interest is fully deductible. A business loan is one that you make only if you're protecting a trade or business. This can include the trade or business of being an employee of your company. So, if you make a loan to your business primarily to protect your salary (your only source of income), interest on the loan is fully deductible as business interest.

➤ Investment loans. Interest is deductible up to the amount of your dividends, interest, and other investment income. Generally, loans to start a business are viewed as investment loans, not business loans. This is because you don't yet have a salary from the business that's worth protecting compared with the cash investment you've made.

➤ Passive activity loans. Interest is deductible to the extent of passive activity income (income from other passive activities). Passive activities, in general terms, are businesses in which you don't participate on a day-to-day basis but, rather, are only a silent partner. So this rule would limit interest deductions for any silent partner you bring in.

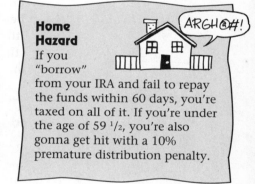

Home Hazard

If you "borrow" from your IRA and fail to repay the funds within 60 days, you're taxed on all of it. If you're under the age of 59 $\frac{1}{2}$, you're also gonna get hit with a 10% premature distribution penalty.

➤ Retirement-plan loans. Interest on a loan taken from your 401(k) or other retirement plan to invest in your business may not be deductible. The loan is treated like an investment loan so that interest is deductible only to the extent you have investment income, such as dividends and interest. (Even this break doesn't apply to key employees who borrow from their retirement plans.)

The Least You Need to Know

➤ Personal savings is the best kind of money to use.

➤ Borrow against your securities instead of selling them to raise cash.

➤ Credit card borrowing is the most expensive form of financing.

➤ Use your home equity for your business.

➤ Borrow from your retirement plan only if you're starting a sideline business.

➤ Interest on loans from your personal resources may be fully deductible, partially deductible, or not deductible at all.

Chapter 12

Swimming with the (Loan) Sharks

In This Chapter

➤ Using a personal loan to start your business

➤ Getting a business loan from a bank

➤ Being Small Business Administration material

➤ Getting special breaks if you're a woman, a member of a minority, or a person with a disability

---

Okay, so you're not a Rockefeller flush with cash. You've decided you just don't have the personal resources to get the business started on your own so you have to look to Chase, Citibank, and other commercial loan sources for help. You might be able to borrow from these banks, even getting favorable terms under special loan programs sponsored by the Small Business Administration (SBA). There are also organizations that make loans just to small businesses.

In this chapter you'll learn about the difference between a personal and a business loan. You'll learn how to do the application two-step to get a commercial business loan. And you'll understand what it means to get a handout from Uncle Sam in the form of an SBA loan and find out about special SBA loan programs, one of which might just be right for you.

Getting a Loan: Personalize It

Your house is already mortgaged to the hilt, your credit cards are tapped out, and your selfish spouse isn't willing to work four jobs just so you can start your business. Don't get discouraged. Although banks are usually for standing in line and getting dinged with bounced check charges, maybe in this case your friendly banker can actually help. Think about going for a personal loan to start your business.

There are two things a bank looks for when it makes a personal loan:

➤ A good personal credit rating.

➤ The ability to repay the loan. If you continue on a job but want the loan to start a sideline business, your salary may be enough to convince a bank to give you a loan to start up.

Business Buzzword

An *unsecured loan* is one in which you don't have to put up your car or other property as collateral (security for the loan) that the lender can keep if you don't keep your promise to repay the loan on time.

Home Hazard

If you don't repay the loan, the lender can sue you and get your personal assets (if you have any) to satisfy the loan. If you don't have enough assets to pay off the debt, the lender can use a judgment against you to garnish your salary if you have a job. Garnish is nothing so pleasant as parsley. It's basically a way to grab your paycheck out of your hands. The judgment can stay on your credit history for a very long time.

Both commercial banks and savings and loan associations make personal loans. To get the personal loan paperwork in gear, ask your local bank or credit union for an application. Generally they'll ask you to list your assets and work history. You have to state the purpose for the loan—to buy a franchise, for example. The lender generally doesn't need to know that you have a Ph.D. in baking and great ideas about opening up a gourmet bread franchise. The lender doesn't need to see your business plan (though this shouldn't stop you from making one). And the lender doesn't need to see proof of how you spent the money.

Here's the bad news: Interest on a personal loan is higher than the interest rate charged on home mortgages (or even car loans). That's because the loan is *unsecured*. You're not putting up your little split-level home so the banker can easily take it out from under you to get his money back. The lender is advancing you the money based only on your promise to pay (and what it considers your ability to do so).

Now that you know all about a personal loan, I'm going to talk you out of it. You're probably better off with a business loan because it offers lower rates and the business repays it (as you'll see in a minute).

But having said all that, many individuals apply for personal loans because they're too darn lazy or uninformed to write a business plan and convince a loan officer they've got a great idea. Also, some individuals are more comfortable dealing with their local savings and loan than with a big commercial bank. But now that you've read all the sage advice in this book, you won't be lazy or uninformed. You've got what it takes to get comfortable with the bank that can really help you.

Let Your Business Do the Borrowing

The business of banks is lending money. Whether you need just a few thousand dollars or tens of thousands of dollars to get your business started, you might just want to think about a commercial loan. It's important that you apply for a loan with the bank that you have the best chance of getting a loan from. Take a moment to think about which kind of bank is your perfect match.

The Educated Entrepreneur

Joe's Bank for Savings doesn't make commercial loans. So the savings and loan association that's holding the mortgage on your home or the one where you have your personal checking account isn't the one to look to for a business loan. The same is true of credit unions you may have put money in through your work. Credit unions don't make commercial loans.

Commercial banks make commercial loans; it's just that simple. You can easily locate a commercial bank in your area, if you don't already know one, by looking in the Yellow Pages under the heading "Banks" and steering clear of any listing in which the word "Savings" appears. Major commercial banks include Bank of America, Chase, Citibank, and Wells Fargo.

Commercial banks make money by lending it out to businesses and receiving interest on their money. So, in theory, commercial banks should be more motivated to make loans to businesses, right? Well in practice, they may not be motivated to help you. The reason is the cost involved in processing loans. It's expensive for a bank to review your loan application. In years past if you only wanted to borrow a small amount, say $5,000, it simply didn't pay for most banks to even consider your application. The lender may only have been interested in making loans of $50,000 and more.

But the times they are a-changing. Some lenders are now *offering* loans to the same small businesses they used to turn their noses up at, and other commercial lenders are expected to follow suit. Here are some ways to quickly learn which bank may be receptive to your application:

131

➤ Ask other small business owners in your area which bank they've borrowed from.

➤ Call the SBA's Small Business Development Center for a referral to a lender in your area willing to make small loans for starting up a business. For the center nearest you, call 800-827-5722.

➤ Look for loan offers. Wells Fargo has aggressively sought small business loans by offering lines of credit as small as $5,000. It has sent out thousands of invitations to small business owners explaining its one-page application that cuts preparation time to as short as 15 minutes.

➤ Talk to your chamber of commerce. Ask for advice on where your best chances of getting a loan in your area might be.

Plodding Through the Paperwork

You think it took paperwork to get your home mortgage? You ain't seen nothin' yet! Be prepared for paperwork like you've never seen before. The bank wants to know everything about your business and you. You'll have to supply this information as well as contracts, sales agreements, and other documents they ask for. Understanding what's in store for you means you're prepared, which, in turn, should help make the process go more smoothly.

Step 1: Prepare the Paperwork

The first thing to do in applying for a commercial loan is to get all necessary papers to the bank. For this you may need a shopping cart or a strong back.

➤ Loan application. This form, which you get from the bank, asks basic information about the business and its owner—you. The length of the application, one page to many pages, varies from bank to bank.

➤ Loan proposal. The bank wants to know *why* you want the loan. You have to explain the *type of loan* you're asking for and the *reason* you want it. For instance, you want a line of credit (type of loan) to start up your business (reason for the loan).

➤ Business plan. You generally have to attach your business plan to the loan application. The plan describes your business and outlines your strategy for the next several years.

➤ Repayment plan. It's not that it doesn't trust you, but the bank has this tendency to want to know how and when it's going to be repaid. If the business plan projects significant profits—more than enough to cover loan repayment—the lender may be satisfied. You may not need a separate repayment plan. But if your business will take some time to get rolling, you may have to give a separate explanation of how you intend to repay the bank until the business can make the payments.

➤ Personal profile. Apply for a loan and suddenly you're fascinating: The bank wants to know as much about you as it does about the business. Your business background, as well as your personal financial picture, all can make or break getting a loan for your business. Your business background may be explained in the business plan. Your personal finances aren't, so you need to get that together. The bank might ask questions about your personal finances on the loan application, or you may have to provide an additional statement to go with the application.

➤ Other documents. You might be asked to give supporting documents, such as letters of reference, contracts, or vendor quotes.

➤ Collateral. Gone are the days when you could use your good name to guarantee a loan: The bank wants to have something concrete to repossess if you can't repay the loan. The bank holds stocks, bonds, or equipment as *collateral* until you pay off the loan. Sometimes you're allowed to hold the collateral but you can't sell it without the bank's okay. When the loan is paid off, the collateral is returned to you (if it was held by the bank).

> **Homegrown Tip**
> Ask *up front* before you prepare your application what supporting documents the bank wants you to provide. They won't even begin processing your loan until every scrap of paper is in. Giving them everything at once will save you time. But don't give them *more* than what they want because it may delay the process, or worse, divulge information that may hurt your application.

Step 2: Follow-up

Okay, you spent your summer vacation collecting enough paper and filling out enough forms to sink the *Titanic*. What's next? The bank will review the papers you've submitted. They will probably want to talk to you—in person or over the phone—about certain things like, you know, that time back in '77 when you were three days late paying a credit card bill. Be prepared to answer questions about the information you've included in your papers.

Step 3: Approval or Rejection

Under the Equal Credit Opportunity Act a bank has to give a small business (start-ups and existing companies with revenues of $1 million or less) an answer to a loan application within 30 days. They can call you on the phone or write you a letter, but however they do it, you must get an answer—yes or no. The 30 days start from the day on which you finally submit the last piece of information the bank asks for.

If you don't get loan approval, find out why. The bank has to state in writing the reason for rejecting your loan. The reason may be anything from a bad credit history to not enough collateral. (It cannot be just because they don't like your face.)

But as with folks who don't pass their driver's license test the first time, you can go back as many times as you like until you get approved. The bank keeps the application and other documents on file for one year. During this time, you can try to correct the reason for the loan rejection and win approval of a reapplication.

If you're rejected by one bank, this doesn't mean you can't get a loan. Banks have different standards. Your failure to get a loan from one bank doesn't prevent you from going to another and meeting its standards. Don't get discouraged. For one guy I know the fourth time was the charm: Rob got a loan for his diet supplements business after four tries with four different banks.

The Educated Entrepreneur

If you were turned down for a loan and believe it was because of your sex, race, national origin, or marital status, you can get help from the federal agency that supervises the bank you dealt with. If you sue because of discrimination and win, you can get money for damages, including punitive damages against the lender, attorneys fees, and court costs.

Home Hazard

Your home and other property is at risk when you give your personal guarantee. If the business can't pay off the loan, the bank can sue you personally and try to get the money back from your personal assets.

If you're rejected on a commercial loan, the bank may advise you to reapply under an SBA program discussed later in this chapter.

You're on the Hook, Too

If you get the loan, you'll be asked to give your personal guarantee for repayment. This means you get to sign the loan application on two separate dotted lines—once as the business owner on behalf of the business and again as an individual co-signing the loan.

Help from Big Brother

Although it may not always seem that way, government policy supports business. To do that, they've created a federal agency that's in the business of small business—the Small Business Administration.

You can't exactly get an SBA loan. That's because the SBA doesn't make loans. It sponsors loan programs. The loan programs work like this: Chase makes a loan and the SBA guarantees a portion of that loan. The SBA guarantee for small loans (up to $100,000) is generally 80% of the loan. The percentage is 75% on larger loans and even less on some other loan programs. This means that the lender can't lose more than a small percentage of the money it has loaned out under the SBA loan program, so it's more generous with its money.

Finding an SBA Loan Program You Can Love

The SBA is constantly changing its loan programs and adding ones that are more helpful to current business needs. Here's a rundown of the SBA programs open to small businesses right now:

➤ Fa$trak loans. A two-year pilot program that started in February 1995 allows commercial banks to make loans without first getting SBA approval. The bank simply follows the SBA guidelines for making a loan. The bank uses its own application form. Since the bank doesn't have to wait for the SBA to review the loan, it can act quickly—on a Fa$trak, get it? The SBA guarantee to the bank under this program is 50% of the loan. Fa$trak can be used for loans up to $100,000.

➤ Microloans. This is a program especially for very small loans—under $25,000. The loans are made through nonprofit organizations, not through commercial banks.

➤ Capital term loans. If you're buying a franchise or just starting up a business, you can get a loan for operating capital, called (logically enough) a capital term loan. Typically you have up to seven years to pay back what you've borrowed. These loans are given through commercial banks.

There's a special type of loan called a *Low Doc* loan. Low Doc stands for low documentation, which means you can get rid of the wheelbarrow. These loans are designed to simplify the loan application process. These loans can be used for most SBA loan programs for loans up to $100,000. Low Doc loans aren't a loan program by themselves: they have a

> **Homegrown Tip**
> Find the right SBA loan program for you by calling the SBA at 800-827-5722. Also get loan program information on the Internet at http://www.sbaonline.sba.gov.

135

one-page application form that you attach to your business plan. The bank may also ask for other information, such as your personal financial statement.

Knowing When You're Special

In addition to commercial banks that make loans under SBA-sponsored programs, there are special programs to explore. Small Business Investment Companies (SBICs) are privately managed firms licensed by the SBA to make loans to small businesses. Instead of straight loans where you pay back the money, these lending programs generally give the SBIC firms options to buy stock in your company. They may also involve something called convertible debentures—bonds that can be changed into stock under certain conditions.

Homegrown Tip
To find one of the 175 SBICs across the country, call the National Association of Small Business Investment Companies at 703-683-1601. To find an SSBIC, call the National Association of Investment Companies (NAIC) at 202-289-4336.

And if you're not confused by all these options yet, Specialized Small Business Investment Companies (SSBICs), also licensed by the SBA, make loans to businesses that are mostly owned by socially or economically disadvantaged individuals. Financing under the SSBICs generally involves only equity arrangements (you take them in as a partner); there are no straight loans.

SBA Loans: Can You Make the Grade?

Want an SBA loan? Here's what's required:

➤ A "reasonable stake" in your business. This is kind of a "hey, you first" approach: The SBA doesn't want to stand behind a loan to you if you haven't first put your own money into the business. You must have already invested between 25% and 50% of the amount you want to borrow. So, if you want to borrow $30,000, you have to sink between $7,500 and $15,000 into your business (depending on the lender and the loan program you want).

➤ A good business plan. Didn't I tell you a business plan was important? The SBA wants to be sure that you understand the business you're in and have thought things through so your business will succeed (and you'll repay the loan).

➤ A good personal credit rating. Since you have to give your personal guarantee for an SBA loan, you have to show that you aren't a deadbeat. The bank will run a credit report on you and include this information in your file for the SBA. Also, the SBA may look at your work history and even ask for letters of recommendation to back up your personal standing.

➤ A plan to repay the loan. Just like any commercial loan, you have to show how you plan to repay the money you borrow. Your business plan should show that the business will have enough cash flow to make the monthly loan repayments.

Getting a Break: Women, Minorities, and People with Disabilities

Most bankers want you to fit a cookie-cutter mold, but here's where it pays to be different. A number of government and private loan programs are designed to encourage business ownership by women, minorities, and people with disabilities—groups that, until recently, were underrepresented in the business world. For example, the National Association of Women Business Owners (NAWBO) joined with Wells Fargo Bank to offer loans to existing women-owned businesses that want money to expand (for information, call 212-916-1473).

For some government programs, it pays to get certified as special. Not all labels are bad. If you get labeled as a business owned by women, minorities, or people with disabilities, it can open up special money doors for you. The SBA gives certification called W/MBE—women or minority business enterprises. While each bank may have slightly different standards for certification, here are some guidelines to show you the strictest requirements you may be asked to meet (you may find less demanding banks out there, if you're lucky):

➤ Ownership by women and/or minority members of at least 51%. More than half of your business must be owned by a woman and/or a minority individual. If, for example, you're a woman who forms an equal partnership with a man (who's not a member of a minority), then your business doesn't meet the 51% requirement.

➤ Management of the business is by women and/or minority members. You have to answer the phones, push the buttons, and meet the clients on a day-to-day basis. You must also be involved in making decisions. You can't be mere investors.

➤ Investment must be "real and substantial" by women and/or minority members. This requirement is designed to weed out women and/or minority members who act as "fronts" for non-women or non-minority owners (a growing and sinister criminal class, I hear).

➤ The business must be "independent." The business can't be too closely tied to a non-women or non-minority business (under the control of another business). If a business has only one client who happens to be a non-women or non-minority company, it may not be considered "independent."

There's also special certification for people with disabilities and for businesses that serve the needs of people with disabilities. A person with a disability is one who has a permanent physical, mental, or emotional impairment, defect, ailment, disease, or major disability that keeps the person from competing equally with a non-disabled competitor.

Special certification for a business owned by a person with a disability is called HAL-2. For this certification you meet the following:

➤ The business is 100% owned by one or more people with a disability.

➤ The person with the disability manages the business. Again, the individual can't be an absentee owner.

Special certification for a business that serves the needs of people with disabilities is called HAL-1. Qualification for this status must be shown by the business' by-laws, incorporation papers, certificate of tax-exempt status by the IRS, or recognition by the U.S. Secretary of Labor or a state vocational rehabilitation agency. Besides producing a product or providing a service, it must operate for the benefit of people with disabilities. This means that at least 75% of the direct work involved is done by people with disabilities. Finally, the net income of the business can't go to benefit any stockholder or other person.

The Least You Need to Know

➤ Using a personal loan for your business is a less complicated process than going for a commercial loan, but it's not necessarily the best loan for you.

➤ Go to commercial banks that are eager to make small business loans.

➤ Master the commercial loan application process so things will go smoothly for you.

➤ The SBA doesn't make loans directly but sponsors many different loan programs.

➤ Some SBA-sponsored loans have easy applications and quick approval for small business.

➤ There are special loan programs for women, minorities, and people with disabilities.

Part 4
Let's Get Physical: Setting up Your Office

Up to now you've been thinking about what kind of business to start, whether to incorporate or take on a partner, and how to find the money you need to get going. Now it's time to get physical and decide how you're going to turn your cozy three-bedroom ranch house into the ideal working space.

First, if you plan to run your business out of your home, you'd better make sure you can do that without breaking the law. Once you determine whether your home business satisfies local zoning laws, you have to think about your space and equipment. Do you need storage space for inventory or samples? Is your home office a place you'd be proud of or ashamed to bring clients or customers into? Do you have enough phone lines and the right kind of electrical outlets to power your business?

In this part of the book, you'll figure out the physical stuff: zoning rules and how you can get around some restrictions (legally), how to lay out your office space, and how to get the equipment you need to run a business.

Chapter 13

Office Space in Your Place

In This Chapter

➤ Operating an office that's legal

➤ Running your business from a cooperative apartment

➤ Laying out your work space

➤ Planning for visits from clients and customers

Your home is your castle: familiar, comfortable, and convenient, but can you run a business there? Sure, you'd like to. That's why you want to run a home-based business (and that's why you bought this book). But before you put in the time and money to set up a home office, make sure you find out whether you're allowed to do so *legally*. Your city or town may have rules that say certain kinds of businesses just don't mix with residential areas.

But let's assume your business is A-OK with the zoning types. Now you have to set up your office. This may not seem so difficult. In fact, you may have already done it whether you know it or not. A desk that's been used for writing household bills and personal letters can be dubbed the "office desk," and it becomes the centerpiece for your home office.

But some people may not see right off the bat where they're going to put their office. It might take a little furniture rearranging, or more. This might be especially true if your business has inventory or samples you have to store. You may also have to make your little oasis attractive to visitors—clients, customers, suppliers, and others.

In this chapter you'll learn about zoning restrictions and how to get around them—legally. You'll also learn that a home office has physical needs, too. You'll discover ways to make your space the perfect place to do business.

Zoning Out

In the early 1900s when cities began to spread into farmland and noxious factories encroached on neighborhoods, a new type of law, called zoning, began to evolve. Cities and towns wanted to control the type of development—commercial, residential, industrial—taking place within their borders. They wrote zoning laws to say where people could do what.

Today, zoning laws in most places have rules about what businesses can be run from home. The problem in some places is that these laws were written in the Dark Ages. This was before the computer age when home offices looked very different. Back then, zoning laws were meant to prevent the introduction of industrial work (called piece work) into the homes of America. The city fathers wanted to limit the size of professional offices so traffic from patients or clients didn't disturb neighborhoods. Some places have modernized their rules or are in the process of doing so. Others haven't. If you want to run a business from home, find out the rules that apply to you and be sure you follow them.

Doing Business in a Residential Zone

If you don't operate within the law, you may be sorry. My friend Melanie ran a nationwide medical referral business quite successfully for several years from the basement of her home in the suburbs outside New York City. Neighbors ignored the comings and goings of the cars belonging to her five employees because there was no noise. But when one of the employees was fired, she turned Melanie in to the town zoning board. The business, which was in violation of zoning law, had no choice but to move out of Melanie's basement and start paying rent. And the business had to write a big, fat check to the city for penalties on zoning violations.

The same thing can happen to you if your business irks the zoning powers-that-be. An angry neighbor or even a customer may turn you in and report you to the local zoning board. If someone files a complaint, your city or town will investigate. If they decide you've broken the law, you'll pay, literally, several hundred, or even several thousand, dollars. The good part is that with a little knowledge and planning you can avoid this kind of problem.

Do You Live in an Entrepreneur Zone?

How business-friendly is your town or city? Will it let you run a business from your home? If you don't know, you'd better ask somebody. You don't want to break the law and have to pay penalties and fines. But even if a reading of the rules makes you think you can't run the kind of business you plan to from home, you might be able to get permission if you go about it correctly.

To find out the zoning rules in your area, check with your city or town. Of course, they don't make it easy for you: Each place has a different name for the office that oversees zoning. In some places it's simply called the zoning board. In others it may be called the building code, code compliance, or something else. But don't worry: After seven or eight phone calls, you're bound to stumble on the right office.

Once you've found the right person to ask, then be sure you ask the right questions. Ask hypothetically, "If I were to run a mail-order business from my home with one employee who doesn't live with me, would this violate the zoning law?" Be sure to lay out all the variables that apply to you—the nature of your business, the number of outside employees, the frequency of visitors, parking issues, signs, noise, deliveries, and anything else you can think of.

There are special rules for professional offices. For example, in most towns no more than two parking spots are allowed for patients or clients. Customary home occupations also have special rules requiring that all of the business activity be conducted in the home and not smack dab in the middle of the front yard. There is a limit on the number of employees who don't live in the home. The business can't have noise, odors, or hazards that go outside the walls of the home (odors that stay put are fine). A sign with the name of your business? Maybe yes, maybe no, maybe just a teensy one—one foot or two feet square (every place has a different rule!).

If you're told that you can't do what you planned because of zoning rules, ask which zoning rule covers your situation. What's the sticking point that would

Business Buzzword

When looking into zoning rules you may see mention of professional offices and customary home occupations. *Professional offices* are for doctors, dentists, chiropractors, attorneys, and certain other designated professions that have traditionally been allowed to operate from home.

Customary home occupations include seamstresses, music teachers, and other kinds of businesses that have traditionally operated from home.

Homegrown Tip

If you're told that there's no problem running your business from your home, ask which zoning rule covers your situation and write it down. Get the name of the person who gave you the information and write it down. After all, you're putting a great deal of reliance on this (no doubt reliable) civil servant's word.

make your proposal violate the rules? Maybe it's just a limit on the number of outside employees. You want two; the rules say one employee who doesn't live with you. You might be able to modify your plans. Maybe one employee is all you'll need to get started from home. Or maybe you can contract out a portion of your work so you don't have any employees in your home. Maybe there are some legal steps you can take to get special permission to run your business from home.

Once you've cut your way through all the rules and restrictions, you may find you don't have any zoning concerns. As a practical matter, if your business is just you working in your home office and you don't bring in outsiders—employees, customers, or others—no one's going to care. As a freelance writer sitting at a computer screen all day, I certainly don't create a zoning problem for the neighborhood. Even though my business may not fit the language of the zoning code, my town doesn't care about me doing my kind of work from home. Most other areas probably won't care, either, and will simply ignore you. But it's still a good idea to check it out.

Be sure to find out whether you have to pay any fee for a permit to run a business from home. An increasing number of localities are more than happy to allow businesses to operate in residences—as long as they cough up some cash (which can be as much as a few hundred dollars).

Aren't You Special?

Okay, so you can't fight city hall; but if you know how, you can get it to bend a little. Let's say you've asked about your proposed business and were told that you'd violate existing zoning rules. Don't give up. You may still be able to go ahead with your plans and not get hit with fines or penalties—if you get special permission. This is called a *variance* or a *special use permit*.

Business Buzzword

A *variance* is a change or alternation of a zoning rule granted specifically for one person.

Let's say your business doesn't meet the definition of a professional office or a customary home occupation as defined by your local government.

If you don't fit the zoning rules, you usually have to make a formal application to your city or town government to get special permission to run your business from home. Make sure you follow the procedures in your area. Here are some of the things you should know before you ask for special permission:

➤ Where to make your application. Generally there's a zoning board or other group of government officials tucked away in some city office building whose job is to consider individual requests for changes in or exceptions to zoning rules. Ask at your town hall or other local government offices.

➤ The procedures for making a variance request. If you've ever tried to get anything done at city hall, you learned that towns are very independent creatures: Each town and city has a special way it handles requests. There are specific (and sometimes seemingly arbitrary) steps you have to go through before you'll get a decision, one way or the other.

You may have to inform your neighbors about your business and find out whether they've got objections. (They may have to put them in writing, or they can simply consent by not objecting at a public hearing.) There are also specific time periods for

making requests. You want to be sure to get your request in at the right time—if you don't, it may be weeks or even longer before you'll have another opportunity to approach the board. You may have to show up in person when the board meets and answer questions about your request. At that time, the board will also listen to your neighbors' gripes, if any.

➤ Find out what the board wants to see. Sometimes you have to show architectural drawings or other documents that the board can look over to decide on your request.

Homegrown Tip
You may want to work with a lawyer who regularly handles zoning issues. The lawyer will know the procedures and what's required to get a positive answer to your request.

Co-op Owners Beware

If you live in a cooperative apartment and want to run a home office there, city hall may be the least of your problems. Even if the government says it's okay to run a business from your unit, your co-op board may have another opinion. Cooperative apartment boards are allowed to regulate the activities that go on in their buildings and have the right to make their opinion stick.

Make sure you ask your co-op board whether your planned home business is permitted under the rules. If the board says no, find out whether you could make changes to your plans to satisfy the board members. If not, maybe this is the perfect time to rent a U-Haul.

A Space in Your Place

Artist, medical billing, plumber, mail order, children's clothing. All businesses are not created equal, and the space they need is also different. The nature of your business dictates the kind of space you need. You may be fine at the kitchen table, or you may need to use a spare bedroom, the family room, or the den.

Homegrown Tip
For other pointers on planning your office space and furnishings, check out http://home-office-center.com, as well as *The Home Office Book* by Donna Paul (Artisan/Workman Publishing) and *Home Office Design: Everything You Need to Know About Planning, Organizing and Furnishing Your Work Space* by Neal Zimmerman (John Wiley & Sons).

Think about what you need to run your business—elbow room, a good view, whatever you think it takes. Then pick the right part of your home to use for your business.

You'll be happy that you took the time to plan your physical setup. After all, you'll be spending a lot of time there. The more details you can work out in planning, the more comfortable you'll be in your home office.

The cost of setting up your space is entirely up to you. If you already have what you need, your cost is zero. If you need to put up a partition in a room or buy a desk, carpeting, and light fixtures, your costs can run into thousands of dollars.

Above all, have fun with your plans. Decorating an office can even add to the value of your home, if your budget allows you to go for it.

Desk Space

There's an old saying that clutter expands to fill the space you have: The larger the desk the more junk you can fit on it. To arrange your home office, you have to know two things: your available space and what furniture and other office equipment you need to put in it. What are your home office options? Do you have a spare bedroom? Do you have part of a family room or finished basement available for your business? Can an attic, basement, or garage be converted into office space? Look around and decide where you can fit your home office.

In selecting your office space, consider the stuff you'll want to pile in there. List the items that you *must* have in your office. These may include some or all of the following:

➤ Desk

➤ Desk chair

➤ Copying machine

➤ Bookcases or shelves

➤ Daybed for those "inspirational" naps

➤ Chairs and/or sofa for clients or customers

➤ Drafting table

➤ Fax machine

➤ Computer

➤ Basketball hoop above your wastebasket

The Educated Entrepreneur

If you want to order furniture by mail, you have a number of options, including national chains like Office Max, 800-788-8080; Reliable Home Office, 800-869-6000; and Staples, 800-333-3330. Even if you don't plan to buy via mail order, you may still want to look through these catalogs. The furniture listings have dimensions that you can use to plan your home office.

Of course, you may not be an office type. Maybe you need an artist's studio for your design business. Or perhaps you grow orchids for sale. You can still accommodate these activities in your home and treat the space as your home office. Perhaps you can use an attic, converted garage, or greenhouse for your business. (Of course, you should check the zoning on these unique space arrangements.)

The key is understanding your business needs and choosing the space that will suit them.

Getting It on Paper

A picture is worth a bunch of words. Once you've picked the right space in your home and have an idea what you'll need to put there, it's time to lay out your floor space. You can do this best on graph paper. Or you can use the grid that follows to help you lay out your space. Figure each box equals one foot. So if you have a 10-foot square room that you're using for a home office, count off 10 squares across and 10 squares down for your space.

Think about where you're going to put all of your equipment. You can draw in your office furniture and equipment in pencil. Using pencil lets you "move" furniture around easily, trying out one arrangement and then another. Here are some general measurement guidelines for placing your office equipment:

➤ Desk: three feet by five feet

➤ Chair: one foot square

➤ Bookshelf (freestanding): one foot by three feet (or longer)

➤ File cabinet: 1 ½ feet by 2 ½ feet

➤ Drafting table: three feet square

➤ Printer stand: 1 ¹/₂ feet by 1 ¹/₂ feet

➤ Credenza: two feet by four feet

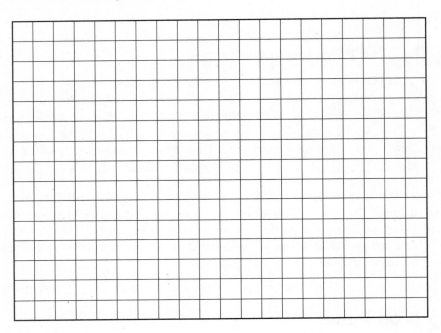

If your space is limited, look into space-saving office furniture designed to fit a lot of equipment into a small space. And don't forget where electrical outlets and telephone lines are when placing your desk in your room plans.

Homegrown Tip
In deciding where to put your office, read up on the tax rules that allow you to deduct the costs of your home office (explained in Chapter 22). After reading them, you may decide to change your plans.

Instead of pushing a pencil around graph paper to map out your home office, you can use a computer and software to do the same thing high-tech style. Half a dozen different software programs (costing $35 to $70) allow you to fiddle with furniture placement, add lighting, and even try out different wallpaper, carpeting, and paint. This helps you envision what your office will look like after you remodel.

You may find that your space just isn't big enough for all your stuff. Your choices at this point can be difficult. If you own your own home you may be able to add on a room, convert a garage to office space, or expand an existing room. This alternative requires a substantial investment, so weigh it carefully. If you can't afford to remodel (or don't want to make the investment until your business is profitable enough to help pay off the cost), then you either have to give up the idea of working entirely from home or somehow scale back your office plans. Sure, these are tough decisions. But it's better that you make them now, not once you've left your day job and suddenly find you're too cramped to run your new business properly.

A Place for Everything and Everything in Its Place

If you're a consultant or provide a service, you don't have any inventory that needs to be stored. Your storage needs are limited to your office supplies and client files.

But if your business depends on inventory, think hard about where you're going to put it. Depending on the product or products you sell, you may need a little or a lot of space.

After taking measurements, you may find that you'll have to call on the local Storage-R-Us outlet. What's this going to cost you? Find out the cost of this off-site storage space (and remember, it's deductible). What's it going to cost in terms of your time getting to and from your off-site inventory?

Homegrown Tip
If you use a spare bedroom as an office, consider converting the closet into storage space. Invest in file cabinets and shelves to deck out the closet. Or use closet organizers to customize your storage needs. You'll find other organization tips in Chapter 24.

Paving the Way for the Public

If you're a freelance writer working alone, you can skip this part; you won't be having many guests in your home office. But if you have outsiders—clients, patients, customers, suppliers, or even an employee—coming into your home on a regular basis for business, what does it mean to you? Some businesses can't run without contact with the public. If your business is one of them, can your home take it?

There are three main concerns about visitors to your home office: space, appearance, and safety:

➤ Space. Where are you going to put everyone? You need to have a place for visitors to sit and transact business.

➤ Appearance. If you're the only person using your office, your paper clutter, your children's toys,

Homegrown Tip
If you install ramps, handrails, or make other changes to your home to accommodate business visitors who have disabilities or are elderly, you're probably eligible for special tax benefits you'll learn about in Chapter 22.

and your pets may not be a big deal. But if you have business visitors, they may not appreciate pet hair on their clothes and Mighty Morphin' Power Ranger dolls underfoot. You want your home office to look professional and businesslike.

➤ Safety. You may think your house is as safe as a church, but if you have regular business visitors, you have to make sure that your entry and office space are hazard-free. You may need to install handrails by the steps into your home. You may want additional lighting in your driveway. The last thing you need is a client breaking an arm by slipping on your front step and all the associated lawyers, insurance people, and general chaos that can ensue.

The Least You Need to Know

➤ Check out local zoning rules to avoid penalties down the road.

➤ If zoning rules prevent you from running your business from home, you might be able to get special permission.

➤ Check with your co-op board if you want to run any kind of business from your cooperative apartment.

➤ Setting up and decorating your home office can be fun but requires planning and attention to detail.

➤ Make sure you plan for business visitors so you'll have enough space and no safety hazards.

Chapter 14

Lines of Communication

In This Chapter

➤ Having multiple phone lines to keep in touch

➤ Using a toll-free number for your business

➤ Taking messages when you're out to lunch

➤ Paging the home businessperson

I've often thought that Alexander Graham Bell should be voted the patron saint of home-based businesses. As a home-based business owner, the telephone is nothing less than your lifeline to the world. There's no way around it: It's an essential piece of equipment and you can't do business without it, regardless of whether you sell a product or provide a service.

When you set up your home office, you need to pay special attention to your telephone setup because the way you receive and handle phone calls is a key part of your business image. You have a number of options that can add to your effectiveness. But of course, these options cost money.

In this chapter you'll learn about your phone options. You'll also find out how to stay in touch with your office, your clients, your customers, and other business resources when you're away from home with technology like paging and e-mail.

What's My (Phone) Line?

Whether you're writing a cyberspace newsletter, sending out a mail-order catalog of educational toys, selling super vitamins direct under a network marketing arrangement, or tutoring acting students in your home, your telephone is perhaps the single most important piece of equipment for your business.

Gone are the days when a single phone line could meet the needs of even the typical family, let alone one with a business in the basement. Odds are the existing phone line to your home may not be enough (especially if there's a teenager around the house). You may need additional lines or special services.

There are several alternatives, and no single solution is best for every business. The way you set up your phones depends on things like the nature of your business, your family's penchant for gossiping long distance, and your bank balance.

The Educated Entrepreneur

In the future you'll be able to have full service communications via your cable lines. You'll get tele(vision) phones, with both local and long-distance service, more rapid Internet access, and traditional cable service from the same company. Expect to pay as much as $200 to $300 a year for this additional service (over and above your regular monthly cable bill). Sound like science fiction? Guess again. It's already being test marketed.

Keep It Personal

Obviously, adapting your personal phone service to business use is the least costly way to go. However, this option works best if your business doesn't involve a lot of phone contact. Of course, your situation can also change over time: I was as happy as a clam using my personal line for business—until my children got old enough to monopolize the line.

Homegrown Tip

If you haven't already done so, be sure you're paying for unlimited local calls. This type of phone service is, in almost all cases, most economical for home-based business owners.

You can convert your personal phone line into a *faux* second line by getting something called *call waiting*. You've probably encountered call waiting before. Remember chatting with Aunt Fanny when you heard that tiny little click on the line? Suddenly Fanny went over to the second call and you were left twiddling your thumbs, basically on hold, while she dealt with the other caller.

Call waiting is a special service provided by the phone company for a flat monthly fee in addition to your regular bill. Call waiting lets you know when there's another call coming in (that's the click). Instead of getting a busy signal—the last thing you want to have a business contact hear—the caller gets through to you. You have to put your first caller on hold while you attend to the second caller. You can make arrangements to call one of them back or juggle two conversations by going back and forth. Just be careful not to mix up the banker with your boyfriend!

Home Hazard
If you have only one phone line in your home office, you can't deduct the basic monthly costs of service. You can, however, deduct your long-distance charges for business calls and the business portion of the cost of any special services (such as call forwarding or call waiting).

Bite the Bullet and Add a Business Line

If you use your phone regularly and continuously for business, one line just won't do. You may have no choice but to bring in a second phone line despite the added cost. Your new line is strictly business; your old line is for you and your family to use.

There's an important advantage to having a phone line just for business. You can get a listing in the classified section of your Yellow Pages so potential customers can let their fingers do the walking to your home-based business. With a single personal line you can't advertise your business in this easy and familiar way.

You also gain the tax advantage of being able to deduct *all* of the costs of the business line. What's more, having a business line doesn't prevent you from deducting any business calls you make on your personal line. You can get a separate telephone for the business line. Or you can get a two-line phone to handle your personal and business line.

Homegrown Tip
Having a two-line phone in my office is something I couldn't do without. It saves space (I don't need to have two phones sitting on my desk). It may also make sense (depending on the layout of your home) to do as I did and have another two-line phone installed in a room like the kitchen. This allows me to field business calls when I'm "out" of the office eating chocolate cake.

Bringing in a second line involves not one, but three separate costs:

➤ Telephone equipment. You need to have a new phone for your business line. This can be a second one-line phone, or you can get a two-line phone for your business and personal lines.

➤ Telephone installation charges. You have to pay the telephone company for running a second line to your home. If you have the business line run to more than one room in your home, your installation charges are even higher. Be sure to keep in mind that the phone company charges higher installation fees for business lines even though there's no additional work involved. Why? Because they can.

➤ Telephone monthly charges. The monthly costs of a business line run higher than comparable service for a personal line. While this may make sense only to the phone company, you just have to write it off as one of life's little injustices.

In looking at the cost of the monthly charges, don't ignore the separate cost of long-distance charges (if you use them in your business). Having a business line means lining up a long-distance carrier. These carriers have different pricing structures. Many offer special deals for small businesses. And trade and professional associations offer special discounts to members for some long-distance carriers. Check around before selecting the carrier for your business line. Don't hesitate to switch carriers if a better offer comes along (and believe me, they will, usually around dinnertime every other evening).

How Many Lines Is Enough?

Just when you'd adjusted to the idea of two phones in your home, I'm going to shake things up again. Believe it or not, a separate business line to your home may not be enough for you to run your business efficiently. You may need a third or even a fourth line. I'm up to three already!

If you have a fax or modem, you may want to have a *dedicated* line—one used exclusively for online stuff. All large companies do it, and maybe you should, too. If you run all your equipment on the phone line you use to talk to clients, customers, or suppliers, you'll have telephone logjams when calls and equipment compete for the line. You have to stop your telephone conversation every time you want to receive or send a fax.

You also can't talk and use your computer's modem at the same time, so your clients might get that lethal busy signal when you're online. The cost of a dedicated line for your fax or modem can be less than $15 a month.

If your business is heavy on phone calls, you may also want extra lines. This becomes very important if you have an employee or two who work from your home office. They may need separate lines to use the phone for business if you, too, are using the phone for business.

Paying the Toll: 800 Numbers

Do you need to have a toll-free number for clients and customers to reach you? Again, the type of business you run will provide the answer. If, for example, you have a mail-order business that invites customers to place orders by phone, you may have no choice but to offer a toll-free number (if you want to be competitive). It costs to provide one, but that cost can easily be repaid by increased orders.

The Educated Entrepreneur

Today, existing toll-free numbers are denoted by 800 instead of an area code. But the long-distance carriers have virtually run out of these numbers. They now offer toll-free numbers denoted by 888. These new toll-free numbers act the same way as the old 800 numbers.

Toll-free numbers are offered by long-distance carriers. Phone numbers starting with 800/888 are called "toll free" but this is only half true. The calls are toll free to the caller, but you, the receiver, pay for them. The cost of having these numbers varies from one carrier to another. Here are the three types of charges you should ask about when investigating a toll-free number:

➤ Installation fee. Some companies (such as MCI) have them; others (such as AT&T) don't. The installation charges, however, generally are modest (such as $10).

➤ Monthly fee. You pay a flat monthly fee for the privilege of having a toll-free number.

➤ Per call charges. You're charged a set amount per minute for all calls made to you via your 800/888 number, even wrong numbers and crank calls. Some carriers offer a single per minute charge. Others have different charges for in-state versus out-of-state, and peak versus off-peak calls.

Homegrown Tip

Here are phone numbers for major carriers for 800/888 numbers: Allnet, 800-783-2020; AT&T, 800-222-0400; Cable & Wireless, 800-486-8686; LDDS, 800-737-8423; MCI, 800-444-2222; Sprint, 800-877-2000.

To give you some idea about costs, look at the table below. Just remember that the numbers reflect costs as of the date this book was published; expect that costs will change.

Comparison Chart of Toll-Free Charges

Carrier	Installation Fee	Monthly Fee	Per Call Per Minute Charge
AT&T	No charge	$5	26¢ in-state (28¢ out-of-state)
MCI	$10	$10	28–30¢ peak; 23¢ off-peak
Sprint	No charge	$5	19¢

Be In When You're Out

The telephone can be used to connect you to the outside world even when you're not at home. And even if you're in the office, there are times when you just may not be taking calls. Still, you don't want your business callers to get turned off by busy signals or a phone that rings and rings. The good news is you can easily stay in touch even when you're not available to answer the phone.

An Old-Fashioned Answering Machine

I bet you already know about this one: The simplest and least expensive way to be sure to get phone calls when you're unavailable is to hook up an answering machine to your telephone.

Any decent answering machine allows you to get your messages when you're out of the office. These machines have a unique remote access number. When you call in and press that access number, the machine plays back any messages.

Here's the good news: The cost of a good answering machine—one that records the time and date of calls, displays the number of messages, and allows you to access your messages from an outside line—can be well under $100.

E-Mail Your Way to Success

Welcome to cyberspace! An increasingly popular alternative to phone calls is to stay connected to business contacts via your computer. Instead of calling up on the telephone, you use your portable computer to receive and send messages with e-mail (electronic mail).

To use e-mail, you need certain equipment—a computer, a modem, and an online provider (such as America Online, CompuServe, or a local Internet provider). However, it takes two to e-mail: Even if you have what it takes for e-mail, it will do you no good if the other person doesn't have e-mail, too.

There are several advantages to e-mail:

➤ Convenience. You can leave detailed messages of virtually any length when it's convenient for you and your contact will get them the first time, instead of leaving a trail of voice messages to call each other back. I'm a morning person on New York time; one of my publishers is in California. E-mail means I can leave lengthy messages for my editor at 6 A.M. that he picks up when he gets in the office, four hours later.

➤ Cost. E-mail is a lot cheaper than long-distance calls. If you regularly speak with business contacts long-distance, whichever long-distance carrier you use, you still pay for long-distance service. But with e-mail, your online provider is generally only a local call away. Thus, even if the guy you're calling is in another state or even another country, you pay only for the local call to your online provider. Of course, getting messages from e-mail means you have to place another phone call via your computer to access them, but it's still a local call. You also have to pay a monthly fee to your provider, which may or may not include unlimited online time (depending upon your service provider).

➤ Time savings. E-mail is a serious time-saver. You avoid the personal, but time-consuming, aspects of calling and just get down to business. You can send the same message to numerous people with ease (and with a time savings to you). While e-mail may at first seem cold and impersonal, your business contacts will also appreciate the time savings.

➤ Written record. Unlike phone calls, which don't leave a trace of their contents (unless you're in the CIA), you get a record of your communications with e-mail. You can print your e-mail messages and keep them on hand for future reference.

The chief downside to e-mail for some people is that they feel as impersonal as HAL's voice in *2001: A Space Odyssey*. You can't pick up cues from body language or tone of voice as you go. A lot of people prefer to speak directly to another person and don't like the more formal, correspondence feel of e-mail, even when it's tempered with "emoticons" (those annoying little smiley symbols, the Hallmark cards of computer speak <g>).

Voice Mail

Want a solution to allow your business callers to leave recorded messages without ever getting a busy signal? Consider a messaging service. This is a service you can get through your local telephone company. Thus, even if you're on the phone, your second or third caller can leave a voice message for you. You can then access your messages at any time, seven days a week, 24 hours a day. Voice mail is rapidly becoming the messaging alternative of choice.

There are numerous add-ons (special features) to enhance voice mail. These include the ability to leave automated information messages for your callers, signals to your personal pager (discussed later in this chapter), and more. Donna, who ran a one-person cleaning company from her home, appeared to outside callers as a large operation. The reason: She had a feature called Multiple Mailboxes. When one of her accounts called in, the

Home Hazard

Currently, voice mail may be limited to those who live in urban areas. If you live outside of a metropolitan area, you may not have easy access to voice mail at this time. For an alternative, consider an old-fashioned answering service.

customer heard a message that said "To speak to the billing department, press 1 now. To schedule a cleaning, press 2" and so on. Her customers assumed the company had a dozen departments when, in fact, Donna was a one woman wonder.

The cost of voice mail can be rather modest—as little as $5 to $18 per month (depending on the features you select). Then, too, you must figure in the cost of your local calls to access your messages, unless you pay for unlimited local calls. To check out voice mail service, call the company listed in the table below that services your area.

Basic Voice-Mail Messaging Service

Telephone Company	Voice Mail Service	Phone Number
Ameritech	Voice Mail	800-650-LINK
Bell Atlantic	Answer Call	Call local office
BellSouth	MemoryCallAnswering	800-356-3094, ext. 3
Nynex	Voice Messaging	212-890-2350
Pacific Bell	The Message Center	800-503-7500
USWest	Business Voice Messaging Service	800-603-6000

Answering Services Could Be Your Answer

In ancient times, before answering machines and computer-based messages, an answering service was the only way someone could get messages when they were not in. You can set up your phone calls to "roll over" to the answering service. Today, answering services are still around. For some businesses, they still make sense.

An answering service gives the caller the opportunity to speak to a human being and leave a personal message. This can make some callers feel warm and fuzzy. The answering service can respond to the caller's needs more intimately, saying things like "Mr. Smith will be right back" or "Mr. Smith will be out of the office all day but will be calling in for messages; is this an emergency?" Of course, the service has probably never even met Mr. Smith and may have no idea what kind of business he runs, but his customer doesn't know this.

An answering service also gives the business a veneer of professionalism. The caller doesn't have to know that she is speaking to a service. Instead, the caller can believe that she has reached your office and is speaking to your incredibly efficient staff.

Cellular Phones for Everyone!

An increasingly popular device for telephoning is the portable phone, or cell (cellular) phone. These days the guy in front of you in line at the bank, the lady in the next booth at the IHOP, and the kid in your neighbor's sandbox all seem to have cell phones. You can carry a cell phone with you just about anywhere. It's a convenience because it means you don't have to find a telephone booth or other phone line to place or receive your calls.

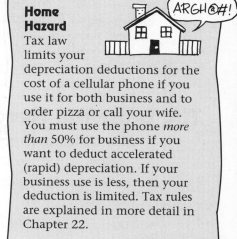

Home Hazard
Tax law limits your depreciation deductions for the cost of a cellular phone if you use it for both business and to order pizza or call your wife. You must use the phone *more than* 50% for business if you want to deduct accelerated (rapid) depreciation. If your business use is less, then your deduction is limited. Tax rules are explained in more detail in Chapter 22.

But although they're trendy, beware: Cellular phones are expensive to operate. (For example, a $30 monthly minimum whether you make any calls. This minimum may cover only 30 minutes of phone time; you'll pay more for additional use.) They are helpful primarily to business owners who need to stay in phone contact with business callers when they're out of the office. They don't make sense, from a cost perspective, for business owners who make only occasional portable calls.

Pagers Find You Anywhere

If you're out in the field a lot, you may need to stay connected to your home office in a more immediate way. Business clients, customers, or others may need to contact you NOW; they can't wait until you choose to retrieve messages from voice mail or an answering machine. For these impatient callers, a simple solution is a personal pager, or "beeper."

Here's how it works. You give John Customer the telephone number for your pager. When John needs to speak to you, he calls that number and keys in his phone number. Your pager beeps (or vibrates or whistles the "Star Spangled Banner") to let you know that a call has come in. Your pager displays John's phone number and you return the call.

The cost of using a pager includes the cost of the pager itself (a modest expense whether you buy or lease the pager) and the cost of the monthly monitoring company (about $20 per month).

Some pagers have become as sophisticated as a Stealth bomber. They're no longer just numeric, displaying simply a phone number and the time of the page. Instead, they're alphanumeric, capable of displaying short, or in some cases, even lengthy, written messages. Older pagers just showed you your caller's phone number (like you have all your customers' numbers memorized and know who the heck you're calling back). Nowadays, a pager can also display your caller's name.

The Educated Entrepreneur

Although there are now more than 2,000 nationwide, all monitoring services are not the same. There are local, regional, and national services. Some have 24-hour-a-day, 365-day-a-year service, while others keep banker's hours. Of course, you get what you pay for, so if your business is entirely local, why pay for regional or national service? You may be able to get temporary national service at a small cost if you travel. Shop around and pay only for the service you need.

The Least You Need to Know

➤ The telephone is probably the most important piece of equipment for a home-based business.

➤ Using your personal phone line for business saves money but may not be right for your business needs.

➤ You may need a dedicated phone line for a fax or modem.

➤ A toll-free number may be necessary for some types of businesses.

➤ There are many different ways to retrieve messages taken in your home office when you're away.

➤ A pager can help you stay in touch with your office and business contacts when you're out in the field.

Going High-Tech

When I started working at home 15 years ago, who would have thought that I (and everyone else) would soon have a computer? Back then, only scientific nerds in giant think tanks needed one, or so we thought. But today nearly every business under the sun uses computers.

Naturally, some businesses are completely dependent on computers—not only computer consultants but also writers, graphic designers, stock analysts, and newsletter publishers. Even if your business isn't tied into technology, you may find it difficult, if not impossible, to run your business without one. Today the computer is used for most mainstream business-type stuff: keeping books and records, printing out invoices, writing correspondence, faxing, and even sending and receiving electronic mail (e-mail).

The computer isn't the only piece of equipment you may want or need for your line of work. There may be other high-tech items to help you run your office efficiently, like a fax machine or a super high-speed copier. In this chapter you'll learn about the computer and what model is right for you. You'll also see whether it pays to buy or lease a computer or other equipment.

Which Computer's for You?

Buying a computer is like buying a car—you have to think about how much you'll use it and for what kinds of things. Do you need a rugged, expensive pickup truck for a small construction business or a used motorcycle for an around-the-town courier service? Does your computer run your business or just spit out six invoices at the end of every month?

Homegrown Tip
This chapter only provides some general advice about fitting computers into your business lifestyle. For more details about using computers, you can look at *The Complete Idiot's Guide to PCs*, Fourth edition, published by Que.

You may be a consultant who's completely dependent on a computer—it's the heart and soul of your business. Or you may be a jewelry designer who uses a computer only as a tool to help you with billing, writing letters, and bookkeeping. What you want your computer to do for you will affect, to some extent, the type of machine you get.

If your business is focused on the computer, you want to get the best machine you can for your money. Judy, who puts out a monthly newsletter, needs a computer that has enough memory to support her desktop publishing software. Don is an economic forecaster who runs his business from home. He needs to continually crunch numbers, which requires both memory and speed. His computer has to be top of the line.

Homegrown Tip
If you already own a computer that you've been using to balance your checkbook and play solitaire, you don't need to buy a new one for business. Just "convert" your computer to business use, upgrading its memory and processing speed to handle more work if necessary. But if your mate and/or kids regularly use the computer, you may want a separate computer for your business. That way you'll always have access to it (and the kids won't accidentally trash that 50-page report you just finished while playing Intergalactic Space Nerds).

On the other hand, Jane only uses the computer to do a few everyday clerical things (for bookkeeping or letter writing); she can get by with a slower, less expensive model. Someone like Jane might be able to buy a used computer for her home-based business. Used machines can cost only a few hundred dollars, much less than the several thousand it costs for a new computer. You can even buy used computers from a reputable dealer and get a warranty.

Computers Made Simple

Fifth graders today can sit down at a computer and whip through some new program they've found in two seconds flat. Some people—especially kids who've grown up in the computer age—are very good with computers. You may be one, and if you are, you certainly don't need this book to tell you about the ins and outs of computers.

But if you're just starting up a home-based business and you've never worked with a computer, you may not be so well informed. If you don't have a clue about how to work a computer and what it can do for you, you need to learn so you can make an informed decision on the model you buy or lease.

If you're shopping now for a computer, decide in advance how much you expect to use it. Rank how great your demand will be for speed and storage, then use one of these sample hardware scenarios as you wander the store aisles. Don't let some computer store clerk intimidate you: Pick the level of computer you need, then hand the guy this book and point to one of these:

➤ High demand: A 586 Pentium, 200 mhz machine with a built-in CD-ROM drive, fax/modem of at least 28.8, 32MB of RAM, and a 2 gigabyte hard drive. Expect to pay around three grand or more for this baby.

➤ Medium usage: A 486, 133 mhz processor with a built-in CD-ROM drive, fax/modem of at least 14.4 bps, 16MB of RAM, and at least a gigabyte hard drive. You might find one of these for around $2,000.

➤ Low usage: At least a 386 with 75 mhz processor, external CD-ROM drive if needed, fax/modem of 9.6, 8 MB of RAM, and 810 megs of hard drive memory. (This would probably be a used machine and cost somewhere in the neighborhood of $1,000 to $1,500.)

How do you know if the computer you're thinking about is going to keep your business humming? Back into your computer decision by first looking at what you need to do and the software programs you'll need to run to do those things. Then pick out a computer with enough space and power to do them.

You wouldn't buy a car without reviewing consumer reports and checking out the list of features on the sticker, so get educated before you choose your computer, too. You can learn about computers by visiting computer superstores and asking questions. You can read up on computers in books and magazines. And you can ask other people who already own computers and use them for business what they like and don't like. Or, you can go to the real experts: Ask your kids!

Buy or Lease?

Don't feel like laying out thousands of dollars at the moment? Relax, you don't have to *buy* your computer. You can lease one. There are compelling reasons to go one way or the other:

Homegrown Tip
It's a good idea to take a service contract for repairs and maintenance on your computer. It's pretty cheap. (Dell offers one on their computers for less than $100 for on-site—in home—service for three years.) And you know you'll get quick service—an essential since a computer that's down can mean you're out of business until it's repaired.

Homegrown Tip
There's not much difference in terms of total dollars between buying the computer over time (financing the purchase) and leasing it (although the lease alternative may be slightly higher). The monthly payments are about the same. This is because the life of a computer is rather short. So your cash flow can be helped with *either* buying over time or leasing.

➤ **Buying.** If you buy a computer, you own it. You can purchase the computer with one payment or finance all or part of it. Obviously, with financing, the interest you pay raises the total price of the computer. Once you've paid off what you've financed, the machine is yours free and clear. Dream systems, with all the features you could want, run upward of $5,000; budget systems that perform adequately are less than $2,000.

You can ease the sticker shock if you buy used equipment. There's an increasing market for pre-owned computers. In fact, today one in ten home office users buys used systems. The reason for this is simple: cost. The cost of reconditioned computers is about 40% less than the cost of new ones. Most pre-owned computers bought from companies that recondition them come with a warranty ranging from 60 to 90 days, parts and labor. Almost-new may be good as a second system (for use if something goes wrong with your new computer or if you have an employee who needs something to work on occasionally).

➤ **Leasing.** If you lease a computer, you have the right to use it for the period or term of the lease. At the end of the lease it's bye-bye computer (unless you exercise your right to buy it at that time at a fixed price). With leasing, you generally don't have to pay much up front (just a deposit of a month or two). Your monthly cost (depending, of course, on the system you select) can be less than $100. So cost is the main attraction of leasing. The cash you don't have to put into the computer when you lease it (as opposed to buying it) is available for other business needs—advertising or payroll, for example.

Leasing equipment doesn't let you off the hook for keeping it in good repair. You also have to take out insurance to cover the cost of the computer in case it's damaged or stolen. If you have any questions about a lease it's a good idea to have an attorney look it over for you.

> ### The Educated Entrepreneur
>
> Computers go out of date faster than hemlines. According to some statistics, businesses should expect to replace their computers every 27 months. This is because technology's been moving so fast that older computers become almost obsolete in no time. Businesses that want to keep up with the Joneses (and be able to handle new software applications) must replace old computers with faster and better ones. I've replaced my computer about every three and a half years.

Leasing Made Easy

If you've ever tried to read the fine print on a car lease, you know they're written by and for lawyers. The same is true of leases for computers. But if you know what you're looking for, it can help you get the best lease terms and not get trapped by the fine print.

➤ **Lease term.** Typically, computer leases are for three- to five-year terms, but you may be able to negotiate for shorter or longer leases. Since a computer becomes "old" in less than three years, don't take a lease for any longer than that.

➤ **Documentation fees.** They get you coming and going. There are fees to write up the lease and then there are fees to wind up the lease. These can be as modest as $50 or a whopping 2% of the lease itself.

➤ **Security deposit.** To make sure that you make the lease payments on time, the company giving you the lease will usually require a security deposit. Typically this deposit covers two months of the lease (some may only require a one-month deposit).

Home Hazard
Signing a lease is like signing a pact with Lucifer—it can't be canceled or shortened once it starts. If you want to pay off the lease early, there may be prepayment penalties. If you go bust, you're still responsible for paying off the lease. Even if your business is incorporated, you may be personally responsible for payments on the lease. Most companies won't lease equipment to a small business unless you, the owner, co-sign or guarantee the lease payments.

➤ Buy-out option. Most leases give you the chance to buy the computer at the end of the lease. Your buy-out price is set in the lease, but you may still be able to negotiate a lower price when it comes time to make the decision at the end of the lease.

Software: It Makes Your Computer Go

A computer's only a machine. The thing that makes all this hardware work is software. There is operating system software like Windows or OS/2 that basically tells your computer how to wake up in the morning, buzz, and whir; then there is software that you use to get things done, like word processors or spreadsheet programs. The operating system software is probably already on your computer when you buy it and you don't have to worry your head about it; the other kind of software is where you've got some decisions to make.

Homegrown Tip When you buy a computer today, you usually get the computer operating system, such as Windows 95 or Windows 3.1, *and* a software package, such as Microsoft Works, factory installed so you have everything you need to get started.

Home Hazard Don't copy software from Bill, your next-door neighbor, just to save a few bucks. Not only is it illegal (it's called copyright violation), but your computer may catch a nasty virus.

Which software you get depends on what your business needs. Today, there are several "office packages," called software suites, that include word processors, spreadsheets, and more. Microsoft's® MS Office Professional includes Word (a powerful word-processing program), Excel (a spreadsheet application), PowerPoint (a business presentation application), and Access (a database program); Corel's® WordPerfect Suite includes WordPerfect (another word-processing program), QuattroPro (a spreadsheet application), and Corel Presentations. While these office suites don't come cheap, they're integrated, meaning you can easily take files from one application and use them in another.

If you're the type to choose one item from Column A and one from Column B on Chinese menus, you can put together your own set of software by buying separate products to meet your needs as they arise. For example, you can get Microsoft's® Word for your word processing and add Intuit's QuickBooks® for your accounting software to keep track of your invoicing, bill paying, receivables, and payables.

Who You Gonna Call?

Computers, like any other machinery, can have problems and will eventually break down. But unlike the broken faucet in the bathroom, you may not have the tools or knowledge to repair them. You may have to rely on experts to service your computer.

Be sure you understand what you've got coming to you in the way of service when you buy or lease a computer. Will the store stand behind it and provide technical support? For how long? If you buy your machine through mail order, what recourse do you have? Will you have to go back to the manufacturer for help?

Many computer problems can be handled over the telephone. More often than not the problems stem from software. Sometimes the way the computer is *configured* (that just means the settings you use to make it run) is the problem. These things can be tweaked to correct the problem, and a phone conversation might do the trick.

Homegrown Tip

The stuff you put into your computer is vital to your business. Protect it by backing up files (see more about this later in the chapter). Store your backup in a safe place. Use a fireproof safe in your home office or store your backup off-site (such as in a bank safe deposit box).

Most computer manufacturers have technical support over the telephone. Software companies also provide telephone support to handle problems in their software. In the past, telephone support was typically a toll-free number, but now you'll find that you usually have to pay for it. What's more, if you're put on hold (an occurrence as common and inevitable as ants at a picnic), the cost of the call and the waiting time can be expensive. But the phone cost is certainly less than the cost of a house call by a technician. Even if you've paid for an on-site service contract, the tech won't come until *after* you've gone the telephone support route.

Peripherals R Us

Just when you think you've got it all in hand—the computer and the software—there's more. There's something called *peripherals,* which includes all computer-related equipment except the guts of the computer—the processor and the memory. All computers need some peripherals to operate them—a mouse, cables, and a keyboard, for example. Other peripherals are pretty essential: It's hard to live without surge protectors (gizmos to keep electrical surges on the line from damaging your computer) and a printer.

As for other peripherals—scanners or back-up drives—it's your call. What's your business need? What can you afford to buy?

Pretty in Print

How do you get what's in your computer out? A printer. A printer can cost as little as a few hundred dollars or as much as several thousand dollars.

The Mercedes Benz of printers are *laser* printers. They have speed and the best quality reproduction of images on the page. They're also very quiet when they're running. Like

Mercedes, laser printers cost the most because you get the most in terms of reproduction. If you print a newsletter with a lot of graphic images and embossed text effects, you need a laser printer. The same is true if you print pictures.

Ink jet (also called deskjet) printers are the next best thing to laser. They also have a fairly high quality of reproduction. They don't run as fast as a laser printer and their quality isn't as good, but they cost less (as low as $250).

The Yugos of printers are *dot matrix*. If you still own a black-and-white TV or a rotary phone, you'll love these. Of the three types of printers, this is the nosiest, slowest, and has the poorest output quality. However, it's also the cheapest (around $150). If you're only printing out invoices, a dot matrix may do. But for my money, an extra hundred bucks to spring for a deskjet is a good investment in your business image.

What a Great Picture!

Monitors are like TV screens for your computer, only you can't tune into HBO. Monitors come in black-and-white and color, although all computers but low-end laptops now use color monitors. Like TVs, monitors come in all sizes, from as small as 13-inch screens to 17-inch screens or even larger. If you're doing desktop publishing and use your screen to get a good look at a design layout, you want as large a screen as you can afford.

Monitors also use different resolutions, which is a fancy word for how clear the image is. Consider looking into flat screen monitors, which cut down on glare (but usually cost a bit more).

Cost depends on the quality of the monitor, resolution, and size. The better the quality, and the larger the screen, the higher the cost.

Back Me Up!

Many years ago, on a day almost as earthshaking as the stock market crash of 1929, my hard disk "crashed," wiping out everything that I'd put into my computer. I was devastated. Getting the data back was as impossible as finding a parking space in New York City. Fortunately, I'd saved some of my important files on floppy disks. Once I was up and running again, I just reloaded my files. The files I hadn't backed up were lost forever.

There are several ways to back up (keep a separate record of) the data in your computer:

➤ You can save your files on disks. With high density disks you can now store a lot of information on a single disk. For example, all the words in this book were saved to just one disk! But if you have big files, especially graphics, storage on disks might not be for you.

➤ You can get a special peripheral called a tape backup, which allows you to record your computer's information on tape. This device is becoming largely obsolete today since there's a newer type of device available.

➤ You can back up your computer data onto a Zip drive, the name used for the device by the leading manufacturer, Iomega. The information is recorded on a disk that looks a lot like a floppy disk in a thicker plastic box. The Zip drive can be installed in the computer (internal) or hooked up on the outside (external).

CD-ROM

Not all software comes on a disk. Some now comes on a compact disk that looks like an audio CD. CDs can contain a vast amount of information—the contents of an entire encyclopedia can fit on a single CD!

A CD is read-only, which means you can't add any information to it or change it in any way. What you see is all you get. But much of today's software is now on CD-ROM. For instance, if you want to use a program to prepare your tax return, you'll probably use CD-ROM–based software.

CD-ROM software requires a special CD player (typically installed inside the computer). CD-ROM players are described by speed: 2X (two-speed), 4X (four-speed), 8X (eight-speed), 12X (12-speed).

Music and Pictures

Any software programs that contain sound as well as visual effects, whether on CD or a floppy, require a sound card in your computer to translate the sound information. There are different sound cards (with different prices). And on top of that, you'll need speakers to hear the sound.

If you want to play the neatest video game, you also need a video card to handle all those pretty pictures. New computers will all come with a built-in sound and video card and the software (called drivers) to run them.

Faxes and Modems Keep You in Touch

The American patriots had Paul Revere; you've got your computer to keep you in touch with the world. Communication from a home office to the outside world is essential for running most businesses. To stay in contact, you need to be able to communicate with other computers as well as other people. Two ways to communicate are faxing and e-mailing.

Only a decade ago friends meeting casually over coffee said "Phone me." Nowadays you're as likely to overhear somebody stirring cappuccino say "Fax me." A fax lets you send images to another fax machine over telephone lines. The fax mechanism can be *internal* to your computer in which case it sends the fax using your computer's modem. A software program lets your computer act as a fax machine to transmit information. *Stand-alone* fax machines are discussed later in this chapter.

A modem lets your computer communicate with another computer not only to send faxes, but also to get online. Today, a modem is becoming an essential piece of equipment because you need it to get onto the "Information Superhighway" called the Internet. Small businesses can use the Internet to get information, buy and sell goods and services, and communicate with other business owners. You can also use e-mail to leave messages for clients, customers, and suppliers.

A modem can be either internal or external. An external modem takes up a little bit more desk space but can be used with your next computer when you upgrade your equipment. Of course, the modem may also become dated since newer models have faster speeds. Currently, the newest models have speeds of 50KB. This may be more speed than you need since most transmissions at present don't exceed 28.8KB. But the faster you can upload and download files, the less time you're online, saving you online charges.

Scanning Your Way to Fame

Remember that flyer some guy left on your windshield last Tuesday? It had a couple of photographs mixed in with the text. How did the guy do it? With a scanner. This is a machine that's connected to your computer by a cable. It transmits any image into your computer. Once that image is in your computer, if you have software that can handle it, you can work with it like any other computer file, making changes, resizing the image, and so on.

Scanners can also digitize text—words on a page—into a computer file to save you typing it all in again. But to read the words you need a special program, called OCR (optical character recognition), which lets you edit the text you've scanned into the computer. Do you need all this? If you're not a graphic designer or marketing type, probably not. But at least now you know what it is!

Office Equipment You Can't Do Without

Today, a well-equipped home office has just about the same type of equipment as any office of General Motors. In addition to a computer, your home office should also have a copier and a fax machine (if you don't have one on your computer).

Copiers

How did businesses operate before there were photo-copiers? I can't imagine working without one. The type of copier you get depends on the number of copies you expect to make each month. If you're like me and don't plan to make many copies, you can get by with a personal-type copier. (My first one lasted 13 years!) If you expect to make a lot of copies each month, you'll want to look at a more sophisticated model.

Like computers, you can buy or lease. The same benefits and cautions discussed earlier for buying or leasing computers also apply to copiers.

Homegrown Tip

Whether you buy or lease your copier, check out whether you're covered for servicing of the machine. Copiers, especially the more complex ones, notoriously break down and need servicing, usually when you've got a serious deadline staring you in the face.

The price of copiers runs all over the place, depending on the complexity of the machine. A simple, personal-type copier is only a few hundred dollars. The bigger and better ones can run amuck at several thousand dollars.

Machines That Wear Many Hats

Today you can buy all-in-one machines that act as a fax, a copier, a scanner, and a printer. The upside to getting this type of machine is saving money. The cost of one multi-function machine is less than the total cost of three separate single-function machines. It also saves space.

The downside to getting a multi-function machine is total dependency on just one piece of equipment. If something goes wrong—say, for example, the fax portion of the machine malfunctions—you can be out of business until it's repaired. Forget copying or printing anything until the service guy shows.

The Educated Entrepreneur

If you're a weaver, roofer, or sculptor, a computer may be handy for your billing and record keeping, but the core of your business requires other equipment. You need special tools to ply your trade.

Since these tools are the foundation of your business, you don't want to cut corners here. Expect considerable wear and tear on your tools, and buy the best you can afford to get the longest use possible.

Extend the life of your tools by keeping them in good condition. Set up regular service schedules to keep your tools in good repair.

The Educated Entrepreneur

There is good news: The cost of buying your office equipment can be offset by some tax savings. For example, you can deduct the cost of the equipment you buy up to a certain dollar limit each year. In 1997, the limit is $18,000 (but you need to show income from your business in order to use this tax deduction). Tax rules are explained in Chapter 22.

The Least You Need to Know

➤ Almost all home-based businesses need a computer and other equipment to run professionally and efficiently.

➤ The computer you use for your business depends on the type of business you're in *and* on what you can afford.

➤ You can buy *or* lease most of your office equipment.

➤ Lining up service support for your computer, copier, and other equipment will let your business run smoothly even if you run into mechanical problems.

➤ The peripherals you select depend on the type of work you do in your office.

Part 5
Running Your Business

Having an idea for a business and launching that business is no guarantee that you'll succeed. Robbie Burns didn't say the best laid plans of mice and men oft go awry for nothing. He probably had a failed home business in his past. It's up to you to learn how to run your business so that you can get beyond the start-up phase and watch your business blossom.

There are many aspects to running a business. Being a small business owner means you have to wear many hats. Large companies have separate departments to handle selling, advertising, collections, accounting, and personnel. But you, as a small business owner, are the boss, the mailroom, the secretarial pool, and the janitor. You create the product, produce the service, generate the business, and lick the envelopes for the bills you send out.

In this part of the book, you'll learn about marketing your business, getting paid for your work, finding help when you need it, accounting, taxes, and insurance—all aspects of running your business. These topics apply to all companies, but you'll see that being a home-based business can present special challenges.

Chapter 16

Marketing Magic

In This Chapter

➤ Mastering the marketing process

➤ Making a can't-fail marketing plan

➤ Promoting yourself on the Internet

➤ Using advertising ideas that work best for a home-based business

---

You're in business to sell your product or service to make money. But how do you go about doing this? For many home-based business owners, it's hard to figure out exactly where to begin. The number one question I get from students in a class I teach on starting a home-based business is "Where do I find clients or customers?" Obviously, you need to learn the answer to this question because without customers, you might as well be doing business on a desert island.

To become successful in selling your product or service, you should understand the marketing process. You need to develop a marketing plan. You can take potshots at success, but to hit a bull's-eye, you need to have an idea of how you want to reach customers and then go out and do it. And once you've found clients or customers, you want to be sure to keep them.

In this chapter you'll learn what marketing is all about. You may be surprised to find that you have some wrong ideas about marketing. You'll find out how to develop a marketing plan for your business. And you'll see how to get your marketing plan off the ground and keep tabs on it as you go along.

The ABCs of Marketing

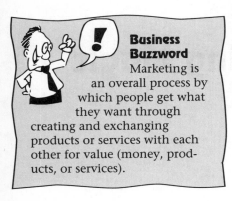

Business Buzzword
Marketing is an overall process by which people get what they want through creating and exchanging products or services with each other for value (money, products, or services).

Many people use the terms marketing, advertising, promotion, and sales almost interchangeably. Each of these terms, which you'll learn the meaning of in a moment, is distinct. Each plays a role in seeing that your product or service reaches the public so you can make money.

The term marketing really covers five separate elements: market research, distribution channels, pricing, advertising, and promotion (the actual selling phase). Let's look at each of these elements so you can develop your own marketing strategy.

Getting to Know You: Market Research

Market research is really just a way to find out if anyone's interested in paying good money for your product or service. Market research is the first stage in marketing. It's also the first stage in developing your business. Don't even think about starting a business until you find out if anyone wants what you're selling.

Some new business owners may think they don't have to do market research. After all, they say, they're small, don't have the time or expertise to conduct the research, and don't know what the research is for anyway. The answer to this attitude is simple: You can't sell anything to someone you don't know.

Market research will help you identify the market you should sell to. Here's what your market research should tell you:

➤ Who are you going to sell to? You want to get a picture of the type of customer you're targeting. Is this character male or female? Is he part of Generation X or a baby boomer? This will help you with your advertising. What's the age group? Level of education? Household income?

➤ How big is your potential market? The potential market includes anyone who might be able to use your product or service. Put your potential market size into numbers. Are there 1,000 or 1 million people in your market? Maybe you'll see that even if you could sell your product or service to everyone in your potential market you wouldn't be able to make a living from it. Say you can sell your house-sitting service to 10% of the market. Well, if the potential market is only 1,000, a 10% share is just 100 people — not enough to make it worthwhile. Then you're back at square one.

➤ What are the geographic boundaries of your market? As a home-based business, you might think you're limited to your neighborhood. Today it's possible to think big even if you're a small business. For example, you can have a national or even international market if you plan to sell on the Internet.

➤ How do you stack up against the competition? Are you the Saks Fifth Avenue of consultants or Filene's Basement?

Distribution Channels: I Can Get It for You Wholesale

If you perform a service, you don't have to worry about distribution channels. You work directly to provide a service to people. But if you're selling products, you need to figure out how you're going to get your products in the hands of people who want to buy them.

There are many different types of distribution channels: retail, wholesale, mail order, direct sales, or selling through sales agents. In a home-based business, you may not be able to sell retail because of zoning restrictions on the amount of commercial traffic to your home. You may be able to sell wholesale, which means putting your product in some other guy's store so he can sell your product to the public.

Many home-based businesses focus on two methods of distribution: mail order and direct sales. Mail-order businesses have sprung up all over the country like weeds after a spring rain. Lillian Vernon started her highly successful mail-order business on her kitchen table in a suburb of New York City. Many other mail-order businesses are also run from home offices.

Direct sales involves face-to-face selling outside of a store or mail order. If you sell cosmetics door-to-door, you're using direct sales. The concept of network marketing is based on direct sales (as explained in Chapter 6).

Homegrown Tip
You can locate fulfillment companies in an industrial directory in your local library. Look under "fulfillment."

As a home business, if you've got big plans for advertising and expect volume business, you may want to think about using a fulfillment company. A fulfillment company can take orders, store products for you, and ship them out for a fee.

Eileen, an account executive with a Fortune 500 company, used a fulfillment company to take her vitamin business from zero sales to almost $2 million in less than two years! She started the business in her garage with money she got by refinancing her home mortgage. She advertised on local talk radio stations and received more calls than AT&T. The listeners were given a toll-free number that, unbeknownst to them, was a fulfillment company that processed the orders. The fulfillment company collected payment on credit-card charges and shipped the vitamins that they stored in their warehouse. The cost to Eileen for each order was a flat charge (around $1 an order).

Pricing Is Everything

Unless you're the only business offering a unique product or service, you have to be concerned about pricing, because the public certainly is. Whatever else you offer, price is the first thing people look at.

Homegrown Tip
In most cases, price is the most important thing to a consumer. Be sure to set your prices high enough to make money, but low enough to attract consumers.

Make your prices realistic. You have to charge enough to make a profit. You can't charge less than it costs you to sell the product or service or you'll be out of business before you know it. Divide your monthly expenses by your monthly units (the hours you expect to bill out for your services or the number of items you plan to sell). This will give you a bare minimum to cover expenses (you'd lose money if you charged any less). Your profit margin—what you add on to each of your monthly units—depends on what you're selling and what the market will bear. You don't want to charge so much that you turn off consumers. You need to be sure that the price for your product or service is not out of whack with the competition.

After determining your minimum price (what you absolutely, positively, cannot charge less than in order to stay in business), compare your price with your competitors. If everyone in your business offers the same price, maybe you have to do the same. For example, if you have a lawn-care business and the going rate in the area for mowing is $25 per week, you probably have to charge the same if you have any hopes of getting customers.

If you see that your price is higher than the competition, you should have a darn good reason for the higher price. Maybe you offer something more for the extra price—special service or a guarantee that your competitors don't offer. Be sure that consumers know that they get a bonus for paying the higher price—"You pay more because you get more."

If you see that your price is lower than the competition, don't assume people will think you're the best deal around. Quite the opposite. The public may think that a lower price means inferior quality or less service. You need to educate the public on the reason for your lower price. Maybe you have a personal connection that helped you buy the products you sell at a lower price than the competition. You can tell the public this—"We pass our savings on to you."

Continue to monitor your prices as your business develops so you can adjust them for shifts in the marketplace or other changes.

Advertising and Promotion: Spreading the Word

Even Thomas Edison had to spread the word about his inventions to capture the public interest. People weren't lined up at his door with a buck and a half for a new lightbulb the first day it became available. You have to let people know that you have something to sell. This means advertising and promotion.

Advertising can take many different shapes. It can be direct advertising where you push your particular product or service—"buy my face cream" or "use my tax preparation service." Or advertising can be indirect. Your entire business image is a form of indirect advertising. Try using a business logo or color on everything that the public sees—your business cards, invoices, stationery, signs, even on a T-shirt. Eventually, you'll build up a business identity that the public will come to recognize, and that translates into indirect marketing and sales.

Word-of-mouth from satisfied clients and customers is just about the best form of advertising you can get. It doesn't cost you anything, and it's highly effective in bringing in new business.

Just advertising, telling the public about your product or service, may not be enough. Here's where promotion comes in. Sometimes you may need to add a little something extra to get the sale. Maybe you have to offer discounts. Maybe you want to offer bonuses. Think of the local bank that gives out a toaster for opening a savings account. You're not a bank, but you, too, can offer a benefit. If you provide a service, you may want to offer a free consultation. Be sure your offer is clear, such as "one hour free." Many people like to test a service before they buy. Just be prepared to give out a lot of free hours before you actually get some paid ones.

Your advertising options are discussed shortly.

> **Business Buzzword**
> *Advertising* means informing the public of the features and benefits of your product or service.
>
> *Promotion* is a way of stimulating an immediate sale, such as offering a discount coupon.

> **Homegrown Tip**
> Give out refrigerator magnets to advertise your business. Bob, an electrician in my neighborhood who runs his business from home, does this with great success. Bob always leaves a magnet on the electrical box when he finishes a job. This way, when there's another problem, his number's always close at hand. And if the homeowner moves, the new owner sees immediately who's been servicing the home.

Sales: Bringing in the Bucks

The last step in marketing is the most important step: the actual selling phase. This is the point at which someone pays you money for your product or service. It's sometimes called closing a sale. All of your previous efforts—market research, advertising, your logo on T-shirts—don't mean a thing if you can't close a sale.

There's a reason good salespeople are as rare as snow in August: Selling is a skill. Some people are born salespeople; others have to learn how to sell. A lot of people are as frightened of selling as they are of major surgery. If you don't feel entirely comfortable in selling, you just have to get over it and get to it.

There are things you can do to become better at selling. Try writing a script for your sales pitch. Write down all the points you want to cover and how you'll present them. Practice the script with family or friends or in front of a mirror until you know it well. Then, as you work with your script in trying to make a sale, you'll be able to add or delete from it to make it even better.

In devising your approach, keep in mind the different parts of your sales pitch:

➤ Identify your customer's needs. What's the situation and how can you make it better (how can you solve your customer's problem)? If you've already been asked to make a proposal, presumably the customer has already told you her needs.

➤ Make a proposal. Tell your customer what you're going to do and how much it's going to cost.

➤ Address objections. Be prepared for an initial "no," but, as the saying goes, never take no for an answer. Discover what objections your customer has and be ready to respond. If price is the only objection, then let's get to the next point.

➤ Negotiate. You may be able to make a sale if you're flexible. With this in mind, you need to put some leeway in your proposal to allow for negotiating.

➤ Close the sale. Get the customer to sign on the dotted line. If, at this final stage in the sale, you meet with just a maybe or even a no, don't give up the ship. Go back to square one and start the process over again. Maybe you didn't properly identify the customer's needs, for example.

Homegrown Tip

If selling's not your strong suit, don't be afraid to bone up with selling techniques you can learn from books, classes, and seminars. Dale Carnegie made a business out of teaching people how to sell.

Your Marketing Plan: Game Plan for Success

So, how are you going to get your business from zero sales to $50,000, $100,000, $1 million? If you don't know where you're going, you won't get there. Develop a game plan that you can use to bring your business along.

The important part of your game plan is not just drawing it up. This is useful because it makes you focus on various points, but the real key is putting it into action. Just sitting back and waiting for things to happen is a surefire way for dust to gather on your inventory.

Set Marketing Goals

How will you measure your success unless you've built yourself a yardstick to measure your progress? Decide your short-term and long-term marketing goals. A goal can be sales, customers, dollars—however you define it. How many sales do you want to make this year, or in the next three years? How many new customers do you want to find in the next month?

In setting your goals, be specific and realistic. Set sales figures you think you can reach, and mark the dates when you expect to reach your targets in red on the calendar.

When setting goals, you should have already performed your market research. You have to know your market size. You need to have strategically set your price.

> **Homegrown Tip**
> If you don't think you're able to create a good marketing plan and have trouble setting goals on your own, try using a canned program for your computer. For less than $150 there are several commercial software programs for marketing plans. Or you can try shareware that can be downloaded from http://www.smalloffice.com.

Size up the Competition

When's the last time you opened the Yellow Pages and looked at the number of companies that do what you do? It goes without saying that for most businesses, the marketplace is very competitive. Find out about your competitors so you can stand out among them:

> ➤ Know the "enemy." Who are your competitors? You can find out just by playing consumer and looking in the Yellow Pages or local ads. You may find there are only one or two businesses in direct competition with you in your area. A direct competitor is one offering the same product or service. For example, if you're an interior decorator, your direct competitors are other interior decorators. Indirect competitors are those offering similar products or services. The local paint and wallpaper stores may offer some decorating assistance, so these stores would be indirect competitors.

> **Homegrown Tip**
> You need to know what kind of advertising your competitors are using. By tracking them down, you'll see what advertising they do and how effective it is. Keep this information handy when it comes time to start your own advertising campaign.

You may find that you have dozens of direct competitors. For example, these days everyone's a Web page designer. So what? If they're all working to capacity or you have a unique feel for design, then there may still be room for you in the market.

➤ Try out the competition's product or service. Be a consumer to test what they're offering. Even if you can't afford to buy one of everything that's out there, at least let them send you their literature and give you their sales talk so you know what they're pitching to your potential customers. Talk to your competitor's customers to learn if they're satisfied and will remain loyal. Talk to local merchants and bankers to find out about the reputation of your competitors. You can also learn about how your industry's doing in general by talking with these sources.

➤ Compare yourself with your competitors. How do you stack up against the existing competition? Use the following worksheet to make your comparison. Find two to five competitors to get a good cross section. Rate each competitor on a scale from 1 to 10 (with 10 being the highest) according to price, quality, service, and other factors (like next-day service, special hours, guarantees). Then rate yourself in each of these categories. The top score for anyone is 40. Be honest with yourself about your weak points and strong points.

Worksheet for Assessing the Competition

You/ Competition	Price	Quality	Service	Other Factors*	Score
You	$_____	_____	_____	_____	_____
Competitor 1	$_____	_____	_____	_____	_____
Competitor 2	$_____	_____	_____	_____	_____
Competitor 3	$_____	_____	_____	_____	_____
Competitor 4	$_____	_____	_____	_____	_____
Competitor 5	$_____	_____	_____	_____	_____

Other factors can include location, hours of business, or other special features.

How'd you stack up against the competition? Were your prices higher or lower? Is your product of better quality? Or worse? Do you offer special service? Do you offer nice little extras? The purpose of the exercise is to let you make adjustments in your business so that you stand out among your competitors. If, after totaling up the scores, you and all the competitors are about the same, you may want to add a special something to bring up your score.

Understand Your Advertising Options

From the time the first caveman advertised his cave for rent at the local dinosaur roast, people have been thinking up new ways to advertise. Advertising can take many forms. The ones you select will depend on what you're selling and the money you have to spend on advertising. Here are some ways to advertise:

Billboards	Radio
Catalogs	Samples
Cooperative advertising	Seminars
Direct mail	Signs
Display advertising	Specialty ads (e.g., journals)
Internet	Sponsorships (Little League team)
Press release	Telemarketing
Print ads (classifieds, magazines, newspaper ads)	TV (network/cable)
	Trade shows
Promotional contests and prizes	Yellow Pages

Some forms of advertising are free. Networking (making personal contacts that can translate into sales contacts) doesn't cost a thing. Networking is a continual and ongoing process. Wherever you are and whoever you're with, there's an opportunity to network. Don't be shy. Talk about yourself and your business. The listener may do the same about her business. This simple conversation has laid the groundwork for future contact. (Networking is discussed again in Chapter 25.)

Planting a story in your local newspaper can also be a great way to advertise your business without spending a dime. Suzanne, formerly a full-time housewife, started up a home-based business as a "custom home designer." According to the blurb in the local paper, she works with the builder and homeowner to pick out tile, carpeting, and other appointments in custom-built homes. The item included her picture and telephone number, and it was listed in the newspaper as community news. This was a great way to publicize a new business at no cost. You can do the same with some event in your business—your grand opening, a new product, a speech you made at a local organization, or record annual sales.

Follow Up

Be sure to follow up on your marketing efforts. You've spent the money and succeeded in getting customer response. Now don't waste it. Maybe it's obvious what you have to do, but here are some reminders for customer follow-up:

➤ Return phone calls.

➤ Schedule appointments.

➤ Fulfill promises made in your ads.

➤ Ask about customer satisfaction.

Your follow-up is as important as the ad itself.

Besides following up on your customers, you should also follow up on your advertising. You want to know whether your advertising efforts are responsible for the customers (or whether they're coming to you some other way). If you advertise in several different ways, find out which one reeled the customer in.

You can find this out in several different ways. You can track ads directly by asking customers "How'd you hear of us?" Or you can use an indirect approach. You make up a name, department, or box number and put it in your ad or on your brochures and promotional coupons. When customers respond and make references to this nonexistent person or department, you'll know immediately that they came to you through your ad. If you find your methods aren't bringing in customers, then you need to change them or review your entire marketing approach.

Understand that advertising, which is the process of informing the public about you, may not translate into immediate sales. People learn by repetition; you've got to repeat your ads until people remember your jingle, your motto, and your phone number. It may be some time before you begin to see results. It's better to have several smaller ads run frequently than one large, expensive ad run once. Frequency, rather than size, is more effective.

> **ARGH@#!** **Home Hazard**
>
> Make sure that you don't have any false or deceptive ads or do anything else that violates Federal Trade Commission guidelines. For example, you can't make promotional payments to only some customers—this is discriminatory. If you're not sure, check with an attorney.

Simple and Cheap Advertising Ideas

Even if you could afford to, you may not be able to use all types of advertising for your business. Zoning restrictions may prohibit you from displaying a large sign or any sign at all at your place of business. The size of your advertising budget may price you out of the range of expensive forms of advertising, like radio and TV. For instance, infomercials, though highly effective, cost thousands of dollars to produce and thousands of more dollars to run.

But there are some types of advertising that just about any home-based business can use. You can't go wrong with having your satisfied customers spread the good word about you. You may want to look into what the Internet can do for your business. And, of course, there are always classified ads and direct mail.

Word of Mouth

Your best ad comes from a satisfied customer. In all my years in business I've never had to run an ad. All my clients have come to me through word of mouth from my existing clients.

You should spend some of your energy and dollars keeping clients and customers happy.

The Educated Entrepreneur

Why spend money you don't have to? It costs 10 times more to bring in a new customer than to keep an existing one. So do everything you can to ensure continued customer satisfaction. A bonus to this is that satisfied customers will tell others about you, bringing in new customers without any added cost.

Use your common sense and good manners. Thank clients and customers for their business. Follow up on problems, and don't let anyone go away unhappy with the results. You may want to send out cards or small gifts at holiday time as a thank-you.

Ask your good clients or customers for referrals. You can even think about offering incentives for referrals, such as $25 off their next order.

Advertising in Cyberspace

If you have a computer, or access to one, maybe you've "surfed the Web" and visited home pages or Web sites of major corporations. The Internet is a place for a home-based business owner to keep up with trends and sell a product or service. The Information Superhighway let's you compete in the marketplace with the big boys.

You can get general information to help you run your business, as you've seen throughout this book (I found a lot of the information for this book on the Internet). You can also get marketing information that you can use for your business. For instance, suppose you want to find out about trade shows in your area of business. You can visit a Web site that will give you information about trade shows all across the country (http://www.tscentral.com).

You can also let the public know you exist via the Internet. Your own Web page can describe your business to thousands of potential customers. You can give information of general interest or specifics about your business. Be sure to list your e-mail address, telephone number, or other ways to contact you.

Here's one way to use a Web page: Henry, an antiques dealer who operates from his home in the Midwest, doesn't bring customers into his home. Instead, he sells his stuff world-wide by displaying pictures and descriptions of it on the Internet. For Henry, the sale is not made on the Internet (the buyer doesn't have to provide a charge card number or otherwise commit to the sale via computer). A person interested in buying an item simply calls him on the phone to get more information and negotiate the price.

Some large businesses spend millions of dollars on designing their sites, but you don't have to spend anywhere near this much. You can spend a relatively small sum (less than a hundred dollars to a few thousand dollars) to have a professional design a Web page for you. The cost of the design depends on its complexity and how many links (cross-references to other home pages) it provides. You can even design a simple page for free if you subscribe to an online service (America Online gives you one free home page per subscriber as part of your monthly fee).

Another cost of having a Web page is a hookup fee, a one-time connection to a storage service (typically about $100). This is the location that mans your Web page 24 hours a day, 365 days a year.

Still another cost: the monthly storage fee of about $100 or more. This cost allows your page to be stored in a central computer site so that it can be accessed by those on the Internet.

And don't forget ongoing costs: fees you'll pay to your Web page designer to keep your site fresh (unless you have the skill to do it yourself).

I Saw It in the Classifieds

Perhaps the most familiar way to advertise what you have to sell is to place a classified ad. You can place the ad in newspapers, in magazines, in the Yellow Pages, or even on computer classified services. Classifieds can be cheap, but highly effective.

The Yellow Pages may be a good place for you to advertise your business. You don't have to rely solely on your telephone listing to bring in business. You can have a featured ad in the section of the Yellow Pages for your type of business—under "cabinet makers," "calligraphers," "carpenters," or "caterers." Check out the cost of running the ad as well as the cost to prepare it. When making the ad, be sure it's catchy. You might want to use a second color (despite added cost) to increase responses. Showcase your specialty (quality, service, low price, guarantee). Be a problem-solver for customers (state how your product or service will be of help). Include your vital information (your hours, whether you accept credit cards, professional accreditation). Depending on the size of your advertising budget you may want to work with professionals (graphic designers or even an ad agency) to design your ad.

The Educated Entrepreneur

You don't have to spend a penny and you don't even need your own Web site to advertise on the Internet. You can climb onto the coattails of another company's advertising efforts. For example, you can place a free ad for your business on the portion of American Express's Web site geared to small business (http://americanexpress.com). The businesses are listed by geographic area and subject matter.

Direct Mail

Many small business owners use direct mail (send an ad right to the mailboxes of potential customers) and you can, too. Direct mail is relatively inexpensive. Your costs include the ad, the envelope, and the postage. You can create the insert yourself (an ad that will go into the envelope) or use a self-mailer. If you get a bulk mail permit (about $85 per year), you can lower your mailing costs from 32¢ to 22.5¢ per piece, as long as you meet certain requirements to prepare the mailing. Or you can use a professional mailer (or mailing house) to do the mailing for you. The cost for that service (which includes folding, stuffing, and sorting by ZIP code for mailing) is about 52¢ per piece for postage and the envelope.

But direct mail only works if three things are in place:

➤ You need the right list. You have to know who to mail your ad to. You can buy a mailing list (it's called buying but in reality you're only renting the list because you only buy the right to use it for a limited time).

➤ You need the right ad. As with any type of advertising you have to get the attention of the consumer and make your point. You may want to try including a coupon for a discount off your regular price for a limited time.

➤ You have to do your mailing at the right time. If, for example, you have a pool service in New England, you're probably wasting your dollars to send a mailing out in November. You would want to time your mailing to *drop* (be mailed) just before the pool season (say in the spring).

> ### The Educated Entrepreneur
>
> You may complain about mail delivery, but you won't complain about a free service from the U.S. Postal Service. Yes, the post office can help you develop your mailing list at no cost to you. It will help you put your mailing list on a disk and add the extra four-digit ZIP codes to reduce your mailing costs. It can also provide you with a list of undeliverable mail to help you update your mailing list. To find out how the postal service can help you, call 800-374-8777.

Keep your expectations about direct mail realistic. A typical good response is only about 2%. So if you're mailing to 10,000 households, that's only 200 responses. At 52¢ per mailer, you'd need to recoup $26 from each of your 200 responses to cover your $5,200 direct mail outlay.

Think that direct mail is too expensive? There's a cheaper way to get your message across—co-op your direct mail. It's called co-oping because your ad goes out with ads from other businesses in your area. There are many cooperative mailing companies that let you put an insert into their mailing envelopes, which are then sent to households and businesses in a particular location.

The cost of co-oping is very modest (about $400 to $600 for a two-color ad that is sent to 10,000 households). This is far less than you'd have to pay for just the cost of the envelope and the postage were you to direct mail on your own. And they can help you with your ad design. You probably already know who the cooperative advertising companies are in your area since you've no doubt received their envelopes from time to time advertising carpet cleaning, florists, accounting services, and the local Chinese food take-out.

The Least You Need to Know

➤ Marketing is a multi-step process that involves everything from understanding your market to advertising your product to locking in a sale.

➤ The price must be right in order to succeed.

➤ You should set marketing goals and figure out how you plan to meet them.

➤ The advertising strategies you use depends on the nature of your business and the size of your advertising budget.

➤ The Internet lets a home-based business sell worldwide with only a modest sales expense.

Getting Paid for What You Do

The bottom line in business is getting paid. After all, you're not in this for your health. You've gone through the trouble of telling people about your product or service, stirred up some interest, and made the sale. You've delivered your product. You've performed your service. Now you want the money you've earned. This chapter tells you how to get it.

To make sure that you get what's due you, you'll have to set up a collection system. And you need to decide how you're going to accept payment for your product or service—whether cash, check, charge, or shiny beads. You should also understand your right to sue in small claims court to collect for your work.

In this chapter you'll learn about smart invoicing policies. You'll also find out about the different ways to get paid. And you'll learn about how you can put the screws to those late accounts.

The Ins and Outs of Invoicing

Money doesn't just magically appear in your mailbox when you run a business. Ronald, a management consultant, sends a bill to his clients at the end of each month showing the hours he's spent on their accounts. Fran, who sells antique porcelain over the Internet, sends an invoice to get paid *before* she ships her wares. You also need to present a bill or *invoice* if you want a payday.

In setting your own invoice policy, you should decide:

> ➤ What your invoice will look like.

> ➤ When you'll send it.

> ➤ The terms you'll offer (how soon you must be paid, interest charges for late payment, discounts for early payment, and so on).

> ➤ What you'll do to get prompt payment.

> ➤ What you'll do just in case you don't.

Business Buzzword

An *invoice* is a bill for your product or service. For goods, it's an itemized list of what you've shipped or sold to a buyer, stating the quantity, price, and other terms of sale. For services, it's a description of the work performed along with your fee.

Creating an Invoice That Says "Pay Me!"

Nobody will pay you if you slip him a quick note on a paper napkin. Make sure that the invoice or bill you present is complete and professional-looking. Here are the elements to include:

> ➤ **Who.** Your company name, address, and telephone number. You may want to add your name as the person to contact in case there are any questions about the bill. This personal touch can't hurt and is appreciated by some people.

> ➤ **What.** Describe the items sold or services performed. For products, indicate quantity, size, and any other relevant information.

> ➤ **When (terms of sale).** Say when payment is due—on receipt of the invoice or within 30 days. If you offer a discount for payment within 10 days or have any other special terms, be sure to explain them. You might want to do this if your cash flow is tight or you have to pay your suppliers on delivery.

Homegrown Tip

You took all that time producing quality work, don't blow it now! Make your invoice look good. It's a reflection on your business identity, so use it to put your best foot forward. Include your business logo or use colors to reinforce your identity with the customer. Make sure it's neat, accurate, and professional looking.

➤ Invoice number. To help you keep track of your sales, assign a number to each invoice. This'll help you track payments made to you and follow up on late accounts. Get creative! You can use your mother's initials and start at number 1 or 1,223; it's up to you. But issue invoices in sequence. If you receive payment on Invoice #203 and #205, you'll be able to spot immediately that #204 hasn't been paid.

Need a head start? Here's a sample invoice that you can use if you're selling a product. If your business involves a service, you need to modify the invoice to cut out quantity, unit price, and shipment terms. Instead, just describe the services performed and list your fee. If you bill on an hourly basis, indicate your hourly rate and then multiply it by the number of hours you worked on the job. If you also had expenses that are billed to the client, list them separately from your rate and total the expenses with the cost of your services.

INVOICE

Your company name   Invoice #

Your address

City, state, ZIP code   Date

Your telephone number

Description	Quantity	Unit Price	Amount
_____	_____	$_____	$_____
_____	_____	$_____	$_____
_____	_____	$_____	$_____
_____	_____	$_____	$_____
_____	_____	$_____	$_____
_____	_____	$_____	$_____

Subtotal $ _____

Sales Tax $ _____

Shipping & Handling $ _____

TOTAL DUE $ _____

Payment Terms (due on delivery, net 30 days, and so on)

THANK YOU FOR YOUR BUSINESS

Smart Invoicing

Copier repairmen (or women) who service Xerox machines on the fritz usually present an invoice when they've fixed the machines. For lawn-care businesses, it's more customary or convenient to bill monthly. Only you can decide what's best for your business.

In picking the best time to bill, here are some ideas to mull over:

➤ Stay on top of your invoicing. Make sure your bills go out on time. You can even speed up your invoicing. For instance, if it's customary in your type of business to bill monthly, you might want to bill twice a month if you leave your payment terms open-ended. Your quicker invoicing should pay off in several ways. You may be able to catch the customer's payment cycle. Let's say the customer pays his bills once a month on the first of each month and you send your invoice out at the end of the month. Your bill won't arrive until after the first of the month, missing an entire month's payment cycle. If, instead, you send your invoice on the fifteenth of the month, you never miss a monthly cycle by more than a couple of weeks. Also, the faster you send your bill, the quicker you can expect payment.

Homegrown Tip
If you're in a service business and do contract work, get a retainer or down payment against work to be done. It's not unusual to get paid for, say, 10% or even 25% of the job on the signing of the contract. This retainer is your insurance policy that you won't be completely stiffed for the work you've done.

➤ Do it in stages. If you perform services that can add up to thousands of dollars, you may not want to wait until the job's history to bill for your work. Consider billing in stages. You can bill your work-to-date at regular intervals (weekly, monthly). Or you can bill when you've completed a phase of the job. Break the job into phases and tell the client or customer that you'll be billing at the end of each phase.

➤ Use the bait of discounts to get prompt payment. Your invoice can offer a discount of 1% to 2% if the bill's paid faster than usual.

➤ Discourage late payment by charging interest penalties. Your invoice can charge interest of 1% per month for bills paid after 30 days.

Three Cs of Payment: Cash, Check, and Credit Card

"Cash is king," you may have heard. The reason is simple. Once in hand it can be used by you to pay your expenses. Unless you get passed some counterfeit money you can be sure that once you get the green in hand, the transaction is complete. You've provided your goods or services and received full payment in exchange. But cash isn't the only way to go. There are also pros to taking checks and getting payment by credit card.

The Educated Entrepreneur

In the good old days before money, people paid each other in eggs or a day's work. Some small business owners still barter with others for goods or services they need. A house painter may need some accounting work. The accountant prepares the house painter's tax return in exchange for the painter adding a coat of Robin's Egg Blue on the walls of the accountant's office. No money changes hands. If you think this arrangement saves you taxes, think again. According to tax law, each participant in the barter transaction is taxable on the *value* of the services received. The going rate for preparation of a tax return or painting a room would be treated as income.

The Check's in the Mail...Really

Some types of bills are typically paid by check. Professional services (barring the oldest profession) these days are rarely paid in cash because who carries around that much cash? Even if you're selling a product, some customers don't have the cash on hand to make the purchase. With cash out, checks are in.

If you get paid by check, when, exactly, is the money yours (when can you use it to pay your own bills)? The amount written on the check isn't yours to spend until it clears your account. The rules in your bank say when a check clears. This can be just a few days to as much as a week, depending on whether the check is from the same bank, another local bank, or an out-of-state bank.

If you take checks, be sure you understand how to avoid the dreaded rubber check. Here's how to avoid checks by Goodyear:

➤ Telephone number. Have the client or customer write down her telephone number on the check. More times than not, a bad check is just an oversight or miscalculation on the part of the customer. Perhaps a client deposited a check from her customer that hasn't cleared her account. Although it's about as much fun as falling off a cliff, if you have a telephone number you can contact a client or customer to say that a check's bounced. The client may tell you to re-deposit the check. This simple step may be all that's needed to receive payment. But if this doesn't do the trick, you can tell the client to bring in a new check (written against a different bank account and made of paper, not latex) or to settle up with cash.

➤ Driver's license. Make sure that the customer puts his driver's license number on the check. This information can be your only hope if he has intentionally passed you a bad check. It'll help the police track him down. Of course, you may not be able to get your money back in all cases, but at least you can have the satisfaction of seeing the guy sweat it out in court.

Homegrown Tip
TeleCheck Check Acceptance Guarantee Service, a data- base you can access to eliminate the risk of accepting out-of-state or out-of-town checks, is available at special rates to members of the National Association of the Self-Employed (NASE). For membership information, call 800-232-NASE.

➤ Use a service to check on checks. Access a database that preapproves a check so you'll know it's good.

➤ Prescreen your clients or customers. If you're in the business of providing substantial services or large orders for clients or customers, you may want to check their credit worthiness in advance. You don't want to find yourself in the position of running up a bill for thousands of dollars only to find that the client or customer has a poor credit history and can't pay you. Ask for a credit reference. Or run your own check through Dun & Bradstreet (800-234-3867). It costs about $80.

Credit Cards or Bending the Plastic

When Dustin Hoffman was told in *The Graduate* "plastics," I don't think he was thinking of credit cards. But if he'd had a home-based business instead of spending his afternoons making nookie with Mrs. R., maybe he would have. Depending on what you sell, you may be forced to accept payment by credit card if you want to be competitive and don't want to discourage sales.

Anne, a woman who set up a mail-order business for maternity lingerie, found out that she had to accept credit cards. Her customers were used to paying with plastic when they bought from catalogs. She lost out on sales when she only accepted checks as payment. Eventually, she began to accept credit cards and her business grew.

There are some good reasons for taking credit cards. As a merchant, the credit card company is essentially guaranteeing payment to you. You don't have to worry if the buyer will pay her credit card bill. As long as you receive authorization from the credit card company to accept a particular card as payment for your product or service, the payment's yours, and collection is MasterCard's headache.

Another advantage is ease of bookkeeping. Credit cards can eliminate invoicing if the client or customer pays you on the spot. What's more, the credit card company credits your bank account with payments so you don't have to deposit checks and wait for them to clear.

Of course, you don't get something for nothing. There's a cost to you for accepting credit cards: a per charge fee of between 1.5% and 3% of the amount of the charge. So, if you sell an item for $10 and there's a 2% merchant's fee, you only net $9.80 on the sale; 20¢ is the fee you pay Mr. MasterCard and Ms. Visa.

To accept credit cards, you have to get merchant authorization. This isn't easy to do as a home-based business owner. The reason? Many companies that process charges simply don't grant this authorization to home businesses because there's more room for scam operations from such a location. They suspect that some home business owners will accept payment by credit card but not deliver the goods, thereby using the card companies as a cash machine for their own illegal purposes. Of course, the overwhelming majority of home-based businesses are legitimate and need credit card authorization to be competitive.

There are some companies that see home businesses in a more positive light. For example, Card Establishment Services (CES) in New York City (212-262-5299) handles authorization for the major cards (American Express, MasterCard, and Visa). And you may be able to find merchant authorization through a trade association or an independent sales organization.

Check around for the best deals in merchant authorization. Here are the points to consider:

➤ Per transaction charge. What percentage does the company keep from each sale you make? The fees can vary with the type of business. A mail-order business may have a different rate than a retail business. Of course, large companies (who don't need the money) command better rates. As a small home-based business owner you're not yet in the position to ask for and get better rates (unless you go through a trade association or other group where the group commands the discounts).

➤ Equipment rental fees. To accept credit card payment you need certain equipment, such as an electronic tie-in to the company that'll give you the authorization. You may need to have a modem and special software. Equipment fees can run from $20 to $80 per month, depending on the type of equipment (whether you have to telephone in for approval or can use a terminal, as well as the number of credit cards that you accept).

➤ Other charges. If you don't get direct merchant authorization and instead use an independent sales organization to act as your middleman, you may have to pay a non-refundable application fee (up to $200) to gain approval. There can also be other charges (such as a per statement fee).

After You've Invoiced, Then What?

When you send out a bill and don't receive payment, what do you do? Don't just cry and hope for the best. (And it's really not wise to send in a thug to break a few thumbs.)

You need to take steps—all of them legal—if you want to get your money. Set up collection policies now so that you'll know what to do when the check doesn't arrive. In setting up your policies, you want to keep cost in mind. The principle of it aside, it doesn't pay to spend $10 to collect $5 past due.

Preemptive Strikes

Decide that step one is simply sending out a reminder (another invoice conspicuously marked "Past Due"). How many reminder notices should you send and how often will you send them? Typically, you should send a monthly reminder. But fix in advance how long you'll let nonpayment go on. Can you tolerate 60 days? What about 90 days? Longer?

If, at the end of whatever time limit you set, the check still hasn't shown up, then take other action. You can become your own collection agency. Call the client or customer and ask the reason for nonpayment. Maybe the client's unhappy with something that you can easily correct or there's some problem you don't know about.

Maybe the customer's experiencing a cash crunch but really wants to pay you. Try to work out payment terms. Maybe the client would be willing to send you partial payment in installments until the bill's paid in full. At least you'll be getting something and, with enough patience, maybe everything.

Getting Help to Get Your Due

If your personal efforts to point out to your customers that they're acting like deadbeats don't bring results, maybe it's time you called in a professional. You can turn your past due bills over to a professional *collection agency*.

> **Business Buzzword**
>
> A *collection agency* is a third party that can perform a variety of collection services ranging from sending out reminders to tardy clients to suing delinquent ones on your behalf.

Collection agencies charge according to the services they perform. If they take a minor role, they may charge a flat per account fee (such as $20) to send out duplicate invoices and make personal calls to clients or customers who haven't paid up. If you authorize them to use the full extent of the law, including slapping your client with a lawsuit, to collect unpaid invoices, you usually have to pay a percentage of the amount collected. Roy, an electrician, couldn't collect a $1,000 bill that was owed to him. The collection agency was willing to take it all the way—for

25% of what it could recover, which turned out to be $600. Roy got only $450 ($600 less 25% of $600). Some collection agencies keep as much as 50%.

If you use a collection agency, be sure you understand the charges. You may be able to negotiate more favorable terms than those first offered to you (such as less than 25% of the amount recovered). Also, check out the agency itself. Some states license collection agencies, so look to see if your agency complies with state law requirements.

Tell It to the Judge

Okay, you've cajoled, cried, sent reams of paper marked past due, and still are having no luck getting your money. If you want to take matters into your own hands but find your monthly reminders and phone calls haven't brought results, you can take your case to court. Depending on where your business is located and the amount you're suing for, you can use small claims court. This forum has informal rules (just like the TV show *The People's Court*, though you probably won't get characters as entertaining as Judge Wapner and Rusty the Bailiff) and you don't need a lawyer to represent you. Generally, you can have the court hear your case quickly, one to two months from the time you file it with the court. There may be no appeal from a decision by the small claims court.

Before you tell it to the judge, decide whether the effort's worth it. I've been stiffed only twice in 15 years. Both times I felt the amount was too small to bother with. If the amount that you've been unable to collect is below the dollar limit on small claims court in your area (no state has a limit under $1,500 so any claim up to that amount is sure to be in the jurisdiction of small claims court), it's up to you whether you go to court. It's only costing you your time, plus a small filing fee (from $10 to $50). You can be your own attorney so you don't have costly legal fees.

Make sure that you don't wait too long to bring a case. You can't sue years after the fact to collect on an

Home Hazard
Some states don't allow collection agencies or collectors to sue in small claims court (or they require that they be represented by an attorney). Unless the amount at stake is substantial, if you live in a state that bars collections agencies from court (or ups the cost to you by requiring them to have an attorney) you may have no choice but to take the matter to court yourself.

Home Hazard
If your business is incorporated, you may be prevented from using small claims court to press your case. Some states just don't allow corporations to sue in small claims court even if they're small and owned by one person. Your only option is a regular civil court, which will cost you dearly in court costs and legal fees.

unpaid bill. Ask your local small claims court clerk about the statute of limitations, the time limit for starting a case. Also, find out about other rules of the court. Your court may have a brochure or booklet that explains the rules of the small claims court game.

Before putting in your time and effort in small claims court, keep in mind that winning in court doesn't guarantee payment. You still have to collect on your judgment, which kind of puts you back where you started. If the person or company you're trying to get paid from is broke, you'll only win a symbolic victory in court because you won't get paid.

Bad Debts: Share Your Loss with Uncle Sam

Home Hazard

If you're a consultant using the cash method of accounting and don't receive payment for your services, you can't claim a bad debt deduction for nonpayment. You're just out of luck. There's no tax break to compensate you for your lost time and effort. Say you're a plumber on the cash method who repaired a customer's sink pipe. You charged $50 for the service call and $5 for parts ($55 in total). When the customer doesn't pay, you can't claim a bad debt deduction for your services. But you can deduct the $5 for parts since you had to pay for the item yourself. Sorry, Charlie.

Okay so you've done everything this side of the law to collect for your goods or services but nothing's worked. What now? When all else fails, write it off!

The tax law (finally) gives you a break. You can deduct the unpaid amount against your other business income. The amount of the deduction is the amount you've got on your books as accounts receivable. The value on your books is the amount of your deduction even if the actual value of the receivable—what someone would be willing to pay you for it—may be less. Say you sold a $200 item to a customer who hasn't paid for it. You can't get the item back and your collection efforts have gotten you zilch. Since the item is carried on your books as $200 under accounts receivable, you can deduct $200.

To claim a bad debt you must be able to show the amount of the debt (your invoice will do) and that, even though you've tried everything you could think of to collect with no success, there's no reasonable expectation of receiving payment.

The Least You Need to Know

➤ Adopt smart invoicing policies to get prompt payment.

➤ If you accept checks, be sure to protect yourself.

➤ Get merchant authorization to accept credit cards.

➤ Take steps to see that late or unpaid invoices get collected.

➤ You may want to sue delinquent clients and customers in small claims court and act as your own attorney.

➤ If you can't collect, you may be able to write off your unpaid invoices against your other income.

Getting the Help You Need

Picture the circus act where a man keeps dozens of plates spinning atop poles, running back and forth to keep them all in motion. That's what it's like for many home-based business owners who do it all alone. They market their product or service, close the sale, perform the service, ship the product, send out an invoice, deposit receipts, keep the books, handle correspondence, and more. But some owners just can't do it all themselves. They need or want to have help. If you find you just can't do it or you think you'll need help in the future, you have several options.

In this chapter you'll learn whether you can and should take on an employee. You'll also learn where to find the help you need. You'll find out about other ways to get help besides hiring someone. Finally, you'll see what it means to be the boss—responsibilities, taxes, and all.

When You Can't Do It All

There are only so many hours in a day. Even if you spend all of them working, you simply may not be able to get everything done. Or you may be spending all your time working but not earning any money for all your efforts. Karla is a computer consultant who found herself working all the time but having less than she wanted to show for it. She bills out her consulting at a high hourly rate. She found that she was spending a lot of time on clerical work and wasn't getting paid for that time. So she hired Christine, a part-timer, to do her filing and correspondence and answer the phones. This gave Karla more time to spend on billable hours doing her consulting work. The additional billing she got from making more productive use of her time more than offset the cost of paying Christine.

> **Business Buzzword**
> An *independent contractor* is a worker who contracts to do a piece of work according to her own methods and who's not under the control of the business for which the work is done (except for the results of the work).

Or maybe you only work at your business a few hours a day. You have plenty of time but you never learned to type and haven't a clue about how to keep the books. You, too, need help to do the things you can't do by yourself.

There's more than one way to get the help you need. You can take in a partner to work with you. You can hire an employee to work for you. Or you can use *independent contractors* or outside companies to do certain jobs.

Of course, you can even use a combination of these methods to get the help you need to run your business effectively and efficiently.

In deciding which method will work best for you, keep these things in mind: zoning, space, cost, your business needs, and your personal preference.

Are You in an Outside Employee Zone?

So you're convinced you need an employee. But are you allowed to have someone work in your home? Before you go ahead, make sure you aren't violating any zoning restrictions. Depending on the type of business you run and the location of your home, you may be prohibited from having *any* employees who aren't related to you and who don't live in your home. So, if you hire your teenager to do clerical work for you on a part-time basis, there's no problem. But if you hire your neighbor's teenager to do the same work for you, you may be violating zoning rules.

By now you've probably checked out what you can and can't do in a home office, so you know if you can have outside employees. If you've forgotten, look back to Chapter 13 where zoning rules are discussed.

Fitting Everyone in

Let's say the law says you can have an outside employee. This doesn't mean you should plunge ahead with your hiring plans. Before you do, make sure your office has the space you need. Does it have room for two desks? Do you have a spare phone line so your employee can get his work done? Can you put in another computer if you need one?

You may be able to manage the space issue by using non-office space for some jobs. The kitchen table may be useful for collating reports, doing manual bookkeeping entries, or even wrapping packages for shipping. Lillian Vernon started her mail-order business on her kitchen table.

Home Hazard

If you shift some work into non-office space, make sure your assistant doesn't mind being tucked away between the fridge and dish-washer. Be sure that any employee you hire understands the need to be flexible because your business is run from your home.

To Hire or Not to Hire

Hiring an employee costs money—maybe more than you think. First there's the salary you'll pay to the employee. But that's just the beginning. There are also employment taxes you have to pay to the government. And you'll have additional insurance costs, the time it takes to comply with government rules (filing employment tax returns), and even costs to adapt your office space to make room for another person or two.

Partners in Crime

Think of Astaire and Rogers, Barnum and Bailey, Rolls and Royce. Sometimes the best way to tackle a task is with the right partner. You can keep your costs down by getting help without hiring someone. You and a partner can divide up the work. You can assign jobs that match your relative skills, abilities, and preferences. Bringing in a partner has benefits beyond merely lifting some of the work off your shoulders. You and your partner usually get paid only if the business makes money.

Here are some other benefits to taking on a partner to divide up the workload:

➤ Added capital. If you join forces with someone to share ownership of your business, that person must pay for the ownership interest. The partner must contribute cash, property, or services sufficient to buy the ownership interest. You don't have to give an equal ownership interest to your partner. You can keep control and give only a minority interest to your partner.

➤ Shared responsibility. You can hire an employee, but an employee doesn't have the sense of responsibility that an owner does. If you bring in a partner you can share the responsibility. This translates into more than just a time-saver. It's a psychological benefit. As an owner in business alone it's difficult to get away for vacation or take personal days because there's no one to be responsible for the business. By having a partner, that responsibility is shared, allowing you the freedom you thought running your own business would get you in the first place.

Putting Out a Contract

If you don't want to bring in a partner (you don't want to share responsibility or ownership with anyone), you can still get the help you need without hiring an employee. You can use someone else's employees—independent contractors or companies—to handle specific jobs.

It usually costs less to use independent contractors than employees to do the same work. (Independent contractors and your obligations to them are explained later in this chapter.)

Working with outside companies to handle specific projects may be another way to go. Say you're planning a large promotional mailing. To save time, you can work with a company like Kinko's™ to prepare the inserts and then fold them and stuff them into your envelopes.

ARGH@#! **Home Hazard**

It's extremely difficult, but not impossible, to find temporary employment agencies willing to send workers to home-based businesses. It's the policy at this time of many of the nationally-known temporary agencies *not* to deal with any home business. Some of these will make exceptions if the home business office has a separate entrance, separate bathroom facilities, and a separate kitchen (in effect a unit separated from the owner's living space).

Take the Temporary Route

Another cost-saving way to get the help you need without taking on permanent employees is to use temporary workers. Temporary workers are employed by agencies like Olsten and Manpower. The agencies send the workers to you to perform work at your home office. You pay a flat hourly fee to the agencies; they pay their employees and handle all payroll taxes and insurance obligations. Presumably, they screen workers to determine their ability to do the job and do background checks to find out about their reliability.

Personal Preference

Before deciding to hire an employee make sure you consider your own work style and preferences. You may like to work alone as I do. You don't want to keep regular business hours. You don't want to supervise employees. You don't want to bring outside employees into your home. This is your personal preference and that's fine.

Once again, you can meet your work needs and respect your own desires if you use independent contractors instead of an employee.

Hiring Good Help

The old expression "Good help is hard to find" continues to apply today. It's not easy to find someone who can both do the job and fit into your business, working well with you.

Working in a home office brings up another issue—finding an employee who's comfortable working in your kitchen.

Keep It All in the Family

Good help may be right under your nose. Maybe you can hire your spouse or your child to work along with you. There are some good reasons for doing this:

➤ Keeping it all in the family. By hiring your spouse or child, the money stays in the family. If you pay your teenager to do filing it's like turning his nondeductible weekly allowance into a deductible business expense.

➤ Special tax breaks for hiring relatives. Wages paid to a child may go untaxed. In 1997, a child can earn up to $4,150 without any federal income tax. If your business *isn't* incorporated, then the wages you pay to your child under the age of 18 aren't subject to FICA; wages paid to your child under age 21 aren't subject to FUTA. (FICA, which is the Social Security and Medicare tax, and FUTA, which is the federal unemployment insurance tax, are explained later in this chapter.) If your partner isn't the father or mother of your child, then this exemption from FICA doesn't apply. Wages paid to your spouse are subject to FICA but aren't subject to FUTA. Check for possible state unemployment exemptions as well.

Home Hazard When hiring relatives, be sure to keep good records of the time they put in and work they perform. The IRS uses a magnifying glass to scrutinize family relationships that give rise to business deductions to make sure the expenses are real and not made up.

➤ Intangible benefits. Working together can produce benefits that can't be boiled down to numbers. If you hire your child, you can teach valuable lessons about work and responsibility. You can even teach skills that your child can use in the business world. Many teenagers today are already computer literate. Use that knowledge and have your teenager keep your books and records on computer.

While these reasons for hiring relatives are good ones, there's a downside to hiring your spouse or child instead of using an outsider. Your family becomes tied to the business. Depending on its nature, your family can have trouble arranging vacations and other time away from home. And, there's the question of personalities. Some family members may just not get along in a business environment. Would your mate like taking orders from you? Be forewarned that the arrangement of family members in business together works very well for some but poorly for others.

Where Can You Find Employees?

If you don't have a spouse or child who can do the jobs you need to have done, you'll have to look to outsiders. Finding a good employee isn't as easy as you'd think, and it doesn't happen overnight. First you have to advertise or let the public know in some other way that you have a job to offer. Hopefully people will respond. Then you have to screen job hopefuls, making sure that the person you hire is comfortable with a home office setting and won't disappear with the silverware. Many employees are looking for the social aspect that working can provide, something generally not found in a home office.

Let's begin the search for your employee:

Home Hazard

You generally won't be able to use an employment agency to find an employee. Like temporary employment agencies, it's the policy of most permanent employment agencies *not* to send any applicants to a home-based business. But this could change as the number of home-based businesses multiplies, so check around.

➤ Place a classified ad. In your ad, be clear about the job responsibilities *and* the fact that you're a home-based business. This will help weed out those who aren't willing to work for a home-based business.

➤ Network to find an employee. Word of mouth that you have a job opening may alert an interested person. You may be surprised to find that a neighbor or a friend of a neighbor is looking for work and has the skills you need. Networking is a good way to find an employee because it doesn't cost you any money and the people who contact you know all about your home office location.

➤ Check out your state labor department or its unemployment offices. You can list your job opening at no cost. Some states have even gone high-tech and let you list your opening online.

➤ For part-time help, you may be able to find high school or college students willing to work in a home office. Speak with your local school placement office to see if you can post your job opening on its bulletin board.

Mastering the Hiring Process

Okay, you've found people who want to work for you. But do you want them under your roof? Here are some things you can do to make sure that the person you hire will work out:

➤ Job description. Be clear about what you want an employee to do. What skills or abilities are you looking for? How many hours of work do you anticipate? Will there be any late hours? Weekend work? What're you willing to pay? Are you going to offer any benefits (paid vacation and sick leave)?

Home Hazard
Be careful what you ask an applicant. You don't want to be guilty of any discriminatory practices. Under the Equal Opportunity in Employment law, you can't ask about marital status, children, national origin, or religion. You can, of course, reveal whatever you want about yourself.

➤ Interview. This is a two-way street. Make sure you find out what you want to know about the person, but also tell the applicant what she needs to know about you.

Since you'll be working closely with the person you hire, make sure that she not only can do the job but will also get along with you and isn't afraid of your dog. You don't want to have constant turnover because the people you hire don't like your kids or can't stand your habit of running to the refrigerator every hour on the hour.

➤ References. Be sure to check out prior employment. As a practical matter, former employers generally won't give unfavorable responses even if they're being less than truthful because they don't want to be sued for giving a bad reference. Still, you can verify the type of work the person did and the period of former employment. And you may be able to read between the lines about any problems on the last job. Also, if your employee will be driving your car or truck, ask her permission to run a license check.

Home Hazard
Take your time in hiring. You're not only going to be working with this person, but you're also bringing him into your home where your family and possessions reside. Sure it's a risk. But there's no protection other than caution.

Being the Boss

There is a reason people often say it's easier to just do it themselves. If you think working by yourself is tough because you have so much to handle, it's nothing compared with being the boss. You now have someone to do some of what you've been doing, but now you have a whole new range of headaches. These include:

➤ Supervision. You have to decide what jobs your employee will handle. You have to take the time to train your employee to do things the way you want them done. You may also have to supervise to see that your instructions are being followed.

Home Hazard

If you are self-employed, you pay employer taxes only on your employee's wages. But if your business is incorporated, you pay employer taxes on both employee wages and your own. The tax consequences of being self-employed are discussed in Chapter 21.

➤ Keeping employee records. As an employer, whether you're incorporated or not, you've got to handle the paperwork involved in having an employee, including things like payroll, paying taxes, on-the-job injuries (even minor ones), and performance reviews. This takes time, and if you make a mistake, it could cost you.

➤ Government regulations. The federal, state, and local governments all have a number of rules that you, as a small business owner, must follow. Luckily, many of these rules apply only when there are many more employees than you'll have at your home business, so that let's you off the hook. These rules are discussed more fully later in this chapter.

➤ Managing employees. Being an employer doesn't mean you show the employee his desk and say "go." You need to explain what you want done and how you want it done. This requires time and patience on your part. Use the job description you wrote in finding the employee to guide you. You can't expect an employee to be a mind reader and anticipate what you want done. The sooner an employee understands exactly what he is expected to do, the sooner he can begin to work more independently. Set up periodic reviews to go over the employee's progress. Use these reviews to provide constructive criticism designed to help the employee do a better job.

Home Hazard

Don't be casual about your tax obligations. Even if you hire Uncle Max or your best buddy, you're still responsible for complying with employer tax obligations. If you don't, there'll be heavy penalties and interest to pay.

Paying Payroll Taxes

Here comes the hard part of being a boss—taxes. There are lots of rules, and if you don't follow them, it's going to cost you. As an employer you must withhold some money from an employee's wages and pay it to the government. You also have to pay your share of payroll taxes to the government.

Which Taxes Apply?

If you think April 15 is the only day you have to think about taxes, think again. As an employer, you're up to your elbows in taxes (and not just income tax on your profits) almost all the time.

➤ **Income tax withholding.** There's not much good news about taxes, but here's an exception: Income tax withholding doesn't cost you any money. Nada, zip, zilch. You merely subtract it from your employee's paycheck and pay it to the government. But how do you know how much to take out of your employee's paycheck? Income tax withholding's based on marital status and withholding allowances your employee claims on IRS Form W-4, "Employee's Withholding Allowance Certificate." This form generally isn't filed with the IRS; you give it to your employee to complete and then keep it in your files. Besides federal income tax withholding, there's also state income tax withholding in some states (ask your state tax or revenue department about it).

➤ **FICA (Federal Insurance Contributions Act).** FICA covers both Social Security and Medicare. Employee and employer split this up the middle. The Social Security portion of FICA for both employee and employer is 6.2% of wages up to an annual wage base ($65,400 in 1997). The Medicare portion of FICA for both employee and employer is 1.45% of all wages (there's no wage base limit).

For example, if George, your employee, earns $250, you have to withhold $19.13 from his paycheck to pay his share of FICA—$250 x 6.2% for Social Security plus $250 x 1.45% for Medicare. George's paycheck (ignoring income tax withholding in this example) is then $230.87—$250 minus $19.13. You also chip in the same $19.13, your share of FICA.

FICA applies to most payments you'll make to your employee—not only wages, but also vacation pay, sick pay, and certain benefits. But remember that there's no FICA on wages to your child under age 18 if you're unincorporated.

➤ **FUTA (Federal Unemployment Tax Act).** This is the federal portion of the tax that the guys on the unemployment line are waiting to collect; if you let your employee go, paying this tax ensures that she can join the line. The FUTA tax rate is 6.2% of the first $7,000 of wages (per employee). However, you get a credit of up to 5.4% for your state unemployment insurance (so that your FUTA rate can be as low as 0.8%). And there's no FUTA on wages to your spouse or to your child under age 21 if you're unincorporated.

Homegrown Tip
For complete details on federal withholding and payroll taxes, get IRS Publication Circular E by calling 800-829-1040. Make sure you get the one for the current year!

➤ State unemployment insurance. The federal and state unemployment systems work together: You pay a percentage of your employee's wages to your state to cover unemployment insurance for discharged employees. The rate you pay is based on your "experience" (the amount of unemployment claims by your former employees). Generally, the state assigns you a rate when you first take on workers. The rate's then adjusted annually to reflect your experience (low claims, low rate). To find out your state unemployment insurance responsibilities, contact your state department of labor, employment, jobs, or industrial relations.

Forking Over the Money

The government doesn't make paying the taxes any easier than figuring them. Unlike your income tax that's paid to the IRS, you pay payroll taxes by "depositing" them with an authorized financial institution or Federal Reserve Bank. Depositing these taxes doesn't mean you have to open up a special bank account. It means delivering or mailing the taxes to the bank by their due date, along with a special deposit slip, called IRS Form 8109, "Federal Tax Deposit Coupon." The IRS is so happy to hear you hired someone, they automatically send you these slips when you apply for an employer identification number (this is explained in Chapter 7). If you haven't received your slips by the time you have to make a deposit (it generally takes five to six weeks from the time you applied for your employer identification number), you can get a substitute slip at the bank (IRS Form 8109-B).

You can pay your employment taxes with your return (and don't have to deposit them) only if your tax liability for the quarter is less than $500. If you guess wrong and your tax liability turns out to be $500 or more, there may be penalties.

If you have to deposit your taxes, there are two deposit schedules: a monthly schedule and a semi-weekly schedule. Most small businesses fall under the monthly schedule, which covers employers whose liability in the "lookback period" was no more than $50,000. The lookback period is the first four quarters from July 1 through June 30 beginning 18 months before the start of the current year. As a new employer you're automatically under the monthly schedule for your first year. Deposits under the monthly schedule mean you must make them no later than the fifteenth day of the month following the month when you incurred the tax liability. So your

> **Homegrown Tip**
> Make your check payable to the bank. Because the government needs all the help it can get to keep things straight, include on your check your employer identification number, the type of tax ("Form 941 for income tax withholding and FICA"), and the period to which the deposits relate ("fourth quarter 1997"). If you're using a check drawn on a bank other than the depository, ask whether it'll accept your other check. If you regularly use a local bank for your business account, ask whether it's an authorized depository.

withholding and FICA for November payroll must be deposited by December 15, your deposit for December must be made by January 15 of the following year, and so on.

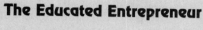

The Educated Entrepreneur

Beginning July 1, 1997, employers with sizable payrolls must pay their employment taxes using their computer to transfer funds from their bank to the IRS. The system's called EFTSA—Electronic Federal Tax Payment System. Even small employers like you can choose to pay taxes by electronic transfer. Don't worry, using it doesn't mean the IRS has access to your computer files. It simply means you can pay your taxes up to the very last minute without ever leaving home.

Just to keep you on your toes, FUTA taxes have a different deposit schedule than income tax withholding and FICA. FUTA taxes have to be deposited by the last day of the month following the close of the quarter. Sound complicated? It boils down to April 30 for taxes in the first quarter of the year.

Filing Returns

Even though the government's got your money, you haven't sufficiently fed their paper monster. Besides paying employment taxes, you'll also have to file tax returns for employment taxes. And you have to give your employee an annual statement showing the wages you've paid and the taxes you've withheld on IRS Form W-2. The form is self-explanatory, as you can see on the next page.

Does filing tax returns sound overwhelming? If you take it day-by-day, it's a little easier. The following is a list of key dates to remind you of your filing responsibilities:

Calendar of Employer Tax Filing Responsibilities

Deadline*	Form	Description
January 31	Form W-2	Give your employee a statement of annual compensation
	Form 940 (or 940-EZ)	File annual unemployment return with IRS (deadline February 10 if tax deposited in full and on time)

continues

Calendar of Employer Tax Filing Responsibilities   Continued

Deadline*	Form	Description
	Form 941	File fourth quarter FICA and income tax withholding with IRS (deadline February 10 if tax deposited in full and on time)
February 28	Form W-2 (copy A) and Form W-3	File with Social Security Administration to report annual wages and FICA
April 30	Form 941	File first quarter FICA and income tax withholding with IRS (deadline May 10 if tax deposited in full and on time)
July 31	Form 941	File second quarter FICA and income tax withholding with IRS (deadline August 10 if tax deposited in full and on time)
October 31	Form 941	File third quarter FICA and income tax withholding with IRS (deadline November 10 if tax deposited in full and on time)

If any deadline falls on a Saturday, Sunday, or legal holiday, the deadline's extended to the next business day.

The W-2 form

a Control number	22222	Void ☐	For Official Use Only ► OMB No. 1545-0008		
b Employer's identification number				1 Wages, tips, other compensation	2 Federal income tax withheld
c Employer's name, address, and ZIP code				3 Social security wages	4 Social security tax withheld
				5 Medicare wages and tips	6 Medicare tax withheld
				7 Social security tips	8 Allocated tips
d Employee's social security number				9 Advance EIC payment	10 Dependent care benefits
e Employee's name (first, middle initial, last)				11 Nonqualified plans	12 Benefits included in box 1
				13 See Instrs. for box 13	14 Other
f Employee's address and ZIP code				15 Statutory employee ☐ Deceased ☐ Pension plan ☐ Legal rep. ☐ Hshld. emp. ☐ Subtotal ☐ Deferred compensation ☐	
16 State Employer's state I.D. No.	17 State wages, tips, etc.	18 State income tax	19 Locality name	20 Local wages, tips, etc.	21 Local income tax

Cat. No. 10134D

Department of the Treasury—Internal Revenue Service

Form W-2 Wage and Tax Statement **1997**

Copy A For Social Security Administration

For Paperwork Reduction Act Notice, see separate instructions.

Do NOT Cut or Separate Forms on This Page

Treat Your Workers Right: Employee or Independent Contractor?

Have you read a hot news story lately about some politician or movie star who didn't pay taxes for his maid or butler? How about the corporation that called all its part-time workers contractors to get out of paying them benefits? It seems the hottest tax issue today is whether a worker's an employee or independent contractor. There are big bucks at stake, for employers, workers, and the government. The IRS estimates that as much as $20 billion in taxes goes uncollected because of misclassifying workers.

The IRS prefers that workers be treated as employees so it can collect income tax withholding and FICA from the employer. The employer (and in many cases the worker) prefers independent contractor treatment since this shifts the tax responsibility (both payment and return filing) to the worker. Also, the employer doesn't have to provide benefits to independent contractors (health coverage or pensions, for example). The worker can deduct work expenses more fully as an independent contractor than as an employee.

Don't get caught in the controversy. If you do and you lose, the penalties and interest can kill you (or at least put you out of business).

Treat your worker right. If you exercise enough control over the worker (how the job's to be done, where, and when), you have to treat the worker as an employee and meet your employer obligations. So if Betty, your neighbor, works in your home office doing clerical work under your constant supervision, using your copying machine, and she's paid at a weekly or hourly rate, then Betty's most probably an employee, not an independent contractor.

Home Hazard

ARGH@#!

The IRS is aggressively looking at worker classification whenever it audits an employer's return. And your state may also come in to question your worker classification if someone who worked for you files an unemployment insurance or workers' compensation claim (neither of which benefit is available to self-employed independent contractors). You can check IRS guidelines for worker classification by looking at its audit manual on the topic, which is used by its agents (you may be able to find it in a law school library). If you're unclear about your own workers, it's best to check with a tax advisor.

Setting the Ground Rules

If you believe that the person you're working with is an independent contractor, make sure that you get things clear from the start. When I do freelance writing for newsletters or magazines, I'm asked to sign an agreement or letter saying that I'm an independent contractor, that I determine the means and method of doing my work, that I'm not supervised or under anyone's control, and that I'm responsible for my own taxes. You, too, should use a similar contract or agreement. While it won't guarantee that the IRS will agree with you, it can prevent a disgruntled worker from later questioning the arrangement.

If you're not sure about how to treat a worker, talk with a tax practitioner. Since this is a big issue and the penalties for making a mistake can be devastating, you can't afford to be wrong.

Following Through

Be sure that you treat your worker as an independent contractor if that's how you want to go. You're required to give your independent contractor an annual information return, Form 1099-MISC, which is reproduced below. This form states the amount of money you've paid during the year. You only have to file it if that amount exceeds $600.

You must give the contractor this form no later than January 31 of the year following the year in which the payments were made. If in 1997 you pay Angela, a consultant, $1,500, you'll have to give her Form 1099-MISC showing this payment no later than February 2, 1998. (January 31, 1998 happens to fall on a Saturday, so you've got until the next business day to act.) You also have to file this form with the IRS no later than February 28, 1998.

Form 1099-MISC

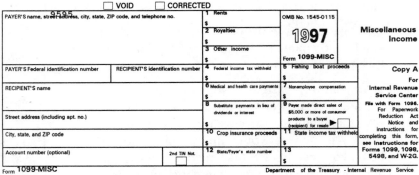

Getting Along with Uncle Sam

Taxes are only one type of government regulation you have to follow if you have employees. There are many others designed to provide safe workplaces, job security, benefits, and more. Fortunately your life's simplified because many of these regulations don't apply to you. The reason? You have only one or two employees. These regulations have exemptions for "small employers"—those with less than 10, 15, or 50 employees, depending on the regulation.

But one rule that applies to all employers, regardless of size, is that you can't hire illegal aliens (and no, this doesn't mean Klingons). You have to document the fact that your worker has a right to a job in this country. The worker must complete INS Form I-9 to verify her legal status. Don't assume that someone who applies for a job is authorized to work in this country. If you guess wrong, it can cost you between $250 and $2,000 ($10,000 if you pull this more than once).

Homegrown Tip

You can get a handbook for employers and instructions for the form by calling the Immigration and Naturalization Service at 800-870-0777.

The Least You Need to Know

➤ Zoning restrictions can prevent you from hiring an employee.

➤ Hiring your spouse or child can have important advantages, but some drawbacks can exist as well.

➤ Keep up on your employer responsibilities.

➤ Payroll taxes have to be calculated and paid, and you have to file forms.

➤ Don't misclassify your workers or you'll pay dearly.

Chapter 19

Be Sure to Insure

In This Chapter

➤ Understanding insurance options for home businesses

➤ Upgrading your homeowner's policy to protect your business

➤ Buying a comprehensive business owner's policy

➤ Saving on insurance costs

A client comes to your home to meet with you about a megabucks deal. The client falls on the front steps and breaks his hip. What does that mean to you? Maybe a lawsuit. Maybe you'll lose. Maybe it's going to cost you thousands or millions of dollars—your home and everything else you own. If you have nightmares about this sort of thing, you're not as paranoid as you think. This stuff happens all the time.

But if you have the right kind of insurance, your worries are over. The insurance company will defend you in any lawsuit. And if you lose, the insurance company will foot the bill.

When you go into business, you hope for the best, but should plan for the worst. Cover yourself by having enough insurance to pay you if your office copier blows up or you get robbed. And get insurance to protect you from liability claims due to accidents or your mistakes.

In this chapter you'll learn about the different kinds of insurance you may need and want to have for your business. You'll see the special problems that arise because your business is home based. And you'll find out about ways to keep your insurance costs down and protect the things that insurance just can't replace.

Business Insurance R Us

Whether you weave baskets or sell soap, there are certain types of insurance you need to carry. What's more, you may be in the kind of business that requires special insurance. And even if you get all the insurance in the world, you should find ways to keep things that insurance can't cover safe.

Insurance comes in more flavors than Lifesavers. Some types are needed by all businesses; others are needed by only a few. Of course, you're the only one who can decide what you need after you've reviewed your options and discussed them with a smart insurance agent. In talking with the agent, be candid and complete. Your agent's not a mind reader. She needs to know about your business operations to recommend the right kinds of coverage for you.

In the following sections you'll get a rundown of the kinds of insurance to consider. Later in this chapter you'll find out how to get what you need at the lowest price.

Help! Fire! Thief!

Property insurance, also called casualty insurance, gives you coverage for damage, destruction, or theft of property. What would happen to your business if there was a fire in your home? Or some bum came in and stole your computer? Are you covered? The answer may surprise you.

You may think you're protected because you've got homeowner's insurance (if you own your home) or tenant's insurance (if you rent). But when you read the fine print you may find to your amazement that you're only partially covered or have no protection at all! The reason: There may be limits or exclusions (items not covered) in the policy, and they always put that stuff in the fine print.

Your policy may cover your computer only up to $3,000, but your machine costs $4,000 (plus the cost of software you've loaded on it). Or your policy may not cover equipment if you take it on the road. So, if your laptop's stolen when you're visiting a client's office, are you covered? If you store your inventory of handmade soft toys in your basement and it floods, who pays for the soggy bunnies?

Oops! (Liability Insurance)

What happens if the UPS delivery guy falls on your steps while delivering a package? UPS (or the delivery guy) sues you. Are you covered? Liability insurance provides compensation for people who break bones on your premises, so make sure you're fully protected.

Most homeowner's (or tenant's) policies don't provide any liability coverage for business visitors—clients, customers, suppliers, and even the UPS delivery guy. A little later in the chapter I'll explain your insurance options for getting this liability protection.

Malpractice Insurance: It's Not Just for Doctors

Are you protected if someone sues you because you didn't do your job right? If you're a professional, you may want to carry a special type of liability insurance called professional liability insurance—more commonly known as malpractice insurance. This type of insurance protects you from claims, by clients or customers, that you caused injury or harm because you did your job negligently. It's not available for all professions, but it's easy to find out if you can get it. Just ask your professional association—the American Institute of CPAs for accountants, the American Bar Association for lawyers, and so on.

Even if you're not a professional, you can still get protection for "errors and omissions (E&O)"—which in plain English means not doing something you should have. Check out E&O coverage through a trade association.

If You Have Employees

If you're self-employed and don't have any employees, skip this section. But if you've got people working for you then you're required to pay for certain insurance:

➤ Unemployment coverage. This type of coverage is called "insurance" because it gives benefits to employees who've been fired or laid off. You don't have any choice about whether to take this kind of coverage if you've got employees. Federal unemployment coverage is collected as an employment tax (remember the last chapter?). States also have unemployment insurance.

➤ Workers' compensation insurance. This type of insurance is also required by states to provide protection for workers who get anything from a splinter to brain damage on the job.

Homegrown Tip
If you're self-employed you can't be covered by unemployment insurance and workers' compensation. So it's a good idea to get your own disability insurance. It's your only protection in case you become physically or mentally incapacitated and can't work. Check out coverage that may be available through a trade association you belong to.

➤ Disability insurance. Like workers' compensation, this insurance provides benefits to workers who can't work—but in this case because of a disability (even though the job didn't cause the disability).

For Your Car, Your Health, and More

Property, liability, and insurance for employees are the main categories of business coverage. But here are some types of optional insurance you can check into:

➤ Auto/truck insurance. This type of insurance protects you for collision and liability (if you run down the paper boy, for example). If you use your car or truck for your business, be sure that the insurance policy includes your business use. If you use a truck for business, you may not be able to get by with a personal insurance policy and may have to take out a separate business policy.

➤ Business interruption insurance. If your house burns down your business stops, at least temporarily. This type of insurance covers your payroll, insurance, utilities, and so on if you can't operate your business because of some interruption, such as a natural disaster like a hurricane or earthquake, or if there's a riot on your block.

➤ Health insurance. If you don't already have coverage (through a current employer, COBRA, or under your spouse's policy), you may want your business to pay for your policy. Even if you're in business by yourself and don't have any employees, you can still get a "group" policy, which will have lower premiums than an individual policy providing the same benefits. Here's where having a C corporation really pays off. The corporation can deduct the premiums it pays to cover you and your family.

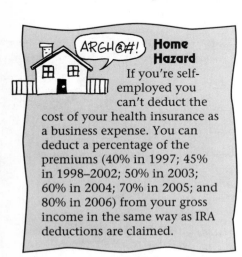

Home Hazard
If you're self-employed you can't deduct the cost of your health insurance as a business expense. You can deduct a percentage of the premiums (40% in 1997; 45% in 1998–2002; 50% in 2003; 60% in 2004; 70% in 2005; and 80% in 2006) from your gross income in the same way as IRA deductions are claimed.

➤ Performance bonds. You say you can do the job but your customer's taking no chances. You can take out special insurance that guarantees your workers' performance.

➤ Umbrella policy. Good homeowner's insurance or car insurance may not be good enough. Today's lawsuits return million dollar judgments—beyond the limits of these policies. But you can piggyback your policy to improve your coverage with an umbrella policy. If your homeowner's policy provides liability coverage up to $500,000, you can get an umbrella policy to cover you up to

$1 million, or even $5 million. The cost for such coverage: about $100 to $150 for each million of coverage (for example, $500 to $750 for $5 million of coverage). But the umbrella policy only protects you for business liability if your underlying home-owner's policy gives you coverage.

➤ Product liability insurance. If you sell a product you've developed, you may want to get product liability insurance. This protects you from claims that your product's unsafe or caused injury. Before you can put your pain-relieving cream on the shelves of a major retailer, you might be required to get a product liability policy. The retailer wants protection in case a customer sues the store because the cream gave him a nasty rash. However, be forewarned: Product liability insurance isn't cheap.

Shopping Around for a Home Business Policy

Like anything else, you have to shop around if you want to get the most bang for your insurance buck—the coverage you need for the best price. It's a good idea to work with a knowledgeable insurance agent. Lay out your needs. Describe your business operations in your home. This information will help your agent tailor coverage to fit your needs.

Use the worksheet that follows to list what you need. You can get separate policies to cover each contingency, or you can buy a package to cover a number of them.

My Business Insurance Needs

Type of Coverage	Separate/Package	Cost
Auto/truck	_____	$ _____
Business interruption	_____	$ _____
Disability	_____	$ _____
Health	_____	$ _____
Liability	_____	$ _____
General liability	_____	$ _____
Malpractice/errors and omissions	_____	$ _____
Property	_____	$ _____
Workers' compensation	_____	$ _____
Other insurance	_____	$ _____

> **The Educated Entrepreneur**
>
> If you don't buy coverage through an insurance agent, you might want to check out what's available through a trade or professional association. These associations offer group rates that can be much lower than the rates charged for individuals on medical insurance, business policies, and more. Some trade associations for home business owners and self-employed individuals are listed in Chapter 25.

Homeowner's (or Tenant's) Policy Plus

Business Buzzword

A *rider* is an addition to an existing policy to cover a specific item or event. A rider can upgrade both property and liability insurance.

An *endorsement* on a policy is a correction or change to an existing policy. A rider can also be an endorsement.

You already have homeowner's (or tenant's) insurance. You can bring your coverage up to snuff for very little cost to get the coverage you need for your computer and other equipment. Some homeowner's policies even allow a *rider* to cover a small amount of inventory ($2,500).

If you have people coming into your home for business, upgrade a homeowner's or tenant's policy to cover your liability for occasional business visitors. I only have a client or two come to my home each month, so a rider for occasional business visitors was all I needed to get protection. The cost of the rider is extremely modest, less than $50 per year.

A Business Policy of Your Own

Not all home businesses can piggyback on a personal policy to get business coverage. You may need a separate business policy, too. For only a few hundred dollars a year, you can get one to cover your furniture, equipment, and inventory. A separate business policy may even cover the cost of data reconstruction if there's damage to your computer records.

Home Hazard

If you run a day care business from your home, be sure to get a special endorsement on your homeowner's (or tenant's) policy to cover your liability vis-à-vis the little darlings.

The same option is available for liability coverage. If a rider to your homeowner's or tenant's policy doesn't cover your situation—you have a full-time employee or frequent business visitors—consider a separate liability policy.

There's no hard and fast rule on when you should use your existing homeowner's policy or a separate business policy to protect your home business. Generally, a separate policy is a good idea if your business owns expensive equipment or stores a lot of inventory or samples. If you store paints or other things that could go boom in the night at your home, then definitely get separate coverage. The same is true if your homeowner's policy limits coverage for other than "incidental business," which it defines to mean income of $5,000—okay if the business is a sideline.

It doesn't have to cost a lot. Jonathan, a friend who's a financial consultant, had a lot of people come to his basement office each month—too many for a rider on his home-owner's policy. Jonathan got a separate business policy, covering his liability and equipment, for only $320 a year!

You can get two separate policies: one to cover property and the other for liability. Or you can get one business owner's package policy to cover everything—with a single premium. For example, for a few hundred dollars a year you can get protection for your office contents up to $15,000, $500,000 per occurrence of liability protection, and $10,000 of data reconstruction (with just a $250 deductible).

> ### The Educated Entrepreneur
>
> You're going to get the best policies in terms of both coverage and price from trade associations that specialize in home office coverage. Inexpensive but comprehensive home business owner's policies are available through the Home Business Institute (914-946-6600) and the Independent Business Alliance (800-450-2422). You'll have to pay a small membership fee in addition to the insurance premium. Coverage from these sources may not be available in all localities, but your insurance agent can find you individual coverage.

Buying Insurance Without Going Broke

Insurance is like dental floss, it's one of those things you don't really want to have around but can't afford to do without. Premiums can be a big expense for your business, especially if you've got employees. But don't feel overwhelmed by cost. There are many simple ways you can bring down your premiums.

> **Homegrown Tip**
>
> If you have any problems or concerns about your insurance policy or your insurance company—you think you're being ripped off or a company won't pay a claim you've made—don't hesitate to contact your state's insurance department for help.

Shaving Dollars off Insurance Premiums

How can you save money on your insurance without giving up the insurance protection you need? Here are some ideas:

> **Business Buzzword**
>
> *Deductible* is the amount of the damage or liability that the insurance company won't cover. You're responsible for the deductible; the insurance company picks up additional costs. So, if your home office suffers water damage of $2,500 and you have a $500 deductible, the insurance company will pay you $2,000 and you have to pay for the rest of the damage.

➤ Ask about discounts. If you don't ask they may not volunteer the information. You may be entitled to a discount for any number of reasons. If you have several policies with the same insurance company, you can get a multiple policy discount. If you're a good driver, there's a good driver discount off your auto insurance premium. Discounts are also given to those who typically drive no more than a certain number of miles each year and to those who've completed a driver safety course. If you have smoke detectors or alarm systems in your home office, ask about a special discount on your homeowner's or separate business policy. If you don't have these devices, it may just pay for you to install them so you can get the discounted insurance and the extra protection that they're designed to provide. Installing an ignition cutoff system to your business car can mean a discount of as much as 15%.

➤ Reduce insurance costs for employees. The cost for workers' compensation, disability insurance, and unemployment insurance for employees may keep them healthy but it can kill you. But you can keep costs down if you're a smart employer. Remember that these insurance costs are based on your experience with employees—how many are hired and fired, get injured on the job, or become disabled. Hire employees that you don't expect will produce problems (go back to Chapter 18 on interviewing and checking references of job applicants). Low turnover means low unemployment experience, which translates into lower premiums. When you first hire employees and are required to estimate your payroll and revenue so that the insurance company can fix your first year's premium, be very conservative in your estimates. The worst that will happen is that you'll have to pay additional premiums when the insurance company audits you (looks over your records) at the end of the first year and makes adjustments to reflect actual payroll and revenues.

➤ Raise your *deductible*. It's a fact that the higher your deductible, the lower your premiums. After all, insurance is designed to cover events that are unexpected and out of the ordinary. You can raise a deductible from $100 to $250, $500, or even $1,000. But before you increase your deductible too much, make sure that you can afford to pay it in case of loss.

➤ Comparison shop. Not all insurance companies charge the same rate for the same coverage (other than for workers' compensation and disability). Shop around and get quotes before you buy. In making your comparisons, be sure that the policies provide the same coverage with the same deductibles.

An Ounce of Prevention

I know, it doesn't seem fair. You've paid all this money just so you can collect on claims, but the fact is that if you never make an insurance claim, your rates will stay down or rise more slowly than rates for people who make claims. So take steps to reduce the need to make insurance claims:

➤ Safeguard your property. Take steps to keep your property from being damaged or stolen. Install fire and security systems to protect your office. Use a central monitoring station to provide an additional measure of protection. Use security devices to protect your business car or truck.

➤ Avoid accidents. If you don't have any business visitors injured on your premises, you can keep insurance costs down. One way to do this is to make your home office as safe as possible. If you have steps into your home, you might want to install handrails to avoid slips. Maybe you need more outside lighting.

➤ Set up safety procedures. If you work with hazardous materials or substances (including paints and other flammables), make sure you store them as safely as possible. If you're a professional, make sure you have safeguards to avoid missing key dates or making other professional errors.

Disaster-Proof Yourself

A tornado hits, taking off the side of your home—the one where your home office used to sit. All's lost. Even if you get the very best insurance you can buy, money can't replace everything. Your company books and records, for example, simply can't be replaced by money from the insurance company. So, get other kinds of protection for things that can't be replaced at any price.

Just because you've backed up your computer files or kept a copy of your mileage log doesn't mean the backup's indestructible. Use a fireproof office safe to store important records and papers. Back up computer data to floppy disks or to a Zip drive. Store your backup in a fireproof safe or off the premises. You might want to store important papers and computer data backups you don't need to get to often in a safety deposit box at your bank.

Here are some other things you might want to make copies of and store off-site:

➤ Client lists. Even if you have them on your computer backup, you'll want to contact key clients as soon as you can after a disaster, maybe even before your computer and office are reconnected.

➤ Inventory information. Keep a list of your regular inventory items, including the name and phone number of suppliers for these items. Also, have a recent report of your inventory and be sure to update this in your off-premises file from time to time.

➤ Tax information. Put copies of your tax returns and tax information in an off-premises file. Include in this tax information your depreciation schedules and other tax items that relate back to prior years.

➤ Photos of your office. This will help you collect the insurance to replace your office and all its contents. The more detailed your records, showing exactly what you have, the more you'll receive in reimbursement from the insurance company.

The Least You Need to Know

➤ Have enough property insurance to cover your business equipment both in your home office and off the premises, as well as coverage for inventory.

➤ Have enough liability coverage to protect you from claims of business visitors who have a spill on your front steps or are hurt as a result of your professional negligence.

➤ Review all your business insurance needs with an insurance agent.

➤ Shop around and use cost-cutting measures to reduce your insurance premiums.

➤ Keep your insurance claims low by adopting safety measures.

➤ Keep your books, records, and important papers, as well as computer data, safe from destruction or theft.

Business by the Numbers

Don't skip this chapter just because you and numbers don't get along. As a home-based business owner you can't afford to ignore the numbers even if you like them about as much as you like root canals. Doing so can doom your business to failure.

If you don't understand numbers, you may be caught short of cash to pay your bills. You won't know whether the business is growing or if you're profitable.

In this chapter you'll learn about accounting methods and accounting periods. You'll also find out how to keep good books and records. You'll learn about cash-flow planning. And you'll discover ways to make the most of if your banking relationship.

You Gotta Have a System

Jean is an artist who couldn't be bothered by the numbers. She threw all her business receipts into a shoe box and spent whatever money she needed on supplies. The only problem was she had no idea whether she was making or losing money. She didn't have any accounting system and didn't keep the kind of books she needed.

The accounting system that you set up provides the framework into which you'll slot your numbers. This lets you keep track of how your business is doing. It also helps you prepare your tax returns (and support your claims in case your returns are questioned). Finally, this information is vital if you need to borrow money in the future to expand your business.

The Educated Entrepreneur

If numbers drive you crazy or if your business becomes complicated, don't hesitate to use an accountant or bookkeeper to handle financial matters—keeping books, filing returns, preparing financial statements. There are accountants who are certified, called CPAs, and accountants who aren't certified, called public accountants. You can find an accountant by word-of-mouth (ask other business owners you know who they use). You can locate a CPA by calling your state CPA society for a list of accountants in your area. For a public accountant, call the National Society of Public Accountants at 800-966-6679. If you use a professional, be clear about the jobs you want done and what it'll cost you.

There are three parts to your accounting system: method of accounting, period of accounting, and how you keep your records.

Accounting Method: Choose Your Poison

An accounting method is a way of reporting when income is earned and expenses are paid. You have two choices for your accounting method: cash and accrual.

Under the *cash method,* you report income when you actually or constructively receive it and write off expenses when you pay them. If you're a consultant or in a service business, you'll probably use the cash method of accounting since it's the easiest way to report your income and expenses.

Under the *accrual method,* things are more complicated. You report income and write off expenses
when there's something called *economic performance.*
This means when all the events necessary to fix the
income or expense have occurred. Sounds complicated? Well, let's look at an example.

Example 1: You sell a customer a gift box for $100.
You ship the box on May 1, along with your invoice
for payment. The customer pays you on May 20.
Under the accrual method of accounting, you enter
your income on the books on May 1 because this is
the date on which economic performance occurred.
You've done everything necessary to secure the
income—shipped the item, determined the amount of payment, and sent an invoice. In
contrast, had you been on the cash method, you wouldn't have recorded the income
until May 20, the date you actually got the money in your hot little hands.

> **Business Buzzword**
> *Constructive receipt* means that you have the income under your control even though you haven't actually received it. So a check you receive is income to you even though you haven't cashed it or deposited it in your bank account.

Example 2: You sign a one-year lease for a computer, with monthly payments of $100
due on the first of each month. Under the accrual method you record this expense on the
first of each month even though you don't actually send out a check until the second
week. In contrast, if you'd been on the cash method, you wouldn't have recorded the
expense until the second week, the date you forked over the cash.

If your business has inventory you *must* use the accrual method. You can't choose to use
the cash method of accounting. Service businesses can use accrual, but most don't because the cash method is easier to use.

Accounting Period: Knowing When to Panic

All good things must come to an end, and so must your business year. You know *when*
you enter income and expenses on your books. But when do you close them? You choose

when your business year will end each year, which is called your accounting period. Having a business year allows you to keep your records and make comparisons from year to year. It's required so you can report your income for tax purposes.

There are two accounting period choices—calendar year or fiscal year. A calendar year kisses your business year good-bye at midnight on December 31. A fiscal year ends on the last day of any other month—June 30, July 31, or whatever month you choose.

Most home-based businesses use a calendar year. It's the easiest thing to do. It's the same accounting period that you, as business owner, use to report your personal income. If you're self-employed and want to use a fiscal year, you then have to use it for reporting your personal income.

Homegrown Tip

If, for business reasons, you use a fiscal year for your business and personal income, then your tax filing deadline changes. For example, if you use a fiscal year ending June 30, you must file your individual income tax return on October 15 (3 ½ months after the close of your tax year).

So why would anyone want to use a fiscal year? Some businesses like it because it jives with their natural business cycles. They find that they wind up their busiest season of the year at the end of March and, so, use March 31 as their fiscal year. In the past, some businesses also used a fiscal year as a clever (and perfectly legal) way of postponing tax on business income until the following year. Here's how deferral worked: A partnership had a fiscal year ending June 30, and its partners reported on a calendar year. The partners' share of partnership income for the year ending June 30, 1997 could, because of tax-reporting rules, be deferred for one year to their 1998 personal tax returns. Today, the use of such deferral is available only in extremely limited circumstances. If you're interested, talk to an accountant.

Keeping Good Books and Records

Homegrown Tip

The rules on tax years and other accounting rules are complicated, as you can see. It's a good idea to discuss your situation with an accountant or other tax professional to see if these complicated rules can be of any benefit to you or whether you're better off keeping it simple.

In Dickens's *A Christmas Carol,* Bob Cratchet spent seven days a week from dawn to dusk entering numbers in the account books of his rotten boss, Ebenezer Scrooge. If you don't have someone like Cratchet to do it for you, then it's up to you to keep track of your income and expenses. It's a chore, no doubt, but a necessary one. How else will you know whether your business is improving or losing ground? How else will you be able to prepare the financial statements you'll need if you want to get a bank loan or deal with a creditor? How else will you be able to prepare your tax returns or stand up to the IRS in an audit? You need to keep account books and save certain receipts and other items (together referred to as records).

But you're not going to get away with only one set of books. Besides your general account books, you also should have special books for your car, travel, and entertainment expenses. Use a diary or log book to keep track of these key expenses. Tax law says that the information must be kept "contemporaneously." This means you should enter the information at or shortly after the time you have the expenses. In the table below, you'll see the kind of information you need to record for these key expenses.

Information for Car, Travel, and Entertainment Expenses

Item	Information
Car used for business	Business miles traveled; purpose of the trip; date of the trip; cost
Entertainment and business meals	Name, address, and location of the entertainment; place where business discussion held (if different from entertainment spot); business reason/benefit for meeting; cost
Gifts to business clients/customers	Name of client/customer and his/her business relationship to you; reason for gift; date of gift; cost
Travel	Date and duration of stay; travel destination; business purpose; cost

Let a Computer Keep Your Books

Bob Cratchet lived (fictitiously) 150 years ago. If he'd had such a thing as a computer he could have asked for Christmas and New Year's Day off. The computer's a modern miracle when it comes to numbers. You can use a computer to keep your books flawlessly, even if you're no good with numbers. Many simple and inexpensive computer programs let you keep track of your income and expense items—QuickBooks®, DacEasy®, and M.Y.O.B.® all cost less than $200. These programs let you prepare financial statements and account reports (which you may need to show investors or lenders). They also tie into tax return preparation programs that pick up the income and expense items and insert them in the appropriate places on the tax return.

You're not just keeping all these books for your health. As a business owner you're required by the government to keep account books. According to the IRS, this obligation is met if you use a computer as long as:

➤ The software you use lets you keep accurate and complete books. It must also have an index to permit rapid retrieval of information. The programs mentioned earlier have what's needed.

Homegrown Tip
Keep your computer backup safe from loss, damage, or theft by storing floppies, tapes, or other backup devices in a fireproof safe. Or you may want to store your backup in a relative's home or a bank safety deposit box.

➤ You've got controls to ensure the "integrity, accuracy, and reliability" of your system. Keeping records (explained later) will show that you've entered all the relevant information and haven't purposely omitted certain information.

➤ You've got controls to prevent unauthorized additions, alternations, or deletions of data. You want to be sure that your toddler or someone else with access to your computer won't come in and zap out your entries for the month of August. You can have adequate controls by backing up your entries onto floppies or using other backups discussed in Chapter 15.

What Records Do You Need to Keep?

Besides the information they give you, there's one other important reason for keeping your records—the government says so, that's why. Your records are your proof of income and expenses if the IRS or your state taxing authority audits your tax returns.

Besides your books, which can be handwritten (the old Scrooge ledger method) or kept on computer, save your receipts, canceled checks, and other papers related to your income and expenses. The guidelines listed in the table below tell you the kinds of records you have to keep.

Records to Keep

Item	Records
Asset purchases	Purchase and sales invoices; canceled checks; depreciation you've claimed
Car expenses	Diary or log book; receipts; credit card slips
Employment taxes	Employee's name, address, and Social Security number; withholding allowance certificates (Form W-4) or other withholding agreements; time slips

Item	Records
Entertainment and meal expenses	Restaurant receipts; other receipts; canceled checks; credit card slips
Other expenses	Invoices; receipts; canceled checks; credit card slips
Travel expenses	Diary or log book; receipts; credit card slips

How Long Is Long Enough?

Your home office may be small and you just don't have much storage space. Records and receipts can pile up. What's a home businessperson to do? Start cleaning out the attic if you have to make room for records and receipts and keep them as long as you need to. How long is that? The answer depends on the records involved. Some businesses keep records forever, storing them away in boxes and forgetting them. As a home-based business owner with limited space, you may not want to keep records any longer than the law requires.

➤ **General rule.** Keep your records to back up your tax return entries. This means saving the records for at least three years after the date your return is due or filed, or two years after the date the tax is paid, whichever's later. Keep your tax returns at least as long as you keep your other records.

➤ **Employment taxes.** If you've got an employee, you have to keep your records at least four years after the date the tax was due or paid, whichever's later.

➤ **Assets.** When you buy a computer or equipment, keep related records for as long as you own it and then some. Apply the general rule to the year in which you sell or otherwise get rid of the assets. So, if you buy a computer in 1997 and then junk it in 2001, keep your records at least through 2005 (three years after the return for 2001 is due or filed).

Homegrown Tip

You don't have to keep receipts for entertainment expenses if they're under $75. So, if you take a client out to lunch and pay cash, you don't need to keep a restaurant receipt if the lunch bill's less than $75. But you still need records of the expenses (when and where you had lunch, and so on).

Home Hazard

ARGH@#!

Just because you don't need your records anymore for tax purposes doesn't mean you should automatically toss them out. You may still need them for insurance purposes or your creditors may require them. So check it out before you toss them.

Go with the (Cash) Flow

When you hear the term "cash flow" do you picture money floating down a stream? Close, but no cigar. Cash flow is basically money going out and coming in to your business. As you begin to run your business, you'll see a pattern develop—you provide your goods or services, buy equipment and supplies (and inventory), sell products or perform services, send out invoices, pay bills, and collect for your goods or services. All of these steps are part of the cash flow process. You want to make sure there's no clog in your cash flow—that you have enough in (or coming in) to pay your bills.

Here's a tale of how cash flow can kill you: My husband, Malcolm, and his partner started up a menswear company in the kitchen. The designs were great and the stores loved them. They had to pay their suppliers on a 30-day basis (30 days from the date of the invoice for materials). But the stores didn't pay for clothing delivered to them until typically 90 days later—sometimes even longer despite being large, nationally-known retailers. So even though they were selling their clothes like hotcakes, the cash flow did them in. They didn't have enough of a cash cushion to back them up to cover their materials. They just couldn't continue to operate and were forced to fold. Their experience isn't unique.

You have to monitor your cash flow regularly (monthly, weekly, or even daily) so that you don't get caught off guard and short of cash. If you project a need for cash, you can at least have the time to try and raise it. If you don't project the need and it arises, you may be out of business before you know what happened.

You can use the worksheet in Appendix B to project your cash flow. Or, if yours is the kind of business that requires you to more closely monitor cash flow, you may want to use a computer program designed for just that. For example, QuickBooks lets you make a monthly cash flow statement showing your accounts receivable, accounts payable, and bank statements for each week in the month. Or you can work with an accountant to stay on top of your cash flow.

Tracking Your Inventory

If you're an interior designer or provide some other service, you're not concerned with inventory (you don't stock Louis IV armoires by the dozens in the back room). But if you sell vitamins, you have to keep a supply ready for those orders that roll in. How do you know how much inventory you should keep on hand? When should you reorder? These are tough questions for any business owner, but even more so for a home-based business owner. The reason? Your storage space is probably very limited. And, as for all business owners, you want to restock your inventory without overstocking it, a mistake that can needlessly tie up your cash and hurt your cash flow (not to mention sticking you with tons of last year's vitamins).

Track your inventory to know what you've got on hand at any given moment, when you should reorder, and how much you should reorder. The best way to do this is by using a computer program designed for this purpose. But not all businesses need the same software. If you sell cartons of skin cream, you need a different kind of program than the one you'd need if you sell rare editions of books (each of which is unique).

The Educated Entrepreneur

You can get free software for your computer to track your inventory by visiting the SBA Web site at http://www.sbaonline.sba.gov. It's good for simple inventories. This software may not be too helpful if you're carrying antiques or other unique items. Here, you may want to invest in special software. It can run you several hundred dollars, but it's probably worth the investment. Check out chat groups online in your area of interest to see if others have suggested any software that works for them.

Financial Help You Can Bank on

If you've never run a business before, then to you a bank's the place you got your home mortgage and deposit your paycheck. But unlike your personal finances, your business can profit from a solid relationship with a bank. You wouldn't let your barber take out your tonsils, so why should you let a personal banker handle your business? Set up a business checking account with Bank of America, Chase, Citibank, Wells Fargo, or another *commercial bank*. It's not a good idea to use a savings and loan or credit union to handle your business banking.

To help you decide which bank to use for your business, ask about the fees you'd have to pay monthly on your checking account. Some banks charge you a monthly fee that's dependent on your average daily balance. Others don't charge any fee if your balance is above $15,000 or some other dollar amount; you may pay only a flat monthly fee if your balance falls below that level. And there are usually charges for making night-drop deposits (if you take in cash and want to deposit it rather than holding it in your home overnight).

Homegrown Tip

Staying on top of inventory isn't easy. If you feel overwhelmed, especially as you're getting started, turn to an accountant for help. If you mess up on your inventory, it'll cost you way more than you'd pay an accountant to get it right.

Also, ask about access to your money and account information. Some banks let you have ATM access to your business account. And you may be able to bank by computer.

Besides checking, check out these services your bank can offer:

➤ Loans. If you need cash to expand or meet a financial crunch, your banking relationship can help you get that loan. Once you get your business up and running, you may want to apply for a revolving line of credit—a type of loan in which you use as much of the money as you need, pay it back when you can, and pay interest only on the part you borrow.

➤ Business advice. Your banker may not know anything about your kind of business, but your bank may still be able to give you some general business help. Chase provides free business advice through its Business Resource Center at 800-334-9294, ext. 850. By calling this number you can get brochures on cash flow and marketing plans or schedule attendance at a free business seminar.

➤ Networking. Your local banker knows your business community. He can put you in touch with resources you're looking for—other business owners, clients, customers, or suppliers.

The Least You Need to Know

➤ Accounting systems have to be set up when you start your business.

➤ An accountant can do the numbers for you if you can't do them yourself.

➤ Keep good books and records to know how your business is doing and to file your tax returns.

➤ Cash flow disasters can destroy your business, so keep close tabs on your income and expenses.

➤ Plan your inventory wisely.

➤ Establish a banking relationship and use it to get advice and financial assistance when you need it.

Sharing Your Profits with Uncle Sam

Say the word "taxes" and some people cringe or go blank. The IRS for many represents an intimidating and baffling presence—but one that every business owner must face. State taxing authorities bring their own brand of paranoia to the mix.

What can you do to face your fears and avoid the wrath of the IRS? Get smart. Learn what you need to know about taxes—the taxes you must pay, the returns you have to file. You'll know what you're up against. And you'll be able to go on the offensive, getting every deduction you're entitled to.

In this chapter you'll learn about the types of taxes you may have to pay as a business owner. You'll also learn about what returns you have to file and when. You'll become familiar with the rules for writing off travel and entertainment expenses and equipment costs and other expenses common to most businesses. And, you'll find out about some limitations the tax law puts on deducting losses from your business.

Taxes, Taxes, Taxes

Homegrown Tip
You'll find a discussion on the special tax rules relating to your home office in Chapter 22. And you already explored the fun world of payroll taxes for your employees in Chapter 18.

As a business owner you hope to be successful. Success generally means being profitable. If you're profitable, the government wants a piece of the action—that's where income taxes come in.

But income taxes aren't the only bad news. There are also sales taxes to collect and pay to the state (if your state has a sales tax). If someone works for you, there's an array of payroll taxes to collect and pay to the federal government, as you saw in Chapter 18.

(There are also many federal excise taxes, but I'll spare you. Most home-based businesses don't have to be concerned with them.)

Not All Businesses Are Taxed the Same

It would be way too simple if all businesses were treated the same. How you organize your business—a sole proprietorship, partnership, limited liability company, C corporation, or S corporation—affects your taxes in a number of ways. It controls what tax return to file, what tax rates you'll pay on profits, and whether payments to you are treated as salary and subject to employment taxes.

Of course, taxes aren't the only factor to use in deciding how you'll organize your business. But it's sure one that hits you where you live—your bottom line.

Working Alone Without a Corporate Name to Your Name

If you operate alone and don't incorporate, you're a sole proprietor (the Lone Ranger minus Tonto). For example, if you're an independent contractor providing consulting services to various corporations, you're treated as a sole proprietor for tax purposes. For federal income tax purposes, the business isn't separate from you, you are one and the same. You report all of the business' income and expenses on your individual income tax return. You explain the business' income and expenses on IRS Schedule C or Schedule C-EZ (a simpler version of Schedule C), which is part of your Form 1040. The IRS releases a new Schedule C and Schedule C-EZ each year just so you won't get bored.

Because you're in this on your own, you're taxed on all of the business' profits. The amount of profits you report isn't affected by any money you take out of the business' bank account for yourself. Of course, money you reinvest in a new copying machine, additional inventory, or other business-related stuff may give rise to tax deductions that reduce your profits.

When you're starting up your business, it's like a new marriage: You may be poor but happy. You may not have any profits to be concerned with. Instead, you may have losses (expenses that are greater than your business income). These losses are deductible against your spouse's salary reported on a joint return, or your interest, dividends, or capital gains, or other income reported on your return. But if you have losses for several years, the IRS may smell a rat and disallow them under the hobby loss rules talked about later in this chapter (this has nothing to do with losing your stamp collection, I assure you).

The Educated Entrepreneur

Sole proprietors are like great big bull's-eyes to the government: They run the highest risk of being audited by the IRS. In fact, a sole proprietor is more than six times as likely to have her return questioned by the government as an individual who has incorporated the business even though the business earns the same amount of revenue. The IRS, in its wisdom, hasn't explained why this is so. They release audit statistics each year, so the risk of audit can vary from one year to another.

So, what other excuse for picking your pocket does the government find? Since a sole proprietor is a self-employed person, the business isn't responsible for FICA (Social Security and Medicare taxes) on earnings. Instead, a self-employed person pays a tax, appropriately called self-employment tax, that's equal to both the employer and employee share of FICA. The tax is applied to net earnings from the business. That is, what's left after you take away all the expenses.

Get a pencil out, here come the numbers. Self-employment tax is figured on Schedule SE, part of your Form 1040. The self-employment tax rate is 12.4% of a base amount ($65,400 in 1997) to cover the Social Security portion of the tax, plus 2.9% on all profit to cover the Medicare portion of the tax. You can then deduct one-half of your tax as a separate item on your Form 1040.

Working Two by Two

If you've got a partner in crime working with you in a business that's not incorporated, you've got a partnership. In many ways a partnership is just like a sole proprietorship from a tax perspective. Partners are self-employed individuals and aren't employees of their partnership.

Homegrown Tip

If you're self-employed, be sure to pay estimated tax on your business income so you won't have penalties and interest. Remember, you're not subject to withholding since you don't have a salary. Your estimated tax should include your self-employment tax.

Also like a sole proprietorship, the business itself doesn't pay any tax. Instead, partners also report their share of partnership income on their individual returns. Each year the partnership tells the IRS all about its income and expenses on an information return called Form 1065.

The partnership income flows through to its owners. If you have nothing better to do with your time you may have seen this called flow-through tax treatment. The partner's share of the partnership income or loss is explained on a form called a Schedule K-1, which is part of Form 1065. Schedule K-1 tells each partner what his share of the partnership's profit or loss, gains, and credits is. Profit or loss isn't broken down into the sources of revenue or expenses. Instead, the net amount (the difference between the cash that's taken in and expenses) is reported as one item on the partner's individual return. Schedule E of Form 1040 is used to report this income. Easy, huh?

Some stuff from the partnership requires special treatment on an individual's return because of limits in the tax law. These items pass through to partners separately, apart from a partnership's general profit or loss. Examples are charitable contributions (which are subject to a deduction limit based on income), a first-year expense deduction (which has dollar and taxable income limits), and capital gains and losses (gains may be taxed as special rates, losses are currently deductible only to the extent of gains and up to $3,000 of ordinary income).

If you're still with me, you may be wondering what tax bracket a partnership is in. The answer is simple—it's not in any tax bracket because the partnership itself doesn't pay any tax. Since each partner reports her share of partnership items on an individual income tax return, the same partnership income picked by each partner can be taxed at different rates.

For example, you and your neighbor Irving form an equal partnership. In the first year the partnership has a profit of $30,000, $15,000 of which you get and report on your individual return and the other $15,000 of which belongs to Irv. Suppose you're in the 31% tax bracket (because you have a working spouse and other income). And suppose your partner's only in the 15% tax bracket. Even though you get the same amount of money, you'll be paying more than twice the tax rate on that income. Lucky Irving.

Another way the government doesn't play fair: You make money, and they're always right there, hand out for a percentage; you lose money and you only get to deduct it up to a point. While income is always taxable, losses from your business may be limited under a number of different tax rules. These rules are designed to limit losses when someone doesn't have a whole lot of stake in the business' finances, or doesn't really play an active role in the business. These loss limitation rules—called the at-risk rules and passive activity rules, if you care—are really complicated and unless you take in Uncle George as a silent partner, avoid them like the plague.

Tax law allows businesses to offer employees medical coverage and other employee fringe benefits on a tax-free basis. Unfortunately, since partners aren't employees of their partnership, they can't enjoy these benefits.

> **Homegrown Tip**
> To find out more about loss limitation rules, check out IRS Publication 925, Passive Activity and At-Risk Rules, which you can get at no cost by calling 800-829-1040.

There's one important difference between a sole proprietorship and a partnership. A partnership has an extremely low statistical chance of being audited. For small partnerships—those with fewer than 10 partners, the IRS can choose to audit any or all of the partners individually. (With larger partnerships, the IRS is required to audit the partnership itself, even though the partnership isn't a taxpayer, and pass any adjustments along to the partners.) Like a sole proprietor, you, as a partner, pay self-employment tax on your share of the partnership's profits plus any guaranteed payments you get from the partnership. However, limited partners who are mere investors in the business and don't do the day-to-day stuff aren't subject to self-employment tax.

Like a sole proprietorship, partners should pay estimated tax for both their share of business income and their self-employment tax.

Inc., Corp., or Ltd.

Once you form a corporation and put those special letters after your name—Inc., Corp., or Ltd., the business is automatically called a C corporation for tax purposes. (Just in case you're thinking of going on *Jeopardy*: the letter C comes from the subchapter of the Internal Revenue Code where the tax rules for corporations can be found.) The corporation is like this little person. It's subject to its own tax, called a corporate income tax. The corporate income tax operates very much like the individual income tax. Like an individual, a corporation files its own federal tax return—Form 1120, Corporate Income Tax Return—to report its income or loss. The federal corporate tax brackets are different from those for individuals. In the following table you'll find the corporate rates, which range from a low of 15% to a high of 35%. Unlike individual tax brackets, corporate tax brackets aren't adjusted annually for inflation.

If Taxable Income Is...

Over	But Not Over	Tax* Is	Of the Amount Over
$0	$50,000	15%	$0
$50,000	$75,000	$7,500 + 25%	$50,000
$75,000	$100,000	$13,750 + 34%	$75,000
$100,000	$335,000	$22,250 + 39%	$100,000
$335,000	$10,000,000	$113,900 + 34%	$335,000
$10,000,000	$15,000,000	$3,400,000 + 35%	$10,000,000
$15,000,000	$18,333,333	$5,150,000 + 38%	$15,000,000
$18,333,333	—	35%	—

Note: The top tax rate is 35%. The rates of 38% and 39% are used to offset the benefit from the lower brackets. A corporation will never pay more than 35% of its taxable income in federal income tax.

Personal service corporations (doctors, lawyers, and consultants who incorporate) are subject to a flat tax rate of 35%. They can't use the graduated corporate tax rates.

Home Hazard There may be state corporate income taxes as well. In some states they're called franchise taxes (even though the business isn't a franchise).

The amount of tax your corporation pays depends on how much you make and how much you take in the form of salary, benefits, and dividends. If you've got a consulting business (which is usually classified as a personal service corporation) and you take out all of the profits as salary, there's no corporate tax—the corporation can deduct the salary paid to you. If you take most of the profits as salary, anything you don't take is taxed to the corporation at the rate of 35%. You pay tax on your salary at your individual income tax rates (somewhere between 15% and 39.6%).

From a tax perspective the key difference between a corporation and any other form of business organization is the potential for double taxation. This is a legalized form of highway robbery. Income earned by the corporation that isn't taken out as salary or other deductible payments is treated as dividends. And dividends aren't deductible by the corporation. So, they're taxed twice—once when the corporation earns them and again when they're paid to you and you pay tax on them.

If you work for your corporation you're an employee (not a self-employed individual). The corporation must pay the employer share of FICA, then you pay the employee share. Owner/employees can be covered by workers' compensation and unemployment insurance so you can go on the dole if the business goes belly up.

If your C corporation is profitable you can take advantage of fringe benefits. This is cool because the corporation gets to deduct its cost for providing them while you don't have to pay tax on them. These include medical reimbursement plans, health insurance, dependent care assistance, and a limited amount of group term life insurance. Of course, corporations are democracies. If you want these benefits for yourself, you'll have to give them to anyone who works for you.

> **Homegrown Tip**
> Careful planning can avoid double taxation. Earnings can be funneled to you and other owners on a tax-deductible basis. Or the corporation can make an election, called an S election, to have income passed through to owners (discussed later in this chapter).

S(pecial) Corporations

Ready to practice your alphabet? It's possible to have the best of both possible worlds—a corporate name and protection from personal liability but no double tax. You can get this by becoming an S corporation, even if you're the only owner. Being an S corporation doesn't change any of the legal consequences of being a corporation, it only affects income taxes. An S corporation is more like a partnership than a C corporation since the corporation's income passes through to its owners and is taxed directly to the owners.

An S corporation files an annual income tax return—Form 1120S, U.S. Income Tax Return for S Corporation. Then, just like a partnership, Schedule K-1 of this form is given to you and any other owner describing your share of each corporate item to be reported on your individual tax return.

> **The Educated Entrepreneur**
>
> Do you like getting headaches? Then, read this. If your business operates as a C corporation before electing S status, there's the possibility that the corporation itself can become a taxpayer, something that can never happen to a partnership. Three different tax rules recoup some of the benefit that a corporation can get from converting from C to S status. This possibility of the S corporation itself paying tax can never arise if a corporation is formed and immediately elects S status. Aspirin, anyone?

As an owner/employee, you're treated as an employee of your S corporation. So, just like a C corporation, an S corporation pays the employer share of FICA and you pay the employee's share. You can also be covered under workers' compensation and unemployment insurance. However, as an S corporation owner you can't get all of the fringe benefits that a C corporation can give. The tax law treats S corporation owner/employees like partners for purposes of various fringe benefits—health insurance, group term life insurance, and more.

Want Choices? Choose a Limited Liability Company

There's a new kid on the block—the limited liability company (if you've forgotten, go to the back of the class and review Chapter 7). As an unincorporated business with two or more owners, this kind of company picks its poison—to be taxed as a partnership or C corporation. If it picks partnership, then it gets pass-through tax treatment for its owners.

Home Hazard
Each state has its own view on S corporations. Check out the tax rules in your state. You may find that you only have to pay a flat franchise tax (for example, $375 per year in New York). But you may have to pay corporate taxes if your state doesn't recognize S status.

In this case, the LLC files a partnership return—Form 1065, U.S. Partnership Return of Income—with members reporting their share of LLC items (as allocated to them on Schedule K-1) on their individual income tax returns. (Only in rare cases would an LLC want to choose corporate treatment, so that's all you'll hear about that.)

Since LLCs are relatively new (the last state to join the bandwagon, Hawaii, did so April 1, 1997), there are no audit statistics for them yet.

As a member in an LLC, you're treated as a partner, not as an employee, and limited partners are not subject to self-employment tax.

Write It Off

So, how do you cut down on the taxes you have to cough up? Repeat after me: Every dollar that I deduct reduces the amount of income I pay tax on. How much a deduction is really worth depends on the tax bracket you're in. If you're a consultant in the 31% bracket, it means that each expense you can write off will save you 31¢ on every dollar (the tax). If you deduct enough expenses, you can even drop down into a lower tax bracket.

Homegrown Tip
Be sure to check on the tax treatment of LLCs under your state law. You may have annual fees and/or tax on LLC earnings.

Most of the money you spend on business-related expenses can be deducted. In the following list you'll find most common business expenses. Certain key items are discussed in greater detail later in this chapter.

Common Business Deductions:

Accounting fees	Lease payments
Advertising	Legal fees
Bad debts	Repairs and maintenance
Bank charges	Subscriptions and dues
Car and truck expenses	Supplies
Commissions and fees	Taxes and licenses
Computers	Travel, meals, and entertainment
Insurance	Utilities
Interest	Wages

In special cases you can claim a write-off. A write-off is better than a deduction—it's a tax credit for certain expenses. A tax credit reduces your taxes on a dollar-for-dollar basis. For example, if you hire an employee who's considered an economically disadvantaged person, you may be able to claim a work opportunity credit of 35% of first year wages up to $6,000 (for a top credit of $2,100). This means that the federal government is basically paying your employee $2,100 (the amount you would have paid in taxes if you didn't take the credit) while you're paying only $3,900.

Home Hazard
Business expenses are deductible only if you've got the proof to back them up. If you don't keep records and receipts, you'll lose out on write-offs you could have claimed.

T&E for You and Me

This might be news to you: Big Brother doesn't completely trust us. The government believes there's a tendency for business owners to label personal expenses, like a meal, as business expenses to write them off. As a result, the tax law has strict rules on deducting travel, meals, and entertainment costs, called T&E expenses.

Here's a rundown of some T&E expenses you may have in your business:

➤ Local transportation costs. The amount you spend on taxis, bus fare, train fare, and for the use of your car or truck for business purposes is deductible. Home-based business owners who leave their office on business can deduct the very first dollar spent on getting to a business appointment. Unlike those who work outside the home, there's no such thing as commuting (which isn't deductible). You'll find the rules for deducting your car and truck expenses later in this chapter.

➤ Travel to another city. Travel away from home, including the cost of your fare (by train, air, or otherwise), hotel lodging, 50% of meals, and incidental expenses (your laundry or use of the hotel fax machine) is deductible. If you combine business with pleasure on a trip in the U.S., the portion of your expenses related to business are deductible if the primary purpose of the trip was business. Suppose you work in Seattle and come to New York City for a week of business meetings. You fly in on a Sunday night and fly back the following Sunday, having spent Friday and Saturday taking in *Cats* and strolling in Central Park. You can deduct all of your airfare as well as the meals and lodging for the days you spent on business. Different rules apply to foreign travel.

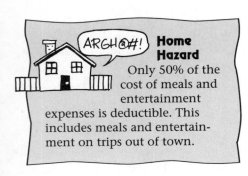

➤ Business meals. Here's where it pays to be sociable. If you take out a client or customer for any meal—breakfast, lunch, or dinner—the cost of both meals is deductible. But if you eat alone, the cost of your meals is not deductible unless you're out of town on business. So, if you leave your office in the suburbs and schedule two appointments for the day, one at 11 A.M. and the other at 2 P.M., in the downtown area, you'll probably eat in between them. Your tuna sandwich and Coke at the luncheonette aren't deductible because you weren't entertaining a client or customer, and you weren't out of town on business.

➤ Entertainment. If you take a client or customer to a Broadway show, a football game, or any other sports or entertainment event, you can deduct the cost of both tickets as long as business was discussed. If you entertain for business at your home, the cost is also deductible.

➤ Gifts. If you buy popcorn boxes as holiday gifts for your suppliers, clients, customers, or prospective customers, you can generally write off your cost. The same is true if you buy a crystal vase for your client's wedding. But there's a dollar limit and it's low: $25 per gift.

While different expenses are deductible, restrictions, some of which you've already seen, lurk everywhere. The following table outlines some of the restrictions to keep in mind.

Restrictions on T&E Expenses

Type of Expense	Restriction
Country club dues	Not deductible
Entertainment	50% of cost
Foreign conventions (those outside the North American area)	Deductible only if directly related to your business and it's reasonable to hold a convention outside the U.S.
Gifts	$25 per gift
Meals	50% of cost
Travel costs of spouse	Not deductible (unless your spouse is your employee and the trip is for business)

Can I Deduct the Spoiler for My Miata?

Do you spend a lot of time running around town in your Chevy? If you use your car for business, you can deduct the business cost. There are two ways to deduct your costs: actual expenses or the IRS standard mileage allowance.

If you use the actual expense method, you have to keep track of your expenses. Use the items below to remind you what's deductible:

Garage rent	Parking
Gas	Repairs
Insurance	Servicing
Lease payments	Tires
Licenses	Tolls
Oil	Towing

Business Buzzword

Depreciation is a deduction of a portion of the cost of a car or other equipment over the life of the equipment (the life is set by the IRS). You can't depreciate equipment you lease, only equipment you own.

Home Hazard

ARGH@#!

The IRS's dollar limits apply only to cars used solely for business. If, as most home-based business owners, you use your car for both business and personal purposes, you'll have to allocate the dollar limits. If you use your car bought in 1996 75% for business and 25% for driving your kids, shopping, and other personal reasons, your dollar limit for 1997 is $3,675 (75% of $4,900).

In addition, you can deduct an allowance related to what you paid for your car, called *depreciation*.

In theory, the cost of a car should be deductible over a period of five years (that's the life of a car in the IRS's view). But logic has little to do with taxes, and in reality, it may take many more years to fully depreciate it. The reason? The tax law puts dollar limits on annual depreciation deductions (dollar limits are adjusted annually for inflation). The more expensive the car, the longer it's going to take to depreciate. A car bought in 1996 for business had the following dollar limits for depreciation: for 1996, $3,060; for 1997, $4,900; for 1998, $2,950; and for 1999 and later years, $1,775. So if that 1996 car costs more than $14,460 it won't be fully depreciated after five years.

Instead of deducting actual expenses, you can use the IRS standard mileage allowance—a cents-per-mile rate that's increased each year to take inflation into account. The rate for 1996 was 31¢ per mile. Using the standard mileage allowance means you don't have to keep track of your gas, repairs, and other costs. You simply look at the number of business miles you drove and multiply that by the standard mileage rate. If you choose to use this rate, you can deduct your parking fees and tolls, too. You don't get to take any depreciation deduction or the complicated computations it requires since depreciation is reflected in the standard mileage rate.

Hold the Phone: Deducting Office Equipment

If you buy equipment that's expected to last more than a year, you're usually required to write off the cost using depreciation. But there's an alternative. You can choose to write off the entire cost in one year if you elect to expense the item. Tax law allows small businesses to expense up to a certain dollar amount of equipment each year.

Year	Limit
1997	$18,000
1998	$18,500
1999	$19,000

Year	Limit
2000	$20,000
2001 and 2002	$24,000
2003 and later	$25,000

There's an important limit on expensing. Your write-off can't be more than your income from the business. So, if you have other large expenses, especially in your first few years, you may not show any income. You can't take your expense deduction. But you can depreciate the equipment so you don't lose out on write-offs, you only delay them.

Get Back When You Get Stiffed

When you sell your goods or perform your services you expect to be paid. Unfortunately, at some time or other you may just get stiffed. Despite all your collection efforts you may not be able to get what's owed to you. Writing off your bad debts is explained in detail in Chapter 17.

Help from the IRS (Finally)

The IRS tries (in its own special way) to provide guidance to small business owners on tax matters. There are a number of different free tax publications you can use to learn more about tax write-offs and other tax questions. You can get these publications, listed in the following chart, by calling 800-829-1040. They're not fun reading, but they're free!

Listing of IRS Publications for Small Business Owners

Publication #	Title
15	Employer's Tax Guide (Circular E)
17	Your Federal Income Tax (For Individuals)
334	Tax Guide for Small Business
463	Travel, Entertainment and Gift Expenses
533	Self-Employment Tax
541	Tax Information on Partnerships
542	Corporations
583	Starting a Business and Keeping Records

continues

Listing of IRS Publications for Small Business Owners   Continued

Publication #	Title
587	Business Use of Your Home
911	Tax Information for Direct Sellers
946	How to Depreciate Property

Homegrown Tip
You can find out what's happening with federal income taxes by checking out the IRS's Web site at http://www.irs.ustreas.gov. You can also order or download federal tax forms and instructions at this site. Tax forms are also available at ftp.fedworld.gov.

If you have nothing better to do, the IRS also offers free seminars to business owners. These seminars cover topics like record-keeping requirements, tax-filing requirements, employment taxes, and federal tax deposit rules for payroll taxes. The IRS also conducts seminars geared to the various types of businesses (sole proprietorships, partnerships). When you apply for your federal employer identification number the IRS will automatically send you information about local seminars. To learn more about what's available, call the IRS's Taxpayer Education Coordinator in your area (listed in the Blue Pages of your telephone book) or call the IRS at its general number listed above.

A Loss Is a Loss, Of Course, Of Course

When you have profits, the government is right at your heel, like a puppy with an itch. But when you suffer losses Uncle Sam may take a powder. Tax law has several limits on deducting losses.

Net Operating Losses

You had some good home remodeling contracts so you bought a new table saw and other power tools and lots of lumber. But you haven't been paid by some of your jobs yet. When you get done looking at your income and expenses for the year, you might find that you're in the red. You may have a net operating loss, called an NOL. A net operating loss isn't a separate loss deduction. It's only a reflection of your other deductions. But, the excess deductions (expenses that exceed your income) can be used to offset income in other years.

How can you benefit from a loss when you don't have income? The answer sounds like double-talk but it's worth knowing about: carrybacks and carryovers. You can use the loss in other tax years. A net operating loss can be carried back three years and forward (over) for up to 15 years. Or you can choose to waive the carryback and simply carry your loss forward for the same 15 years. Bonnie started a greeting card company in partnership with someone else in a garage converted to a studio. In their first year of business they had sizable losses. She was able to use her portion of the losses as a net operating loss, which she carried back to the prior three years. In those years she had been an executive with a Fortune 500 company and had had a big salary. By using her NOL as a carryback, she got a refund of taxes she'd paid. She used the tax refund to help her live until her business became profitable.

Home Hazard Individuals (self-employed individuals and business owners with pass-through income) figure NOLs a little differently than corporations. The rules are complex to say the least, so you may want to discuss them with a tax expert.

You Should Get a Hobby

Even the IRS knows when to stop backing a losing bet. If your business produces a loss year after year after year (something you can afford to do if you have outside income or a hard-working spouse), there may come a time when the IRS says enough is enough and nixes your loss write-offs. You'll fall under the hobby loss rules. These rules came about to stop people from writing off expenses related to their coin and stamp collecting, dog breeding, and other hobbies. Here's how these rules work (and it's full of IRS one-sided logic):

If you have income from a hobby activity, you have to report it. But if you have losses from an activity in which you don't have a reasonable expectation of making a profit, you can't deduct your losses. Of course, your profit motive is really between you and your pipe dreams. But the IRS looks at certain objective standards to make a ruling on your profit motive. The following factors help to show you have a profit motive:

➤ You carry on your business in a businesslike fashion, keeping good books and records. Be sure to have a separate business bank account. A separate telephone line is another indication of a business (versus a hobby).

➤ You put in a lot of time and effort. Being a part-timer or only moonlighting at your home business doesn't mean you lack a profit motive, but it's more convincing if you run your business on a full-time basis.

➤ You depend on your home-based business income for your livelihood. A highly successful doctor gave his wife Paula money to start up an Indian art business from home—something that she loved to do. The doctor was more than happy that the business wasn't profitable because the losses from the business could offset his professional fees. Paula didn't need the business to throw off income because she relied on her husband to pay the house bills. This scenario walks and talks just like a hobby activity, so the IRS might say it is.

➤ You use experts and advisors and change methods in an effort to get profitable. Maybe you don't know it all. But if you turn to experts for help, this shows you want to make your business work.

You may not have to prove you have a profit motive. Instead you can rely on a presumption that you're in the business to make a profit. You are presumed to have a profit motive if you make a profit in three out of five years (and heads up horse breeders: two out of seven years for horse-related activities). So, your first two years in operation are slow but business picks up and by year three you're in the black and you stay there from then on. You're presumed to have a profit motive in your two loss years and the IRS won't bother you. By relying on the presumption, you keep the IRS from saying you lack a profit motive for five years.

> **Homegrown Tip**
> To rely on the presumption, file Form 5213, Election to Postpone Determination With Respect to the Presumption that an Activity Is Engaged In For Profit (catchy, huh?). Usually, you have to make the election within three years of the first year you begin your business. Read the instructions to the form for more details. But even if you don't have the three years of profit, you can always try to prove your profit motive.

Businesses that Never Fly

Suppose you look into a business—check out a franchise or explore buying a company. What happens if the business never gets off the ground? After all your investigations you decide that the business idea isn't worth your efforts or you just can't reach an agreement with the seller. You may have put in money to reach this conclusion—travel expenses to meet with franchisers or others, legal fees for advice, accounting fees to look over the books.

If you only got as far as a general search, your expenses aren't deductible. The tax law doesn't allow you to write off investigatory expenses. However, once you've focused on a particular business (for example, you hire a lawyer to draw up a purchase agreement) but the sale falls through, then you can write off your expenses.

The Least You Need to Know

➤ Sole proprietors (including independent contractors) and owners of pass-through entities pay tax on their personal returns.

➤ C corporations are separate taxpayers, and owners of these businesses only pay tax on income they receive from the business.

➤ There are limits on deducting certain travel and entertainment expenses.

➤ Equipment costs can be fully written off in the year you buy.

➤ As a small business owner you can get help from the IRS with free publications and seminars.

➤ Tax losses may not be deductible in certain cases.

Chapter 22

Home Office Tax Shelter

Congratulations, you're working out of your home! But what does it get you (tax-wise)? Plenty! Whether you rent your home or own it, part of the housing expenses you're already paying may be deductible.

Running your business from home doesn't automatically mean write-offs for a portion of your rent or depreciation on the home you own. Tax law's very strict about which businesses can claim a deduction for certain expenses of operating from home. These tax rules are called *home office deduction rules,* but they apply to any business you run from home—electrical contracting, potter's studio, or catering service.

In this chapter you'll learn about the tax rules for deducting the things that are unique to working from home. You'll see these rules aren't always fair—and often aren't even clear—but you need to understand them if you want to claim deductions.

The Home Office Deduction Two-Step

Everyone knows that tax law's complicated, right? Part of its bad reputation comes from the home office deduction rules. To be blunt, they're as clear as mud and as simple as quantum physics.

You're already paying for your home—whether you run a business there or not. But it's possible to be able to treat some of your personal expenses for the home as a business write-off. This special tax break is called a home office deduction. To fall under the home office rules, you'll have to meet two separate tests. If you fail the first test, don't bother looking at the second because you're out of luck and can't deduct your home office expenses.

Test 1

Test 1 has just one question, but it's a deal-maker or -breaker: What kind of business do you run? The answer affects whether you meet or fail the test.

The home office must be your *principal place of business*. Your home office is treated as your principal place of business if it's the place where you conduct your business. It can be your prime activity or a sideline business. As long as it's the main location for the business, it's your principal place of business. This test's easy for some people. Writers, no problem. Day care providers, no problem.

But if your work takes you all around town, you'll have to decide whether the home office is the principal place of business. So if you're a home contractor, you do the contracting work at the customers' homes and your administrative work in your home office. Which is your principal place of business?

Two key points are used to decide this: the relative importance of the activities performed at each business location (called, appropriately enough, the relative importance test) and the amount of time spent in each location. Look at the relative importance test first and see whether the work you do at home is more important than the work you do around town. Got that beat and you don't need to go on to the time test. But if it's inconclusive, you'll need to look at the relative amount of time spent in each location. Believe it or not, the IRS says it's possible that after you look at both of these factors you'll reach the conclusion that there's *no* principal place of business (so you can't deduct home office expenses).

Over the years irate home businesspeople have fought the IRS over their right to deduct home office expenses. Court decisions have given us some guidance, but the bottom line is the advice Deep Throat gave Woodward and Bernstein—follow the money. Where it's earned is the more important place. If the essence of your business is to meet with people at their locations, or to deliver goods or services at other locations, great weight is given to where the contact occurs. So scheduling appointments, planning, billing, collections, and keeping records at home just isn't enough to make your home your principal place of business. Applying the relative importance test, it's pretty clear that an interior decorator or an electrician whose business is focused on services performed outside the home is out of luck for deducting home office expenses.

Do you bring home a briefcase full of work from your day job on a regular basis? If you run more than one business from a home office, *each* business has to meet the home office requirements in order to deduct any home office expenses. So, if you have a full-time day job but run a sideline business from your home office, make sure that if you do any work for your day job in your home office your employer wants you to do it at home (and you're not doing it there just for your own convenience).

> **Homegrown Tip**
> There's a lot of lobbying going on by home-based business associations and others to liberalize the home office deduction rules so that use of an office for necessary administrative work is reason enough to deduct home office expenses. Keep a watch on developments in Congress.

Did you build a nice little office over the toolshed? There's a special rule for *a separate structure* (that isn't attached to your house or residence) that you use in connection with your business. If you have a separate, freestanding structure on your property, you can treat it as a home office if you use it exclusively and regularly for your home office activity *even if it's not your principal place of business*. A separate structure may be a garage, a studio, a greenhouse, or even a barn.

Let's assume you have a separate structure. It doesn't have to be an actual office for you to deduct home office expenses. The separate structure doesn't even have to be the principal place of your business activity. It only has to be used *in connection with* your business.

For example, Angelo owns a landscaping business and uses his home office to schedule appointments and make up his monthly bills. The home office isn't his principal place of business since the most important activity of the business—mowing lawns and landscaping—is done at the customers' locations. But if he used a freestanding greenhouse on his property to grow flowers that he plants at his customers' locations, he could deduct the expenses of the greenhouse as a home office deduction. Or if he put up a freestanding garage to house his truck, mowers, and other equipment, Angelo could deduct the expenses of the garage.

Test 2

Take a deep breath. You've passed the first test. Now let's see if you can pass the second.

In this test you check to see if the other kids' toys spill over into your playpen. You must use your home office *exclusively and regularly* for business. Exclusive use of a home office means that it's used only for your business and not for personal purposes. So, if you equip a spare bedroom or a den with a computer, telephone, and perhaps a fax/modem for your business, you won't meet the exclusive use test if you also let your family use that room in the evenings to watch TV.

The exclusive use test doesn't mean you have to set aside an entire room for business. You can meet the exclusive use test as long as you clearly delineate a part of a room for business. It must be a *separately identifiable space,* but you don't have to build a wall around it. In one actual case a court allowed a piano teacher who used part of her living room for giving lessons on her grand piano to deduct the expenses related to that part of her living room (that part of her living room was a home office).

There are two important exceptions to the exclusive use requirement: day care businesses (explained later) and storage space for inventory or samples for a retail or whole business run from the home. If you use a portion of your home for either of these purposes, you can claim deductions even though you don't meet the exclusive use test.

Deducting What You're Already Paying for

Congratulations. You've passed the tests and can now figure your write-offs. (For the rest of you, sorry, you might as well jump to the next chapter.)

Figuring what you can write off isn't easy to do, mainly because it involves one of those notoriously well-written IRS forms. You figure your deductions on IRS Form 8829, which is reproduced on the next page.

If you follow the line-by-line instructions on the form you'll come up with your home office deduction. All the separate deductible expenses are added together and subtracted from your business income as one deduction called a home office deduction.

IRS Form 8829

Form **8829**		**Expenses for Business Use of Your Home**		OMB No. 1545-1266

Department of the Treasury
Internal Revenue Service (99)

➤ File only with Schedule C (Form 1040). Use a separate Form 8829 for each home you used for business during the year.
➤ See separate instructions.

1996

Attachment Sequence No. **66**

Name(s) of proprietor(s)

Your social security number

Part I   Part of Your Home Used for Business

1	Area used regularly and exclusively for business, regularly for day care, or for storage of inventory or product samples. See instructions	1	
2	Total area of home	2	
3	Divide line 1 by line 2. Enter the result as a percentage	3	%

• For day-care facilities not used exclusively for business, also complete lines 4–6.
• All others, skip lines 4–6 and enter the amount from line 3 on line 7.

4	Multiply days used for day care during year by hours used per day	4	hr.		
5	Total hours available for use during the year (366 days × 24 hours). See instructions	5	8,784 hr.		
6	Divide line 4 by line 5. Enter the result as a decimal amount	6			
7	Business percentage. For day-care facilities not used exclusively for business, multiply line 6 by line 3 (enter the result as a percentage). All others, enter the amount from line 3 ➤			7	%

Part II   Figure Your Allowable Deduction

8	Enter the amount from Schedule C, line 29, **plus** any net gain or (loss) derived from the business use of your home and shown on Schedule D or Form 4797. If more than one place of business, see instructions			8	

See instructions for columns (a) and (b) before completing lines 9–20.

		(a) Direct expenses	(b) Indirect expenses		
9	Casualty losses. See instructions	9			
10	Deductible mortgage interest. See instructions	10			
11	Real estate taxes. See instructions	11			
12	Add lines 9, 10, and 11	12			
13	Multiply line 12, column (b) by line 7		13		
14	Add line 12, column (a) and line 13			14	
15	Subtract line 14 from line 8. If zero or less, enter -0-			15	
16	Excess mortgage interest. See instructions	16			
17	Insurance	17			
18	Repairs and maintenance	18			
19	Utilities	19			
20	Other expenses. See instructions	20			
21	Add lines 16 through 20	21			
22	Multiply line 21, column (b) by line 7		22		
23	Carryover of operating expenses from 1995 Form 8829, line 41		23		
24	Add line 21 in column (a), line 22, and line 23			24	
25	Allowable operating expenses. Enter the **smaller** of line 15 or line 24			25	
26	Limit on excess casualty losses and depreciation. Subtract line 25 from line 15			26	
27	Excess casualty losses. See instructions	27			
28	Depreciation of your home from Part III below	28			
29	Carryover of excess casualty losses and depreciation from 1995 Form 8829, line 42	29			
30	Add lines 27 through 29			30	
31	Allowable excess casualty losses and depreciation. Enter the **smaller** of line 26 or line 30			31	
32	Add lines 14, 25, and 31			32	
33	Casualty loss portion, if any, from lines 14 and 31. Carry amount to **Form 4684**, Section B			33	
34	Allowable expenses for business use of your home. Subtract line 33 from line 32. Enter here and on Schedule C, line 30. If your home was used for more than one business, see instructions ➤			34	

Part III   Depreciation of Your Home

35	Enter the **smaller** of your home's adjusted basis or its fair market value. See instructions	35	
36	Value of land included on line 35	36	
37	Basis of building. Subtract line 36 from line 35	37	
38	Business basis of building. Multiply line 37 by line 7	38	
39	Depreciation percentage. See instructions	39	%
40	Depreciation allowable. Multiply line 38 by line 39. Enter here and on line 28 above. See instructions	40	

Part IV   Carryover of Unallowed Expenses to 1997

41	Operating expenses. Subtract line 25 from line 24. If less than zero, enter -0-	41	
42	Excess casualty losses and depreciation. Subtract line 31 from line 30. If less than zero, enter -0-	42	

For Paperwork Reduction Act Notice, see page 1 of separate instructions. ✪   Cat. No. 13232M   Form **8829** (1996)

Deductions: One at a Time

What expenses does having a home office entitle you to deduct? As you'll see from the form, the tax law separates expenses into two categories: direct expenses (fully deductible) and indirect expenses (partly deductible).

Just to give you some idea of what indirect expenses you can have, here's a list:

Business Buzzword
Direct expenses relate solely to the home office, such as wallpapering the office.

Indirect expenses relate to the entire home, such as your monthly rent.

➤ Deductible mortgage interest

➤ Real estate taxes

➤ Casualty and theft losses

➤ Depreciation

➤ Rent

➤ Utilities

➤ Insurance

➤ General repairs to the home (such as painting the outside of the house)

➤ Security systems

➤ Snow removal

➤ Cleaning

All of your direct expenses are deductible. But indirect expenses have a different rule. Only the part related to the business use of your home is deductible. How do you decide what this part is? You have to make something called an allocation. Technically this allocation can be made on any reasonable basis. Usually, though, you make an allocation on a square footage basis using this formula:

$$\frac{\text{Square footage of home office}}{\text{Square footage of home}} = \text{Percentage of business use}$$

Take an example. Say your home's 2,000 square feet. Your home office is 10 feet by 20 feet, or 200 square feet. Your home office use is 10% (200 square feet divided by 2,000 square feet).

If the rooms in your home are about the same size, you're allowed to allocate indirect expenses as a percentage of the number of rooms.

Example: You have five rooms in your home, all of which are about the same size. You use one room for business. You can allocate $\frac{1}{5}$ of your expenses, or 20%, for business.

After you determine your business percentage, you can apply this percentage against each indirect expense. So, if your business percentage is 10% and your real estate taxes for the year are $5,000, you treat $500 ($5,000 × 10%) as part of your home office deduction. The balance of your real estate taxes ($4,500) is claimed as a personal itemized deduction if you itemize your deductions.

Casualty losses can be either an indirect or direct expense, depending upon the property that's damaged or destroyed by a fire or storm. So, if just your home office is damaged in a hurricane and your insurance doesn't cover all of your loss, you can claim the entire loss as a direct expense. But if you have flooding throughout the first floor (which includes your home office), you treat the part of the loss relating to your business use of the home as an indirect expense.

If you rent rather than own your home, you can deduct the business portion of rent as an indirect expense. If you own your home, you can't deduct a fictitious rental amount (what you think someone would pay to rent your home office). Instead, you're allowed to claim *depreciation* on your home office.

In figuring depreciation, the deduction's based on the fair market value of the home at the time you first began to use a home office or the original price of the home, whichever's lower. You subtract the value of the land when you figure depreciation on your home because land is viewed as property that never wears out. The rules for figuring depreciation on your home office are explained later in this chapter.

In most cases, utility expenses for electricity, gas, oil, water, trash removal, and cleaning services are treated as indirect expenses. The business portion of these expenses is part of your home office deduction. You can't deduct the non-business part of utilities. However, you may be able to deduct a greater share of a utility expense if your business use warrants it. My home is heated by oil, but my home office, a later extension, has electric heat. I use a lot of electricity in the winter to heat the office I'm in for 10 or more hours each day, so I deduct that additional amount as a direct expense.

The business portion of your homeowner's insurance policy is an indirect expense. But if you also carry extra coverage under your homeowner's insurance just for your home office, then you can write off the additional coverage as a direct expense. Ask your insurance agent for a breakdown of what your premiums cover. You may carry special coverage for the computer or other equipment in your home office. Or suppose you add a

> **Business Buzzword**
>
> *Depreciation* is a deduction that allows you to write off the cost of property over a period of time related to the life of the property. In theory, the property's worn out or used up over the time it's depreciated. (Since land doesn't get used up or worn out like a building, land can't be depreciated.) In practice, property may even increase in value over the same period of time but you're still allowed to depreciate it.

> **Business Buzzword**
>
> *Fair market value* is how much a willing buyer would pay and a willing seller would accept if each knew all the facts and neither had a gun to his head (neither being under any compulsion to act, to you lawyers).

personal liability rider to your homeowner's policy to cover you if a client takes a dive on your front steps. These additional types of coverage are deductible as direct expenses.

Repairs can be direct or indirect expenses. The cost of repairing the boiler for your home is an indirect expense. If you repair a window in your home office it's a direct expense.

A home security system for your entire home generally involves two types of costs. There's the cost of the system itself. You may be able to depreciate the cost of the system related to your home office. And there are also the monthly monitoring fees. A portion of these fees is an indirect expense.

The Educated Entrepreneur

Special rules apply to deductions for your office telephones. Telephone expenses *aren't* part of your home office deduction. The cost of business phone use is separately deductible. But tax law doesn't let you deduct the *basic* monthly service charge for the *first* telephone line to your home as a business expense. You can deduct business-related long-distance calls or call answering, call waiting, call forwarding, or any other special services. You can also deduct the entire phone bill of a second phone line you use just for business, including dedicated fax or modem lines.

Certain expenses can't be deducted even though they relate to your home office. Tax law doesn't let you deduct a portion of the cost of landscaping and lawn care as an indirect expense even though it enhances the appearance of your home and home office.

Special Rules for Day Care Businesses

If you're in the business of watching children, the elderly, or people with disabilities in your home, then you figure your home office deductions differently from all other businesses. Even the IRS realizes that once you let small kids into a building, they're everywhere; you can't confine them to one corner of one room anymore than you can make them eat Brussels sprouts. You don't have to meet the *exclusive use test* described earlier.

This isn't child's play. It's very complicated to figure your deduction. The best thing to do is follow the line-by-line instructions for Form 8829.

Just to give you an idea of the calculations you'll have to make, here's what you've got to do. Allocate the expenses of using your home for business (between business and personal use) by using two special formulas:

Formula #1: $\dfrac{\text{Total square footage used regularly for day care use}}{\text{Total square footage of your home}}$

Formula #2: $\dfrac{\text{Total hours you run your business}}{\text{8,760 hours (total hours in the year)}}$

Here's an example for direct expenses (and you'll use only Formula #2). You run a day care center in your basement, which is 1,500 square feet. Your entire home is 3,000 square feet. You run your business 12 hours each day, five days a week all year (except you take two weeks off for vacation if you're lucky).

For purposes of deducting your direct expenses, apply Formula #2 to your total costs. In your case, the total hours you run your business is 3,000 (12 hours × 250 days [5 days/week × 50 weeks]). Dividing this by the total hours in the year, 8,760, means that you use your space 34.25% of the time for business. So you deduct 34.25% of your direct expenses.

Home Hazard
To be treated as a day care business you must meet state licensing requirements. If you haven't already got one, apply for a license, certificate, registration, or approval as a day care center or as a family group day care home (whatever the law in your state requires).

Here's an example for indirect expenses (and you'll use both formulas). Applying Formula #1, you figure that you use 50% of your home for business (1,500 square feet used for day care divided by 3,000 square feet). So 50% of 34.25%, or 17.13%, of indirect expenses are deductible.

It's obvious that you can use a family room, living room, or basement area for your business. But sometimes you might also use other parts of your home for business. Maybe you've got a laundry room that you use to wash sheets or children's clothes as part of your business. Maybe you have a storage area or garage where you keep toys and equipment. Remember to add in these areas when you figure your write-offs.

Deductions: They're Not for Everybody

By now, if you're still reading this chapter, you've met the home office deduction tests and have figured out your write-offs. You'd think you'd be finished already. Not even close. Now you have to see if there's any limit that may keep you from using your deduction.

Yes, even though you paid for a legitimate home office expense, you may not get any benefit from it for tax purposes. This is because the home office deductions you claim can't be more than your *gross income* from the home office activity.

Business Buzzword

Gross income for purposes of your home office deduction means revenues from your business reduced by expenses that are not attributable to business use of your home, like salary of an employee or office supplies.

ARGH@#! **Home Hazard**

If you've incorporated your business and you lease part of your home to your corporation, your corporation can deduct the cost of the lease. But you can't deduct any expenses related to the home office other than your typical homeowner expenses—mortgage interest and real estate taxes (if you itemize deductions).

If you run your primary business from home and earn a living from it, this gross income limit is probably no problem. As long as the business makes money, deductions are fine with Uncle Sam. But if you have a bad year, just when you need your deductions, they may be limited. The same is true if you're just starting out in business or if your home-based business is only a sideline.

If you earn less (gross income) from your home office business activity than you spent (your total business expenses), your home office deduction is limited for the year. You can deduct the business portion of the expenses you would have deducted without a home office— mortgage interest, real estate taxes, and casualty and theft losses—regardless of the amount of your business income. But insurance, utilities, repairs, and depreciation, items that wouldn't be deductible if you weren't in business, can only be claimed if you have *gross income* from your business to offset it.

Head spinning? Well, I have good news. As a practical matter you don't really have to understand this gross income limitation. It's all worked out for you on IRS Form 8829. When you go through each line of the form, the limitation is automatically applied for you.

If you made too little this year to offset all your home office deductions, you don't lose them entirely. Instead you can carry forward the unused portion. The carry-forward can be deducted down the road if your *same* home business has gross income to offset it.

There's more good news. There's no time limit on the carryforward. You can claim the carryforward even if you move to another state, as long as there's gross income from the same activity to offset the deduction. Be sure to keep great records to back up your carryforward deduction.

Adding on Space, Taking off Depreciation

Suppose you own your home but your existing space just isn't big enough for a family and a budding business? Maybe, if you have the money or can borrow it, you can remodel—converting a garage or unfinished basement or attic into the perfect home office. Or maybe you decide to enclose a screened-in porch and make it into your headquarters. Or maybe you expand an existing room for your entrepreneurial endeavors. If you do undertake these construction projects you can't just deduct your costs in the year you pay them. You can only write off your costs (recover them) through depreciation.

Appreciating Depreciation

Figuring depreciation on your home office involves several steps:

Step 1: Start with your home's *basis* for depreciation. This is the lower of your *adjusted basis* or the *fair market value* of the home on the date you start to use your home office.

Step 2: Subtract the value of the land on which the home sits.

Step 3: Apply the home office percentage representing the part of the business use of your home. This is the percentage you used earlier to figure the deductible part of indirect expenses. This will give you the depreciation basis.

Step 4: Apply the depreciation percentage from the table below. Take the percentage for the month that you begin to use your home for business.

> **Business Buzzword**
> *Basis* is how much you paid for property (called *cost basis*) or some other amount viewed as your investment in the property.
>
> *Adjusted basis* is your original basis increased by permanent additions or improvements to the property and decreased by depreciation you've already taken.

Example: You own a condo that cost you $200,000. In October 1997 you begin to use 10% of the space for business. On this date your home's worth $225,000. (Assume the value of the land is zero.) You start with the lower of your cost or fair market value. Here your cost ($200,000) is less than the home's value ($225,000). Since 10% of the home is used for business, 10% of $200,000, or $20,000, is your depreciation basis. Apply the depreciation percentage from the following table. Since the home began to be used for business in October, 1.177% of $20,000, or $235.40, is your depreciation deduction for 1997. In 1998 and every year after that until the home office is fully depreciated (it takes 39 more years for this), the annual depreciation deduction is $512.80 ($20,000 × 2.564% taken from the following table). A final write-off applies in the 40th year.

> **Home Hazard**
> Depreciating your home office can come back to haunt you when you sell your home. Depreciation reduces your basis in your home, which in turn increases your profit. You may or may not be able to use special tax breaks to offset the profit related to your home office. Planning before you sell your home can let you convert your home office back into personal living space so you'll get all the tax breaks.

Depreciation Table

Year	Jan	Feb	Mar	Apr	May	Jun	Jul	Aug	Sept	Oct	Nov	Dec
1	2.461	2.247	2.033	1.819	1.605	1.391	1.177	0.963	0.749	0.535	0.321	0.107
2–39	2.564	2.564	2.564	2.564	2.564	2.564	2.564	2.564	2.564	2.564	2.564	2.564
40	0.107	0.321	0.535	0.749	0.963	1.177	1.391	1.605	1.819	2.033	2.247	2.461

Special Breaks for Helping Special People

Business Buzzword

Tax credit is a reduction of your income taxes on a dollar-for-dollar basis. Unlike a deduction, which reduces your income before you figure your tax, you take the credit after figuring your tax. Say you spend $500 to put in a ramp to your home office. If you deduct the cost (and are in a 31% tax bracket) the deduction's worth $155 (31% of $500). But if you take a 50% credit for this expense, it's worth $250 (50% of $500), the actual amount of tax savings.

Having people come to your home for business creates potential liability for you. What if they fall on your steps or slip in your hallway? Insurance can protect you, but why not avoid the hazards in the first place and add to your customers' convenience by making your home safer? If you put in ramps or handrails or make other modifications to your home so that business visitors who are elderly or have disabilities have an easier time of it, you can recoup your costs more quickly than using normal depreciation. You have two choices:

➤ You can deduct up to $15,000 when you make changes in your business that will help out the elderly or people with disabilities.

➤ As a small business owner, if you spend at least $250 (but not more than $10,250) you can claim a *tax credit* of 50% of your costs.

The Least You Need to Know

➤ Make sure you meet the tax law tests for a home office before you deduct your office expenses.

➤ Special tax rules apply to day care businesses.

➤ You can claim depreciation for adding on to your home for business.

➤ There are special tax breaks for making your home more accessible to the elderly and people with disabilities.

Part 6
Up Close and Personal Issues

In this part of the book, you'll see what goes on behind closed doors when you work at home. You may have gotten rid of your lousy boss or back-biting coworkers, but home businesspeople have their own challenges: Feelings of isolation and loneliness and the tendency to become a stay-at-home workaholic can be real and hard to deal with. In the chapters that follow, you'll learn about staying connected with the outside world and adjusting to the style of the small home business.

And how do you keep the laundry from spilling over onto your desk and your business proposal from wandering into the kid's room? You'll find out in the chapters that follow how to separate business from pleasure by keeping your family life and your home office in their proper places. Organizing your new life is vital, and organization, the key to any successful business, is especially important for home business owners with limited space and time.

Finally, after all is said and done, you may be so successful your home business just won't fit in the house anymore. You'll see how to recognize that moment and how to make the move out of the home with the least headaches and most rewards.

Separating Business from Pleasure

One of the things that makes working from home so great—having family and business all in one place—is also the very thing that makes a home-based business so difficult to run. Your personal life spills over into your business and vice versa.

This scenario is all too common: A suburbanite with two small children dreams of starting her own business. Her dream turns into a nightmare when she can't figure out how to run her business in between her children's naps, school bus schedules, and other family demands. Then there's the young professional couple that ends up at the marriage counselor because the workaholic husband won't stop answering his business calls in the home office at all hours. There's no such thing as getting away from the office anymore. A home businessperson who doesn't learn how to separate business from family life often can't make the business succeed.

In this chapter you'll learn to identify some key personal issues you'll have to sort out in order to be able to run your business from home. As you'll see, there are many different solutions. You can probably think of your own solutions—if you know what to look for.

Working Just Enough, or Not Too Much

How much time do you want to spend each day on your home-based business? This may seem like a simple question, but you may surprise yourself by not knowing the answer.

You may just say, "I'll spend as much time as I can." If you do, you'll find that there's no time; all of your time is eaten up by looking after your children, doing laundry, grocery shopping, making trips to the cleaners, or just talking to neighbors. Or maybe you're the type who finds you can't remember your kids' names and you've forgotten that Sunday is supposed to be a day of rest. Many home businesspeople work twelve hours, seven days a week without even realizing it.

You need structure. You need to be able to rise above the barking dogs and crying babies and get down to work. But you also need to know when to turn off the light and stop working.

The Educated Entrepreneur

Even if you work full-time, you'll still have to learn to say no to demands made on your time (demands not placed on those who work away from home). Because you work from home, some people simply don't take you seriously. Sure, you work, but they think that's only a sideline—something to do when you don't have anything else going on. They ask and expect you to be able to volunteer for the PTA in the same way as nonworking parents. Or neighbors and relatives may ask you to do favors that take up your time as if you had nothing better to do. If you want to do these extra jobs, great, try to fit them in. But if you don't have the time, learn to just say no.

Set a Schedule to Get Work Done

One of the joys of working from home is that you can do what you want, when you want to. But if you don't fix a schedule, you may never find the time to do any work. Flexibility means taking responsibility for setting up a work schedule. This schedule doesn't have to be rigid. But you have to set priorities. When you need to return a client's call, you may have to put off starting dinner.

Make a tentative work schedule to get you going. In blocking out your time, set specific times for the personal things you have to do, like picking your child up from school or driving your spouse to the train station. In scheduling, you may need to adjust for seasons. If your children are small and off for the summer, you may not be able to put in as many hours as you'd like to for business during that season. Don't try to schedule work when, as a practical matter, you know you won't be able to get to it.

Also block out the time you think you'll have to spend on personal matters. If your children are young but in school, maybe you'll work only during their school hours and be with them once they return from school. Or maybe you'll find you can squeeze in extra hours after they've gone to sleep.

Use the worksheet below to plan your work schedule. It may be a good idea to use a pencil, rather than a pen, since your schedule's bound to change. You may be able to spend some time on the weekends with your business. If you do—as is the case with nearly 35% of all home-based business owners, including myself, according to an AT&T Home Business Re- source Study—then add Saturday and Sunday to your schedule.

> **Homegrown Tip**
>
> When I first started working at home I was concerned with my ability to discipline myself. I knew that the dirty dishes sat waiting for me and the TV called. I thought that if I dressed for business, putting on a business suit, panty hose, and heels, I'd feel more like working. This was all it took for me to get started. After just a few days, I'd already established a routine and didn't need the formal clothes—a psychological tool— to make it work. Jeans and a T- shirt were more comfortable and I got just as much work done.

Work Schedule

	Monday	Tuesday	Wednesday	Thursday	Friday
7 A.M.	_____	_____	_____	_____	_____
8 A.M.	_____	_____	_____	_____	_____
9 A.M.	_____	_____	_____	_____	_____
10 A.M.	_____	_____	_____	_____	_____
11 A.M.	_____	_____	_____	_____	_____
Noon	_____	_____	_____	_____	_____
1 P.M.	_____	_____	_____	_____	_____
2 P.M.	_____	_____	_____	_____	_____
3 P.M.	_____	_____	_____	_____	_____
4 P.M.	_____	_____	_____	_____	_____
5 P.M.	_____	_____	_____	_____	_____

continues

continued

6 P.M.	_____	_____	_____	_____	_____
7 P.M.	_____	_____	_____	_____	_____
8 P.M.	_____	_____	_____	_____	_____
9 P.M.	_____	_____	_____	_____	_____

Of course, what you start with may not be what you end up with. As your business grows, it may take up more of your time—something that you'll just have to work into a new schedule.

When to Call It a Day

Homegrown Tip
In setting up a schedule, be sure to take your personal work habits into account. If you're a morning person, don't plan to work late into the night because you'll never do it or you won't do it well. My neighbor's a talented computer programmer and a night owl. I can see the light on in his home office almost all night, but that's just not for me. Know your personal preference and schedule your work accordingly.

Those same souls who used to come home late from the office can now be seen in their home office late into the night. After all, they now live in their office. Work becomes the prime focus of their day—and night.

When you work at home, there's no division between the office and home so there's a tendency to work just about all the time. Home-based business workaholics have to learn when to quit.

Even if you're not a type-A personality who loves to work all the time, you may have a realistic belief that you can't afford to turn down any work that comes your way. You don't yet have the security of a well-established business to say no, even if it means working longer hours than you'd like to.

This pattern of working all the time isn't good. First of all, it's generally not healthy to work so many hours. Second, if you're working all the time, you're not taking care of your personal responsibilities. And third, most important, your family may resent all the attention you're giving to your business at their expense. They may be able to understand 9 to 5, Monday through Friday. But 7 to 7, seven days a week may be a little hard to swallow. Oddly enough, the answer to overwork is the same as the answer to procrastination, with slight twists: Set a schedule, and keep to it.

If you have a tendency to go overboard in your work hours, having a fixed schedule will help you set limits. Planning your personal activities—scheduling them in much the same way as you would your business tasks—will also help limit your work hours. Each week make a list of the personal things you want to accomplish and then schedule them into your weekly appointment book or other planner.

Maybe you don't need someone to tell you how to spend your leisure time. But if you're like me, work's like a magnet drawing you in. You'll need to schedule time off. Use some of the personal things listed below to give you ideas of what you might want to plan for:

Personal Goals for the Week:

Read a book   _____

Exercise three times
(30 minutes each time)   _____

Do volunteer work   _____

Visit a friend or neighbor   _____

Go shopping   _____

Hear a lecture or seminar   _____

See a movie or show   _____

Sleep (naps or extra hours)   _____

> **Homegrown Tip**
>
> In running a business you have to keep appointments, return phone calls, and more. You can't afford to overlook things. You won't if you write it all down. Use a daily organizer by Franklin Planners (800-869-1776), Daytimers (800-225-5005), or Filofax (800-345-6798), or even a computer calendar to keep track of your appointments and other time commitments.

The Educated Entrepreneur

Working from home gives you the chance to do what you want when you want to. According to one source, 85% of those working from home take breaks during their business day. How do they spend their "off" hours? You name it—running errands, doing housework, or even watching the tube.

As you begin to work at home, some of these planning tips may become second nature. After a while you won't formally have to set aside time for your personal life, it'll become automatic. But in the beginning, the exercise of planning for personal time may be important so you'll have the confidence that you'll be able to fit everything in.

Creating More Time

Whether you find it hard to get to work or hard to extinguish the midnight oil, you could probably do with more time. Sure, there are only 24 hours in a day. But you can convert more of those hours for business if you need to and know how:

➤ Hire help. The days of trying to be Superman or Superwoman are over. Accept it. You can't do it all yourself. You may need help—in your personal life or in your business. Hire someone to clean your house (a job you'd normally do) so that you can spend more time on your business. If the money you earn from your business is more than you'd have to pay for cleaning help, go for it. The same's true for help in your business. Consider hiring clerical help or farming out work to contractors to create more time for you. Even your child care responsibility may have to be delegated. If your children are small and can't be left on their own, you may want to hire a babysitter or ask a willing relative for help.

When I started out at home, I thought I'd be able to care for my one-year-old while running my practice. After only a few days it became apparent to me that irregular nap schedules simply didn't give me enough time for business. I had to bring my daughter to a neighbor's home for a few hours each day to give me the time I needed to concentrate only on work. As my daughter got older and didn't need constant supervision, I didn't need the outside child care.

➤ Use machines. One of the key benefits to machines is saving time. Machines can do the work faster than it takes to do it by hand. If you usually keep your books by hand, automate. Putting your financial information on the computer may save you hours and hours over the course of a year—time you can better use for something else.

Keeping the Family and Business Separate

With your family and your business under the same roof, your family life can easily spill over into your business operations. How do you set boundaries—both psychological and physical? You don't have to build a brick wall between your office and your kitchen; there are less drastic measures you can take.

Teach Your Family and Friends Restraint

If you live alone, there's no one at home to barge in on you. But if you have a spouse, a significant other, children, or a roommate, telling them not to interrupt you is like telling someone not to think of an elephant. Suddenly they're inventing reasons why they've just got to walk in on you. Don't be too hard on them; they probably just miss you. But once you've decided that you want to work between the hours of 1 and 5, you've got to stick to your guns. You have to train them to leave you alone for four hours.

Sound simple? Well, it's not. It means telling them over and over again to hold their questions and solve their own problems while you're working. You'll probably find it's easier to get your kids to keep quiet than to get your spouse to leave you alone. After all, the kids are used to being disciplined, but your poor spouse thinks he has a say in what goes on under your roof.

> **Homegrown Tip**
>
> Keep your sense of humor. No matter how hard you try, it may be impossible to bar your family from your office without a steel door. So when they barge in and interrupt, gently remind them that you need to be left alone—and laugh it off.

Will a closed door stop people from bothering you? Probably not. Will a "Do Not Disturb" sign on the door keep your family out? In my experience, probably not. And although heavy artillery might work, it's probably out of the question. In short, it's up to you to adapt. You have to be the one to set the limits—but be ready to smile when your family crosses the line.

People in your home aren't your only problem. Friends who were used to having their morning coffee with you before you started your business also have to be taught about limits. Tell them that coffee's out and that they have to call after business hours to chat because you don't want to be interrupted during your work time. Of course, you'd probably like an occasional call to break up your business routine. Better that you're the one who makes it when it's convenient for you to talk.

Separate Business from Pleasure—Physically

Just as Virginia Woolf needed a room of her own to write, in the best of all possible home-based business situations you get a separate room with a door. But that's not always possible. You may be forced to share space with your family. When you work on the kitchen table and your son wants to make a peanut butter sandwich there, it's hard to go on working. There's only so much space.

But space isn't your only problem. There are also the psychological intrusions on your concentration. Working in the kitchen, for example, may be a constant reminder of the fancy dinners you're no longer preparing.

It's a good idea to set aside a separate space for business if you can—one that won't be used by your family for other things. If you use part of a family room as your office, try to put your desk in a corner of the room that's away from toys and TV. Keep your supplies close at hand and separate from your family's games and baseball gloves. You don't want your kids poking around your paper clips looking for the pieces to their Monopoly board.

273

Review Chapter 13 to learn about ways to physically set up your office for maximum productivity.

Taking Time for Time Off

Remember those days when you got paid for a two-week vacation? Certainly it was one of the perks of a job. Now you can take all the time off you want—or can you? One of the hardest things for many home-based business owners to do is to leave the office for vacation. There's no one telling you that you can't. But there's concern about what'll happen to the business while you're away. Still, even a home-based business owner needs time off once in a while. Here are some ideas for fitting a vacation in your busy schedule:

➤ Schedule vacations for your slow season. As your business develops you'll be able to see what times of the year are busier than others. Hannah, a financial writer, found out after observing her writing assignments for several years that she was busiest in the summer and fall, slower in the spring, and slowest in the winter. It was clear that migrating to Florida in January was the way to go.

➤ Take long weekends. If a week away would undermine your business, what about a three- or four-day weekend once in a while? Clients and customers are out of communication with you for no more than a day or two instead of a full week.

➤ Hire help to watch the office. While you're away, you can have someone else look after your business. You don't necessarily need someone to run your business as you would; you only need someone to field calls, schedule appointments, and handle simple problems that may come up with customers, clients, or suppliers.

The Educated Entrepreneur

Hiring someone to look after your home-based business while you're away on vacation can have added benefits besides those to your business. Having someone else in your home every day is a deterrent to robbers. The lights are on. The mail and newspapers get picked up instead of being left in the box or on the driveway. The home looks occupied. You can even have the person you hire act as both business employee and house sitter—watching your dog and watering your plants. Hiring someone to look after your business and your home will give you peace of mind while you're away.

The Least You Need to Know

➤ It takes planning to make sure that business responsibilities aren't overshadowed by your personal life.

➤ Make time for personal things so that your in-office time doesn't become all-consuming.

➤ Create more business hours in your day by hiring help and using machines.

➤ Don't fail to schedule vacations away from home and your home office.

HELLO, RESEARCH AND DEVELOPMENT SPEAKING...

Chapter 24

Image Is What the Public Sees

In This Chapter

➤ Getting organized

➤ Developing your professional image

➤ Creating the illusion of a large organization

In planning a wedding, you would probably decide to use professional photographers (you wouldn't want to take the chance that your Uncle Jim's snapshots might not come out). Whatever kind of business you own, the public wants to deal with a professional. They want to know they're in good hands and can trust your work or your product. But working at home poses unique problems in presenting a professional image to the public. Barking dogs, crying children, or the washing machine aren't exactly conducive to the aura of a conventional office. And, as with any business, you face the problem of physical dishevelment: mounds of paper, stacks of samples, overflowing wastebaskets. This is an issue more critical to the home-based business owner because of your space limitations: You don't have a conference room to entertain clients away from the clutter of day-to-day work.

In this chapter you'll learn how to get organized. And you'll discover ways in which you can create a unique and professional image for your business.

Getting Your Act Together

Some people fold towels and straighten pictures like demons, they can't help themselves. Others are more like Charles Schultz's cartoon character Pigpen. They have to make a conscious effort just to stay visible under the papers that pile up around them. Organization is important in presenting a businesslike image to the public. Just because you work from home, you still don't want to have to tell a client who calls to "wait a minute while I find a pen and paper"—a statement that typically isn't heard in a conventional office where pens and paper are as ubiquitous as stale coffee.

One good reason to get organized is to be able to put your hands on information and materials when you need them. If, for example, your desk looks like a junkyard on speed, you'll waste time trying to put your hands on correspondence or other papers that you need.

The Educated Entrepreneur

Paper, paper everywhere (but not the paper you need). Estimates show that the average person (which includes those who work both in or out of the home) spends as much as six weeks out of every year searching for papers that have been mislaid, misfiled, or buried under other papers. Wouldn't you rather spend those six weeks lying on a beach somewhere?

What needs to be organized? Everything. You should organize your time, which you've already seen how to do. But you should also organize your files and your supplies.

Become a Paper Pusher

Remember just a decade ago, when the personal computer came into its own, there was a prediction about a "paperless society"? Well, they also predicted zero national debt, and you know what became of that. Today we handle more paper than ever. But where do you put it all when you work from a home office?

There are only three places where your papers belong—your desk, your files, and the garbage. You'll have to learn to process mail and the documents you create—getting it all from your desk into your files. And, most important, you'll need to be able to trash unnecessary papers.

➤ Your desk. Set up a priority system for your desk. Use the three tray method to process your papers. When mail comes in, it goes into your "in" tray or basket. From here there are only two places for mail to go—into your next tray, "pending," or into the garbage can. Your "pending" tray or basket should be used for mail you have to answer or act on. Once you've done what you have to do, the completed papers should be placed in your third tray or basket, marked "out." The "out" tray is only a temporary holding pen for papers that will be saved permanently in your files.

The Educated Entrepreneur

Before you throw out paper, consider recycling. If you use mounds of computer paper like I do for drafts of proposals or letters, recycle the papers as drawing materials for your children. Or cut the paper up and use the reverse side for sketching rough drafts and as scrap paper for notes. And before you dispose of papers, check with your city or town's recycling rules. Many towns now require "office paper" to be disposed of separately from household garbage or newspapers.

➤ Your files. Set up a file system. Most people need at least two types of files—current files and dead files. Current files contain papers relating to projects you're working on now. These files can also contain materials relating to current projects (like reference materials or brochures). These files should be close at hand—in or on your desk. Dead files are just that: storage for projects you've completed and other material you want to save but won't need to look at for some time, if ever. You should keep all tax-related records and receipts in your dead files to back up tax deductions for past years. Label your files so you (or whoever works for you) can find them easily. How you label your files is an individual choice. You may want to create major categories and then use subcategories for separate files. Try using color-coded labels to quickly identify the categories in which the individual files belong.

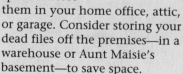

Homegrown Tip
As your dead files grow you may run out of space to store them in your home office, attic, or garage. Consider storing your dead files off the premises—in a warehouse or Aunt Maisie's basement—to save space.

Put in Time to Organize

Organization takes time. Crazy as it sounds, you need to schedule time in order to save time. Develop a daily routine to process your paperwork—read your mail, answer letters, throw away unnecessary paper, and file papers you want to save.

Setting up a routine will let you do several things:

➤ Avoid procrastination. Processing papers can be boring, and many people, under-standably, put off unpleasant tasks. But procrastination in this case just leads to more paperwork buildup, making the job that much more unpleasant. By having a set time each day to tackle the necessary but unpleasant job of going through papers, you can be sure the job will get done.

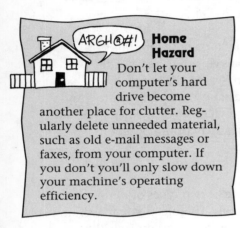

Home Hazard

Don't let your computer's hard drive become another place for clutter. Regularly delete unneeded material, such as old e-mail messages or faxes, from your computer. If you don't you'll only slow down your machine's operating efficiency.

➤ Stay on top of your work. By setting a daily time to dive into paperwork, you can make sure that impor-tant matters will get the immediate attention they deserve. Not answering that letter from your major client because it got lost in a pile could cost you big-time.

➤ Change your habits. You can do away with some paper and the need to file it if you change your work habits. Instead of printing everything from your computer, simply save it to your hard disk or a floppy. If you have an internal fax, you don't have to print out messages before you send them—just send them (with the messages stored on your hard disk).

Homegrown Tip

Use the Internet to catch up on your reading. Instead of saving articles in your file cabinet, you'll save space by jotting down only the name of the article and the magazine it appears in. Then track it down on the Internet when you're ready to read it.

➤ Read your reading matter. If you take the time to read up on trends or news affecting your business in trade publications, magazines, and newspapers—something that's certainly a good idea to do—be sure you don't simply collect the articles and never read them. Plan a time each day or each week when you go through your collection of reading matter. Kathy, a real-estate agent I know, reads her stack of maga-zines while walking each day on the treadmill at the health club. You may find it helpful to clip out articles of interest and discard the rest of the publica-tion. If you want to save any articles for future reference—something I find very helpful—be sure to file them away in appropriately labeled files.

The Supply Cabinet's Full

Paper clips, rubber bands, and staples—you can always find room for these supplies. But if your business uses a lot of paper, like mine, decide where you're going to put it all.

If your business uses more than just office supplies—cleaning supplies for your cleaning business or electrical supplies for your electrical contracting business, for example— storage can become even more of a problem. Put in shelves in your garage or basement to store your supplies. Make sure that the spot you've picked won't drip oil on your Lysol or melt your electrical cables.

Creating a Professional Image

Just because you work from home doesn't mean you're a slouch. You're just as professional as a business owner who pays rent on an outside office. But you need to let your customers, suppliers, and everybody else know it.

A professional image is part of your marketing—it establishes confidence in you and your business. Everything your business does—the letters it sends, the business cards you pass out at a party—reflects on you. Sloppy typing may make people think that your business operations are sloppy, too. Smartly styled materials say, "I'm a professional, I pay attention to details, and I can handle your job."

> **Homegrown Tip**
>
> Where space is limited, store only one extra copier toner, printer ribbon, and carton of paper. When you use your extra toner, it's time to order a replacement. With Staples® and many other office supply stores giving overnight delivery, there's no need to overstock your supply cabinet.

Screening Out Barking Dogs, Crying Babies, and Other Background Noises

Working from home has distractions that aren't ordinarily found in offices. Barking dogs, the patter of little feet, the guy running a lawn mower next door, or other noises may be heard by clients or customers over the telephone. Depending on the nature of your business, these noises can be, at best, a real distraction. At worst, they'll be a serious annoyance to the guy at the other end of the line.

Figure out how you plan to handle these noises. It may be as easy as closing a door. Or you may find that you want to limit your telephone hours to times when these noises are at a minimum in your home—when your children are at school and the neighbor is taking a break from cutting his grass.

A related issue to noise during phone calls is the question of who picks up your telephone. If you use a personal phone line for business so your spouse and children have access to it, your family may rub verbal shoulders with your clients, customers, and suppliers. In many cases this is not a problem. For example, I've regularly dealt with a few different publishers for many years, and I let my children take messages from them even when they were very young (the children, not the publishers). My editors came to know my children and were used to leaving messages with them. This arrangement didn't negatively impact my business relationship at all.

But for some businesses, this casual interaction between family and business may be disastrous. In this case, it's important to separate your family life from your business communications. Limit business calls—in and out—to a separate phone line. Review Chapter 14 to think again about ways to use your telephone most effectively for business.

What's Your Business Personality?

How do you want the public to see you—conservative, creative, high-powered? You can be informal without being unprofessional. Whatever characteristic you choose, it's your business personality. It should shine through in everything you do—your attitude and your written communications.

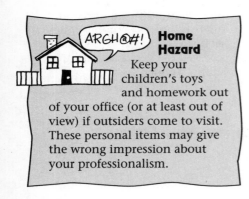

Home Hazard

Keep your children's toys and homework out of your office (or at least out of view) if outsiders come to visit. These personal items may give the wrong impression about your professionalism.

➤ Create something that can be identified with you and you alone. All the big companies do it. "Big Blue" is a well-known alter ego of IBM. Everybody recognizes the red Coca-Cola logo. Use a consistent logo or color on all your written material—letterheads, business cards, envelopes, invoices.

➤ Answer the phone in a consistent way. Decide how you want to impress the caller. Some choose to answer with the number to let the caller know she has reached the right place. Or you may want to answer with the name of your company. Remember that the phone can be the first impression of you for many clients or customers, so make it a good one.

➤ Decorate your office for success. If you regularly bring clients or customers to your home office, make sure it conveys the impression you're trying to establish—professional and businesslike. Hannah, an art appraiser, spent big bucks decorating her home office, with its adjoining powder room, in rich wood built-ins, expensive carpeting, shades, and wallpaper. Because she regularly dealt with a wealthy clientele, she needed a place to match her business.

When Is a Home Business Not a Home Business?

In the not-too-distant past, many home-based business owners tried to camouflage the fact that they didn't have fancy offices at posh addresses. They never divulged the fact that they worked from home. Today, with the growing acceptance of home-based business, this dodge is, by and large, no longer necessary. On the contrary, having a home-based business is (almost) a thing to be proud of.

Still, there are circumstances in which you may need or want to take your business out of the house to function efficiently. You may want to take advantage of a "front" office, a business address other than your own home, for several important reasons.

Creating a "Front" Office

You may live in Podunk, Massachusetts, and think a Boston address would be classier. If you want to use an address that has more national recognition, there are companies that can provide you with an address. Louis sold a beauty cream of his own formula from his home, which was located in a less-than-desirable neighborhood. He wanted to put a glamorous face on the business for marketing purposes. He decided to use an address of Mail Boxes Etc.® in a well-known major business area to create the impression of a prosperous business. He even got a suite number so it looked to outsiders like he had a business located in an office building. When he had to meet with business contacts, he met at local restaurants over breakfast or lunch. Customers and suppliers never had reason to come to his home.

One of the problems that some small business owners face is a prejudice against one-person operations. Clients or customers may not feel secure that there's any backup for you in case of emergency (and there may not be, but you don't want them thinking that!). It may be necessary to create the appearance that there are others working with you who can fill in for you. It's not a question of lying to clients and customers about your business. Rather it's a matter of creating the confidence in them that you've got things covered. You can do this, for example, with automated telephone messaging that identifies separate departments in your business (shipping, marketing, and so on).

Ding-Dong: UPS!

If you get an occasional delivery, it's easy to arrange to be home to receive it. You might even be able to make arrangements with neighbors to help. Depending on where you live, you don't even have to be home to get deliveries—packages can simply be left on your doorstep (if you know they're safe). Leave instructions for Federal Express to leave packages without your signature.

But a home-based business may be no place to send and receive a lot of packages on a regular basis. If you run an inventory business, frequent deliveries may pose a problem. Neighbors may object to the constant UPS trucks or other delivery services at your door. You may find that using a mail receiving service (check your Yellow Pages under this listing) can simplify this aspect of your business as it has for many home-based business owners. You don't have to be home to receive deliveries. You can also take advantage of other services at a mail receiving service. For example, Mail Boxes Etc. offers packaging and shipping. Alternatively, you can use a post office box number for receiving deliveries. A local mail receiving service may have better hours for you than the post office. For example, many Mail Boxes Etc. locations are open until 9 P.M. six days a week.

> **Business Buzzword**
> A *fulfillment company* is a business that takes and processes orders for you. For a flat fee (a charge per item) it will take an order and send out the merchandise to the customer. It generally can accept payment via charge cards.

Another option for some types of inventory-based businesses concerned with both incoming and outgoing packages is to use a fulfillment company.

A fulfillment company was the right solution for Eddie, a home-based business owner who wanted to broaden his market to sell a pain-relieving cream to Hispanic customers. Eddie couldn't even order food in a Mexican restaurant, but he was able to find a fulfillment company with Spanish-speaking operators who could take and process orders. Because of his foreign language limits, he would have been unable to tap this segment of the market without the fulfillment company. And his merchandise was shipped from his supplier directly to the fulfillment company. This eliminated the need to store the cartons of cream in his home.

The Least You Need to Know

➤ Organize your paperwork to save time and to help create a professional image.

➤ Stay on top of reading matter—scan material of interest and discard the rest.

➤ Keep your personal background noise out of earshot from your business telephone line.

➤ Create a professional identity with your attitude, stationery, and office appearance.

➤ Use off-site locations to enhance your business operations.

Chapter 25

Working Alone and Loving It

In This Chapter

➤ Replacing face-to-face socializing when working alone at home

➤ Getting out of the office for business and pleasure

➤ Networking for social and business connections

➤ Joining trade associations for connections to products and services

For most home-based business owners, working at home means working all alone. If you used to have a job in Corporate America, working alone at home is quite a change for you in many ways. Besides the nature of your work, your working social life just shrunk by about 100%. There may be no one to talk to, face to face. The only sound of a human voice you hear all day may be your three-year-old. You may actually begin to miss those meetings you always complained about.

But working alone doesn't have to be lonely. There are many ways to connect to the outside world. You may even come to love, as I do, the solitude and increased productivity that working alone can give you.

In this chapter you'll see how to handle being alone all day. You'll see how you can connect with other people in your area—many of whom may be working out of their homes just like you. And you'll find out about joining trade associations to benefit you and your business in many ways.

When You're the Only One at the Water Cooler

If you used to work at a job in an office or some other place out of your home, you may think back fondly on meeting other people at the water cooler and swapping company gossip. You just can't do this when you work alone in your home (well, you can, but talking to yourself by a water cooler is a sure sign of mental weakness).

Some people, like me, enjoy the peace and quiet in the home office when the rest of the family has left for the day. There are no human distractions to keep you from getting down to business. And there's more time because you're not wasting it socializing. You may be surprised at how much work you can get done every day. You can use these extra minutes for your business. Or you can use your extra time for errands, shopping, and watching Oprah.

But some people don't like being isolated. They get cabin fever, feeling confined to the house day in and day out. They miss the social opportunities that working an outside job gave them. (I don't have any statistics to back me up, but from my observations the overwhelming majority of home-based business owners are married. You think there's any correlation between this and the fact that it's easier to find a date when you're working in a busy office full of other people?)

Some home-based business owners are cooped up all day with young children. They don't have any adults around and when they begin talking in single syllables, they realize they need to get with grown-ups—fast.

You have to decide your own comfort level. If you like being alone and find it helps you do your work, then you don't have to find ways to get out and connect. But if you're the type who needs to bump up against people during the day, there are many ways you can do it while working from home.

Telephone Talk

You knew this as a teenager, but you may have forgotten it: Talking on the telephone is an important way to stay in touch. You've seen how you can use your phone for business. But don't forget you can also use it for social contact throughout the day.

Of course, it goes without saying (but I'll say it anyway) that you need to balance your personal telephone time with your business needs. Tempting as it may be to talk to a good friend about her vacation in Aruba for three hours, you need to set priorities so that your most productive time is not spent socializing. Make personal calls on breaks you schedule between business tasks you need to get done. For example, if you normally spend the first hour of every day going through mail and answering correspondence, slot in a personal call after you've finished your business letters.

Interact with the Internet

Today more and more people are socializing long-distance without ever speaking into a telephone. Instead of meeting face to face, they are talking through a computer. The Internet and commercial online services such as America Online allow you to meet people who may have interests similar to yours without ever leaving your home office. You simply call them up on your computer.

You can enter chat rooms devoted to business topics or you can keep them strictly personal. For example, you can exchange ideas about your home office with others at *Home Office Computing's* Web site (http://www.smalloffice.com), which America Online subscribers can access directly (keyword: soho). Or you can get into chat rooms about gardening, tattoos, or religion.

> **Business Buzzword**
> *Chat rooms* are online areas you can visit to interact with others on a topic of mutual interest. In chat rooms you can just eavesdrop on the conversations of others or you can jump right in and participate.

Get Out and About

You're not the Prisoner of Zenda. Just because you work in a home office doesn't mean you have to stay there. Depending on the type of work you do and where you live, you may find that you spend a good deal of time out of the office on business. You may be visiting clients or customers, meeting with suppliers, or working trade or other business shows.

When I do estate planning, I usually meet with clients in their homes instead of having them come to my home office. The arrangement gets me out of the house. But it also has extra benefits. The clients view my visits as an additional service (because many of my clients are elderly, they don't like to travel). What's more, the arrangement is more efficient since clients have all their records and documents in their home. Meeting there saves them from having to schlep all their papers to my office.

But even if you don't have a business reason to get out of the office, you may find that you have the time to get out for personal reasons. Since you don't spend time commuting to work and since you don't spend time socializing at the office, you have more time for yourself. And you can spend this free time any way you want.

The Educated Entrepreneur

According to one survey, home-based business owners have a lot more "extra" time than they used to when they worked in an office. They use this extra time to exercise, follow up on family activities, do volunteer work, simply run errands, or even do housework.

You can also schedule time away from the office. Once in a while, try to arrange personal or business lunches with your friends or business associates.

Connect Through Networking

Networking's been around forever. The "old boy" network allowed prep-schoolers-turned-Ivy-Leaguers to make important contacts that they used in business for the rest of their lives. The old boy network is still around today, but it's not the only network in operation. Formal networking groups started in the early 1980s, initially to give women the advantages the old boys had. These networking avenues soon expanded to include both men and women looking for business contacts.

Business Buzzword
Networking is word-of-mouth marketing in which contacts are made for the purpose of transacting business together.

Today networking's an important way for all types of business owners to interact with others of their breed. It allows you to swap stories and stay up to speed with your type of business and your business community.

But for a home-based business owner, networking is even more important than for business owners working outside of their homes. Networking's not only a vital marketing tool, it's also a way to break the cabin fever and socialize. Attending a meeting of an organization gives you the chance to get out of your home and mingle with other businesspeople, some of whom may also be home-based.

There are places you can network with other businesspeople. Almost every time you talk with someone presents a networking opportunity to explain your business. Here are some organizations you can use to network:

➤ Become a Lion, Elk, or other networking animal. Networking has long been done indirectly through Rotary, Lions, and chamber of commerce meetings. Luncheons and working together on special projects allow you to get to know other businesspeople on a personal level. Business connections typically are made after personal relationships have been forged.

➤ The National Association of Whatever. If there's an association for your business it may give you a chance to network. For example, I belong to a county women's bar association where I meet with other attorneys to learn about developments affecting the law. There's also a time and place to make friendships through these associations that go beyond business.

➤ Networking organizations. Today there are also special clubs and associations designed especially for networking. You may find networking organizations in your community that meet for breakfast, lunch, dinner, or after dinner most any day of the week (they're a hungry lot) for the sole purpose of exchanging business cards and making contacts. You can choose the meeting that fits best within your schedule. Some of these organizations are open forums; others limit participation to members. Where membership is limited, you might want to join one that restricts the number of members from a certain type of business. Cynthia, an interior designer, didn't want to join a network that had wall-to-wall interior designers. She shopped around and found another group to join.

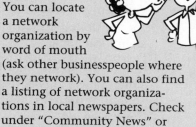

Homegrown Tip

You can locate a network organization by word of mouth (ask other businesspeople where they network). You can also find a listing of network organizations in local newspapers. Check under "Community News" or call your local newspaper and ask where network organizations are listed.

I've Got a Barn and a Great Idea for a Network...

If there's no network organization in your community (or if existing ones don't meet your needs), you may just want to start your own. Decide on your format—open or by invitation only. Fix the time and date for meetings (say, a breakfast meeting at 7 A.M. on the second Tuesday of each month).

Let other businesspeople in your area know about your new organization. If you don't have enough people to invite to your first meeting, place an ad in your local newspaper or get the word out to business owners you know in the area about your new network organization. A local restaurant, community center, or even the public library might be the perfect spot for your new organization to assemble.

Home Hazard

ARGH@#!

It may take time and money to get a group started. Be prepared to give it several months before the group is firmly established. Also be prepared to pay the costs of getting going (advertising, room rental in excess of money collected from attendees). After all your efforts, the group may never get off the ground and you may have to just walk away.

Non-Networking for Connections

Perhaps the most effective way to network is to non-network. No, you're not hearing things, I said non-network. Getting involved in your community without necessarily identifying your business can lead to positive network results for you and your business. People in your community get to know you and, hopefully, trust and respect you. This trust and respect carries over to your business. People want to know what you do and, in an informal setting, allow you to talk about your business.

Non-networking can take the form of membership in your local political club, health club, university alumni association, PTA, or Boy or Girl Scouts, or it can be volunteering for the United Way. Some people coach Little League or soccer; others join the board of their local library.

You pick your area of interest and then jump in. Once my children were old enough that I didn't have to pick them up at school or be in the house with them, I was able to become a volunteer firefighter. Jokes about lawyers following ambulances and fire engines aside, this community service has given me not only a personal challenge and satisfaction but also the opportunity to market my services. I can also find out about the services that others in my community have to offer.

Join a Trade Association

As a home-based business owner, you may feel like a small fish, isolated from the information and buying opportunities that large companies enjoy. You don't have to feel this way any longer. There are a number of trade associations geared specifically for home-based or small business owners. These trade associations let you act like you're a big shot when buying insurance, booking hotel rooms, and more.

Trade association membership, which may cost less than $50 annually, offers you a lot:

➤ Business and personal insurance. Being a member allows you to buy your own insurance at group rates. The types of insurance include medical and dental coverage, special home office business insurance, life insurance, and even car insurance.

➤ Financial services. As a member you may be able to get merchant authorization so you can accept credit cards from your customers (something that's difficult to do as a home-based business owner). You may also be able to get legal and tax assistance on your business questions. You may even be able to take advantage of mutual funds and other investments.

➤ Communications. Membership entitles you to special rates with some long-distance carriers. You may be able to get inexpensive online access to the Internet, e-mail, and other computer-based communications services. Each trade association also has its own newsletter giving you regular news affecting home-based or small businesses.

➤ Products and services. You may enjoy special rates on travel, car rentals, dining, and even relocation counseling. You can buy fax machines, schedule planners, and many other products for your business at discount prices. You may get discounts on overnight delivery and copying services. You may be able to attend local educational seminars geared to small or home-based businesses.

The table below shows some trade associations you might want to check into.

Association	Phone
American Association of Home Based Business	800-447-9710
Home Office Association of America (HOAA)	800-809-4622
National Association for the Self-Employed (NASE)	800-232-NASE
Small Office Home Office Association (SOHOA)	888-SOHOA11

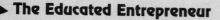

The Educated Entrepreneur

Trade associations may also act as lobbying groups to press Congress for changes that will benefit home-based and small businesses. Trade associations for home-based businesses participated in the White House Small Business Conference in June 1995 and were instrumental in pushing the home business agenda. Now some groups are pushing hard for more liberalized home office deduction rules that will allow tax write-offs for *any* business use of a home office.

The Least You Need to Know

➤ Working alone at home doesn't have to be lonely.

➤ You can use the telephone or the Internet to connect with people without leaving home.

➤ Networking gives you business contacts and social opportunities.

➤ Trade associations give you buying clout and other benefits once limited to major corporations.

Chapter 26

Time to Leave the Nest

In This Chapter
➤ Recognizing when your home office just can't cut it any more
➤ Estimating the cost of moving out
➤ Finding the right commercial space
➤ Making the move without losing your mind (or your business)

Some people, like me, start a business in a home office and work there happily ever after. But for others, a home office is only an incubator—a place to let an idea be nurtured and grow. At some point, the business starts busting out of the home office in several directions at once. More space is needed and, if you don't want to add a new wing to the house, it's time to move out into the world again.

Space isn't the only force that can drive you from your home office. You may need to hire people to help and zoning laws just won't enable you to keep them in your den.

In this chapter you'll see the warning signs of a home business ready to leave the nest. You'll discover ways to stay at home as long as possible if that's your choice. You'll find out how to choose the best location for your new office and how to make a smooth transition to a commercial space.

Warning Signs It's Time to Leave

If you're a consultant or a one-person operation, you may never have to leave home again. I've been working at home for 15 years and don't foresee ever having to make a change.

But not all businesses are the same. Your business may have gotten off to a great start in your home, but you may reach a point when it's time to cut the apron strings. Staying put may stifle further growth to your business.

Sure, after all your efforts to get comfortable in your home office, you're probably cozy there. You love all the positives about working from home—no commute, low overhead, great flexibility, slouching around in sweatpants all day. But if you've been successful and your business has expanded, it may no longer make sense to stay at home. Recognize the signs that it's time to move on so you can make a smooth transition.

Taking on Employees

If your business requires warm bodies to help you out, your hiring is limited by zoning restrictions. Depending on where you live, you may be allowed no more than one employee who isn't a member of your household. Recheck your local zoning rules to find the limits on employees. The zoning rules may have changed since the time you first started your home-based business.

If you need more employees and want to postpone the move, try some of these stop-gap measures. In some cases they may help you avoid the need to ever leave the nest:

Homegrown Tip
Using independent contractors to handle different aspects of your business not only saves space in your home office. It also cuts down on your taxes, as explained in Chapter 18.

➤ Use independent contractors. Farm out some of your work to people with their own businesses. Suppose, for example, you think you need a full-time bookkeeper. Instead of hiring one you may want to use a bookkeeper who's an independent contractor. The bookkeeper has his own business of providing bookkeeping services to a number of clients.

Home construction contractors routinely use independent contractors for different parts of the job. Instead of having a plumber as an employee, the contractor just subcontracts the plumbing work to a plumber with her own plumbing business.

➤ Use employees who work from their homes. If you need someone to devote all of his time to your business and you control how and when the work gets done, you need an employee (you can't just label the worker an independent contractor). But your employee doesn't have to work in your home. You may let the employee work out of his own home. Today there are millions of employees working for large corporations who *telecommute*. If it's good enough for AT&T, why not you?

The Educated Entrepreneur

Want to offer an employee a fringe benefit that doesn't cost you a thing? One thing you can offer an employee you want to hire to work from his home is a tax incentive. Joe or Sally can deduct his or her own home office expenses if use of the home office is *for the convenience of the employer* (that's you). Since you can't and don't provide them with work space in your home office, the arrangement should satisfy tax law requirements for claiming home office deductions.

You can also maximize communication with your employee if both of you have computers with modems. This way, material on one computer can be easily and quickly sent across the street or even to the next town.

If neither independent contractors nor employees working from their own homes is the answer for you, the warning light should go on. It's time to relocate to a regular office in a commercial area.

Cramped Quarters

Remember John Wayne in westerns telling some rustler this town's just not big enough for both of us? That may be how it is with your home business. Even if employees aren't vital to your business, your home just may not be big enough for your family and your business. If you're a graphic designer, for example, as you get more projects and store more artwork, you may need larger studio space than your home can provide.

But before you move your business out of your home office, look into some ways to stay put, if you want to:

➤ Clean up your act. Maybe the reason you're feeling pressed for space is because there's just too much paper around. You're a pack rat; you save everything, even a 1985 directory to your Lion's Club. Learn to clear the decks and make space. Do a spring cleaning on your files. Aim for a paperless office: Don't save paper if the information is saved on your computer (if you have a backup system, such as saving info to floppies). Review the other ideas on organization in Chapter 24.

➤ Hire professional designers. There are professionals who design interior space. Logically enough, they're called interior designers. They look at the space you've got and the space you need and try to make a fit. For instance, putting in overhead storage space (much like kitchen cabinets) can free up floor space for another desk. These professionals (and the suggestions they give to make your space work) don't come cheap. But their bill may be less than it would cost you to move from home and pay office rent each month.

➤ Move a wall, add a room. If you love working from home but just don't have the space anymore, you may want to remodel your home to make it work. Of course, if you rent your home, your landlord might frown on moving walls willy-nilly. But if you own your home, you can make changes. If you have two small bedrooms, you may want to break down a wall to create one large office. I started in a small office, just eight feet by eight feet, off my living room. After two years and not enough bookshelves it was build or move. The old office was torn down and a new office, 12 feet by 25 feet, with plenty of bookshelves, went up in its place. Structural changes are a big commitment on your part. They can cost thousands of dollars (and you have to live through the aggravation and mess of construction). But the price may be worth it to you. It means you can stay where you are rather than moving to a commercial office. And it may increase the value of your home.

> **The Educated Entrepreneur**
>
> You can share the cost of construction with Uncle Sam. If you own your home and make structural changes, you may be able to write off your cash outlays on your tax return through depreciation. (The taxes you save by deducting your costs means, in effect, that the government has shouldered a part of the cost.) Check to see whether you qualify for home office deductions in Chapter 22. But keep in mind that even if you qualify, tax law requires you to spread your write-offs for your addition or improvement to your home over 39 years. Let's see, that's $21.05 a year, times…oh well, you get the idea.

If you've evaluated your space needs and just can't adapt your home office to meet those needs, the warning sign should flash. You've got no choice but to move out.

Where to Warehouse

Consultants and other service businesses usually have more modest space requirements. But if you sell a product, storing the inventory can be a real problem for a home office. Maybe you haven't parked a car in your garage for years because of the cartons of Mama's Homemade Croutons, and still your space is running short. What's an entrepreneur to do?

➤ Take warehouse space. You may find a local warehouse in which you can store some of your products. Of course this costs money, but if your business has grown so that you need to stock so much product, you can probably afford the warehouse rent.

➤ Reevaluate your business. Maybe the way you've been operating can be changed so that you don't have to store cartons in your living room. You may, for example, be able to use a fulfill-ment company to handle your orders. You can have your products delivered directly ("drop shipped") to the fulfillment company instead of to your home. The fulfillment company, not you, has to worry about storage space. Fulfill-ment companies are discussed in Chapter 16.

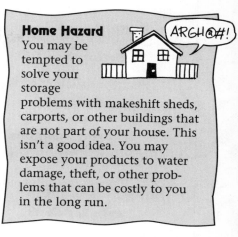

Home Hazard
You may be tempted to solve your storage problems with makeshift sheds, carports, or other buildings that are not part of your house. This isn't a good idea. You may expose your products to water damage, theft, or other prob-lems that can be costly to you in the long run.

Storage may not be your only problem. If the UPS or Federal Express truck is always at your door, your neighbors may start to complain. You may have zoning issues to deal with. But before you move on account of pick-up and delivery, see if you can't make other arrange-ments with carriers to cut down on the traffic. Some options are discussed in Chapter 24.

If you can't use warehouse space because you don't want to split your business (you're in one place and your products are in another), you can't use a fulfillment company, or you can't solve your delivery problems, again, read the writing on the wall. It's time to move out into more suitable space.

Can You Afford to Move?

You may be cramped where you are and want to move. But can you afford to do it? Make an educated guess about the cost of moving your office from your home to a commercial site. Write down the things you'd need to buy or pay for if you move, using the items in this worksheet to remind you.

Expenses to Move

Expense   Amount

    Getting New Office Ready

Wiring $_____

Decorating $_____

continues

---

continued

Expense	Amount
Getting New Office Ready	
Phone installation costs	$_____
New furniture	$_____
Moving Company	
Packing	$_____
Moving office equipment and furniture	$_____
Printing Costs	
New stationery	$_____
Business cards	$_____
Bank checks	$_____
New location announcements	$_____
_____	_____
Total	$_____

Moving's only the first cost you face in running your business from a commercial space. Be sure you know what you're getting into once you unpack the boxes. Use this next worksheet to make an educated guess about the monthly costs you'll have running your business from leased commercial space that you didn't have in your home.

Monthly Expenses of Operating from Commercial Space

Expense	Amount
Personal Costs	
Commuting	$_____
Eating out	$_____
Special clothing	$_____

Expense	Amount
Office Space	
Rent	$_____
Parking fees	$_____
Utilities	$_____
Extra phone lines	$_____
Cleaning services	$_____
Miscellaneous	
Answering service	$_____
Secretarial staff	$_____
Total	$_____

Add up the amounts you must pay just to make the move. Then add in what you'll be paying each month to run your business from outside your home. Make sure your business can survive the move before you make it.

Relocation Rules

So you've tried everything but you just can't stay in your home office. You've tallied the numbers of a move and faced the fact that it's time to call the moving company. But where will you go and how will you make it happen?

You want to make a smooth transition to new quarters so that you don't disrupt your work and lose business because of it. You want to find a new office that's convenient to you and your clients and within your budget. And you want to keep your sanity in the process.

Homegrown Tip

In figuring your moving costs, be sure to get three estimates from moving companies so you'll know that the price you're paying is reasonable. Get the estimates in writing, along with their guarantees in case of damage or loss of your property. You may want to use a moving company that specializes in office moves, even if they charge you more than household movers. These companies are experienced in moving computers and other electronic equipment.

Keep Your Head When You Make Your Move

Remember, you're moving because you've made it. Your business has prospered and you need more space. That's great. But don't get in over your head when you make your move.

➤ Keep commuting in mind. As a home-based business owner you've been spoiled by not having to commute. Now things will change. Unless you live above a storefront or office, you'll have to spend time getting to your new place of business. In choosing an office, keep the commute in mind. Maybe you'll be able to recoup your commuting time with added productivity (maybe you won't spend as much time watching TV or playing with the dog).

➤ Keep clients and customers in mind. Your existing client/customer base was used to your home office. Getting them geared to a new location may not be so easy. The closer you stay to your home, the easier it may be for them to reorient themselves to your new office. And you don't want them to start to use someone else's services because you moved out of convenient range of their offices.

➤ Keep costs in mind. Just because you've succeeded to the point of moving doesn't mean you can stop counting pennies. After all, it was cost consciousness that helped you become successful. Figure out how much space you need on a square-footage basis. Check out commercial rents (which are generally quoted on a square-footage basis).

In deciding *where* to move, there are some things you should avoid. Review this list of don'ts for relocating:

➤ Don't rent more space than you need now (or can reasonably expect to need in the near future). You'll only be throwing rent money away. If there's an opportunity to rent more space than you currently need at a great price, you may be able to sublease the unused part. That extra space may come in handy in the future should your business continue to expand.

➤ Don't pay for fancy space if you don't plan to bring in clients or customers (for example, you're strictly mail order). It may be great for your ego but hard on your pocketbook.

➤ Don't ignore traffic if you're taking retail space. You want to be where people are drawn to, such as a popular shopping area. The cheap rent for a store on a quiet block is cheap for a reason.

➤ Don't forget to check on the location of your competitors. You don't want to be next door to your biggest rival.

➤ Don't overlook parking availability. Neither you nor your clients or customers want to have to park blocks away or pay for expensive parking garages.

You may be able to find a special rental situation that's halfway between your home office and regular commercial space. There are special office suite arrangements in which you get your own office but share common spaces, such as a reception area, copying room, and conference room. These special rental setups generally are less expensive than individual office space—and you get the benefit of sharing a copier and some other equipment as well as a receptionist.

Last Minute Reminders for a Smooth Transition

Moving a business, like moving your home, requires more planning than D-Day. The more you plan, the less surprises you'll face.

For example, you may want to schedule the move on a weekend so that you don't miss a beat in your business. Of course, there are bound to be snags. But here are some things you can do to make the move go as smoothly as possible:

➤ Telephones. Make sure the phone lines for your new office are in place. If you're moving to an office that's close to your home, you may be able to keep your same phone numbers. If not, be sure that the phone company message on your disconnected line tells the new number to those who call. Keep in mind that your Yellow Pages listings may be several months behind your new location.

➤ Computer lines. Have your electrical wiring completed before you move in your computer and other equipment. Make sure the wiring is adequate for your needs. Be clear with your landlord on who's responsible for the cost of wiring.

➤ Announcements. Let your clients, customers, and suppliers know about your new location. Send out announcements, giving your new address and phone number.

➤ Stationery, business cards, and so on. Make sure that your new address appears on all your correspondence, including your invoices and statements. You may also have to change your address on your bank checks. Getting all this printed might take several weeks or more.

> **Homegrown Tip**
> Send announcements not only to your current mailing list but also to former clients and customers. Your new location, which may show that you've come up in the world, can inspire former clients or customers to renew their business relationship with you. If nothing else, it gives you an excuse to remind them of your existence.

The Least You Need to Know

➤ Think of moving to commercial space when you need more employees than your zoning laws enable you to have at home.

➤ Think of moving to commercial space when you can't fit your files, employees, or inventory into your home office.

➤ Before deciding on a move, figure the cost of the move and the ongoing cost of renting commercial space.

➤ Make your move a smooth one with good planning.

State Economic Development Offices

Your state economic development office can provide you with free information on loan programs, tax incentives, the marketplace, business plan critiques, and other information to help you start your home-based business. Call the central number for your state to find an economic development office near you.

State	Phone
Alabama	205-263-0048
Alaska	907-454-2018
Arizona	602-255-5374
Arkansas	501-682-7500
California	916-445-6545
Colorado	303-892-3840
Connecticut	203-566-4051
Delaware	302-736-4271
District of Columbia	202-727-6600
Florida	904-488-9357
Georgia	404-656-6200
Hawaii	808-548-7645
Idaho	208-344-2470
Illinois	312-917-7179
Indiana	317-634-1690
Iowa	515-281-3251
Kansas	913-296-3483
Kentucky	502-564-4252
Louisiana	504-342-5359
Maine	800-872-3838
Maryland	301-333-6975

continues

continued

State	Phone
Massachusetts	617-727-3221
Michigan	517-373-6241
Minnesota	612-296-3871
Mississippi	601-359-3449
Missouri	800-523-1434
Montana	406-444-3923
Nebraska	402-471-3782
Nevada	702-855-4325
New Hampshire	603-623-5500
New Jersey	609-984-4442
New Mexico	505-827-0300
New York	800-782-8369
North Carolina	919-733-4151
North Dakota	701-777-3132
Ohio	614-644-8748
Oklahoma	405-843-9770
Oregon	503-373-1225
Pennsylvania	717-783-5700
Rhode Island	401-277-2601
South Carolina	803-737-0400
South Dakota	605-394-5725
Tennessee	615-741-1888
Texas	512-472-5059
Utah	801-581-7905
Vermont	804-828-3221
Virginia	804-786-3791
Washington	206-753-5630
West Virginia	304-348-2960
Wisconsin	608-266-1018
Wyoming	307-325-4827

Financial Worksheets

When you write your business plan, you'll need a lot of numbers. Use these worksheets to estimate your expenses, your sales, and other figures that are important to include in your plan. Some of the worksheets contain space for six months. You may want to extend your projections for 12 months (just add on the months you'll need). It's a good idea to work in pencil as you play with the numbers or make copies of these worksheets to work out several scenarios.

Projecting Start-Up Costs for a Home-Based Business

Start-Up Item	Estimated Cost
Equipment	$_____
Computers, telephones, copiers, faxes	$_____
Office furniture and fixtures	$_____
Inventory (for product-oriented businesses)	$_____
Supplies	$_____
Stationery, business cards, office supplies	$_____
Professional fees	$_____
Legal fees to set up a corporation or obtain a special zoning permit	$_____
Accounting fees to set up books and accounts	$_____
Insurance	$_____
Fire or liability insurance on property/products (separate or add-on to homeowner's policy)	$_____
Workers' compensation for employees	$_____
Disability insurance for employees	$_____
Licenses/permits (for example, day care facility; home contractor)	$_____
Utilities	$_____
Advertising and promotion	$_____
Occupancy costs	$_____
Miscellaneous and unanticipated expenses	$_____
Personal living expenses	$_____
Total start-up costs	**$_____**

Projecting Income

Income	January	February	March	April	May	June
Total revenues	$____	$____	$____	$____	$____	$____
Cost of goods sold	$____	$____	$____	$____	$____	$____
Gross income	$____	$____	$____	$____	$____	$____

Projecting Fixed Expenses

Expense	January	February	March	April	May	June
Insurance	$____	$____	$____	$____	$____	$____
Loan repayment	$____	$____	$____	$____	$____	$____
Utilities (additional to home use)	$____	$____	$____	$____	$____	$____
Licenses/permits	$____	$____	$____	$____	$____	$____
Depreciation	$____	$____	$____	$____	$____	$____
Miscellaneous	$____	$____	$____	$____	$____	$____
Total	$____	$____	$____	$____	$____	$____

Projecting Variable Expenses

Expense	January	February	March	April	May	June
Wages	$____	$____	$____	$____	$____	$____
Payroll taxes	$____	$____	$____	$____	$____	$____
Advertising	$____	$____	$____	$____	$____	$____
Office supplies	$____	$____	$____	$____	$____	$____
Travel and entertainment	$____	$____	$____	$____	$____	$____
Legal and accounting fees	$____	$____	$____	$____	$____	$____
Miscellaneous	$____	$____	$____	$____	$____	$____
Total	$____	$____	$____	$____	$____	$____

Projecting Net Profits

	January	February	March	April	May	June
Income	$____	$____	$____	$____	$____	$____
Less expenses	$____	$____	$____	$____	$____	$____
Gross profits	$____	$____	$____	$____	$____	$____
Less taxes	$____	$____	$____	$____	$____	$____
Net profit	$____	$____	$____	$____	$____	$____

Projecting One-Year Cash Flow

	January	February	March	April	May	June
Cash on hand (first month)	$____	$____	$____	$____	$____	$____
Cash in bank	$____	$____	$____	$____	$____	$____
Petty cash	$____	$____	$____	$____	$____	$____
Cash sales	$____	$____	$____	$____	$____	$____
Receivables (amounts to be collected)	$____	$____	$____	$____	$____	$____
Total cash in	$____	$____	$____	$____	$____	$____
Disbursements (payments for expenses)	$____	$____	$____	$____	$____	$____
Cash balance (difference between total cash in and disbursements)	$____	$____	$____	$____	$____	$____

Personal Financial Statement

For the period ending _____, *199X*

Assets		Liabilities and Equity	
Cash	$_____	Notes	$_____
Notes	$_____	Mortgages	$_____
Stocks and bonds	$_____	Unpaid taxes	$_____
Real estate	$_____	Life insurance loans	$_____
Cash value life insurance	$_____	Other liabilities (itemize)	$_____
Retirement plans	$_____		
Car/other personal assets	$_____		
Other assets (itemize)	$_____		
Total assets	**$_____**	**Total liabilities and equity**	**$_____**

Business Balance Sheet

For the period ending _____, *199X*

Assets		Liabilities and Equity	
Cash	$_____	Accounts/notes payable	$_____
Notes/accounts receivable	$_____	Other current liabilities	$_____
Stocks and bonds	$_____	Long-term liabilities	$_____
Depreciable assets	$_____	Owner(s) equity	$_____
Intangibles	$_____		
Other assets	$_____		
Total assets	**$_____**	**Total liabilities and equity**	**$_____**

Glossary

Accrual method   Accounting method often used by businesses with inventory; with this method you report income and deduct expenses when the work's done (you've done all the things you have to do to get paid and all the expenses have been incurred).

Advertising   Informing the public about your product or service.

Basis   The amount you paid for property (called cost basis) or other amount treated as your investment in property. Adjusted basis is basis increased by additions or improvements and decreased by depreciation.

Business opportunity   A non-franchise arrangement in which you buy a concept for a product or service.

Business plan   A written report describing what a business is all about and where the business is heading in the future.

C corporation   Corporation organized under state law and taxed as a separate person (a regular corporation).

Cash flow cycle   Time over which inventory is ordered, paid for, sold, and money is received.

Cash method   Accounting method often used by service businesses. With this method you record income when your client pays you and deduct expenses as they come up.

Chat rooms   Locations on the Internet in which people interact with each other on a particular topic or area of mutual interest.

Closely held corporation   Privately owned corporation whose stock is not traded on any public exchange.

Collection agency   Business that performs collection services, including sending reminders to late payers and suing delinquents on your behalf.

Commercial loan   Borrowing from a bank or other financial institution that specializes in business lending.

Constructive receipt   Cash basis businesses must report income when it's under their control even if they haven't actually got the cash in hand (a check is income when received even though you haven't deposited or cashed it yet).

Cost of goods sold   Cost of inventory items such as materials, labor, and packaging.

Credit   *See* **Tax credit.**

Debt   Financing a business by borrowing money. The borrower is called the debtor; the lender is called the creditor.

Debt service   Repayment of a loan (including principal and interest).

Depreciation   Deduction of a portion of the cost of a car or other equipment you own over the life of the equipment (the life is set by the IRS).

Employer identification number   Number assigned to a business owner by the IRS after you file IRS Form SS-4. This is used for identification purposes on tax returns, bank accounts, and retirement plans.

Entrepreneur   Someone who organizes and directs a start-up business, assuming the risk in the hopes of making a profit.

Equity   Financing a business by bringing in investors; ownership of a business. Home equity is the value of your home (after subtracting the mortgage balance, if any).

Escrow   Arrangement in which a third party (usually a lawyer) holds funds; when certain conditions are met, the funds are paid out.

Fair market value   What a willing buyer and willing seller would pay, if neither is being forced to buy or sell and each understands all the facts and circumstances of the deal.

FICA (Federal Insurance Contributions Act)   Social Security and Medicare taxes on wages (paid by both the employer and the employee).

Financial statement   Information about income, expenses, sales figures, and other number-oriented items (for example: cash flow statement, balance sheet, profit and loss statement).

Franchise   A business arrangement that gives you the right to sell a product or service in a particular area. The company selling the concept is the franchisor; you are the franchisee. The right to a large territory is called a master franchise.

Fulfillment company   Business that takes and processes orders for you, including acceptance of payment by credit card. Generally a fulfillment company charges a flat fee.

FUTA (Federal Unemployment Tax Act)   Federal unemployment insurance tax paid by an employer on an employee's wages.

Grants   Money from government sources or private foundations to start or run a business that matches the goals of the grant maker; grant money doesn't have to be repaid.

Gross income   Generally, income before deductions. For purposes of the home office deduction, gross income means money from business minus expenses that don't relate to the use of the home (such as office supplies or the salary of an employee).

Hobby loss rules Tax rules that prevent an individual from deducting business expenses that are greater than business income where there's no reasonable expectation of making a profit from the business.

Home office deduction The total of deductions from business use of a home office, including depreciation on the office or a portion of rent as well as the portion of utilities and insurance related to the home office.

Independent contractor Person who contracts to provide work according to his own methods. This person isn't under the control of the person or business for whom the work is being performed; not an employee.

Internet A worldwide collection of computer networks that you can access with a computer, modem, telephone line, and an online service provider or Internet service provider.

Invoice An itemized list of products you've sold to someone, stating the quantity, price, and terms of sale; a bill for services rendered.

Limited liability company Type of business organization formed under state law that gives owners protection from personal liability but treats them as a partnership for tax purposes.

Limited partnership Partnership in which one or more partners has limited personal liability and can't participate in the day-to-day operations of the business.

Low doc loans Special loan programs with simple application processes (short for low documentation because there's not much paperwork).

Marketing How people advertise, publicize, or otherwise inform each other of their product or service with the goal of exchanging products or services with each other.

Member Owner of a limited liability company.

Multi-level marketing *See* **Network marketing**.

Net operating losses Business expenses in excess of business income; business losses that can be carried back three years and forward 15 years; also called NOLs.

Network marketing Direct sales to consumers with distributors getting money from both direct sales and a percentage of the direct sales of other distributors they bring into the network. Also called multi-level marketing.

Networking Word-of-mouth marketing in which contacts are made to try to drum up business.

Overhead Cost of monthly expenses, including electricity, telephone, insurance, and salaries of employees.

Partnership   Two or more people working together in a business with the intention of making a profit.

Personal service corporation   Corporation subject to special tax rules; corporation engaged in the fields of health, law, accounting, engineering, architecture, actuarial science, performing arts, or consulting and that meets certain ownership and service tests.

Promotion   Stimulating an immediate sale with special offers, such as discount coupons.

Publicly held corporation   Corporation whose stock is traded on a public exchange (such as the New York Stock Exchange).

Rider   Additional clause to an existing contract or insurance policy to cover a special item or event (usually an upgrade to a policy); sometimes referred to as an endorsement.

S corporation   Corporation organized under state law that elects to have business income taxed to its shareholders (also called a Subchapter S corporation).

SBA (Small Business Administration)   Federal agency that sponsors loan programs and other assistance to small businesses.

SBICs (Small Business Investment Companies)   These are privately-managed firms licensed by the SBA to make loans to small businesses.

Shareholders   Owners of a corporation whose ownership interest is in the form of a stock certificate (also called stockholders).

Sole proprietorship   Unincorporated business owned by one person.

Start-up phase   The period in which a business begins (generally the first three months).

Tax credit   Reduction in income tax on a dollar-for-dollar basis.

Test marketing   Introducing a product or service to a limited area, measuring sales interest, and then projecting what demand would be if the product or service were available to a larger area.

Turnkey business   A business that is ready to go into operation, with all materials, processes, and equipment in place to produce a product or service.

Variance   A change or alteration of a zoning rule granted specifically for one person.

Venture capitalists   People or companies that invest in businesses (often technology-related) with the expectation of realizing big profits in the future.

Index

C

F

P

Q-R

U-V